£5

WINGS OF WAR

WINGS OF WAR

PERSONAL RECOLLECTIONS OF THE AIR WAR 1939–45

MARTIN W. BOWMAN

The History Press

First published 2016

The History Press
The Mill, Brimscombe Port
Stroud, Gloucestershire, GL5 2QG
www.thehistorypress.co.uk

British Library Cataloguing in Publication Data.
A catalogue record for this book is available from the British Library.

ISBN 978 0 7509 6758 7

Typesetting and origination by The History Press
Printed and bound in Great Britain by TJ International Ltd

CONTENTS

INTRODUCTION

When Britain declared war on Germany in September 1939 RAF front-line bombers were mainly twin-engined types like the Hampden, Whitley and Wellington, but after suffering heavy losses by day these were used only on night operations which proved no less dangerous than the 'daylights' had been. 'Lady Luck' decided if they lived or died on 'ops'. Fear, sweat, tension and dreaded bomb runs made most aircrew realise that the chance of survival and completing a tour before the Reaper caught them was slim. This was reflected in their unofficial anthem:

> Lift up your glasses ready
> For the air crew up there in the sky,
> Here's a toast to the dead already
> And here's to the next man to die.

Bomber Command sank 55 per cent of the German merchant fleet, and together with Coastal Command, sank three-quarters of the U-boats lost by Germany. In 1942 Sir Arthur Harris became commander of Bomber Command. He began massive raids, which did not cease until the final surrender of Germany. By early 1944 fierce air battles involving four-engined Lancasters and Halifax aircraft raged over the skies of Germany and Reich territory. Approximately 125,000 aircrew served in the RAF, RAAF, RNZAF, RCAF, Polish squadrons and the operational training and conversion units. Most were plucked from Civvy Street where the sight of devastation made many feel that at least they had joined the right service because only Bomber Command was capable of attacking the enemy. It was also refreshing to many young minds to know that soon, with good luck, they would be in a crew that would be dropping bombs on the enemy.

The vivid, poignant and descriptive personal experiences of the bomber crews carrying the war to the enemy in the night bomber offensive in the Second World War are recounted, mostly at first hand, sometimes in wartime broadcasts to the nation.

Of the 7,953 Bomber Command aircraft lost on night operations during the Second World War, an estimated 5,833 fell victim to German night fighters. Nearly 60 per cent of Bomber Command aircrew became casualties. Approximately 85 per cent of these casualties were suffered on operations and 15 per cent in training and accidents. Fatal casualties to aircrew totalled 55,500 and 9,838 were taken prisoners of war and 4,203 were wounded in flying or ground accidents in the UK. Total aircrew casualties numbered 73,741.

I have pieced together official data and the words and memories of the RAF and Dominion pilots and aircrew, detailing many unique experiences during the night bombing raids that were hurled against Hitler's war machine. This collection of first-hand accounts gives a really good feel for the variety of the RAF's bomber war, from the earliest limited attacks of 1939 to the overwhelming raids of 1944–45 and a good cross section of what happened between.

Each chapter is the result of meticulous research and, in many cases, converting the anonymous into real people. Some of the stories emanate from wartime publications that were censored and so their names, units and actions were generally anonymous and unknown to the British public until long after the war. Although the actions covered were real many of the names applied to these actions were fictitious.

Recent years have seen an upsurge in the popularity of the memories and experiences of the ordinary man at war. Perhaps this is down to a realisation that, as time passes, their memories might be lost. Their accounts are stirring, gripping and memorable, and not preoccupied by strategy or tactics, but rather the emotional aspect of war.

The storytellers are an eclectic mix of pilots, navigators, bomb aimers, wireless operators and gunners who flew on operations in heavy bombers. It conveys the terror of being coned by German searchlights over the target, attacks by Luftwaffe night fighters, often catastrophic damage to aircraft and the ensuing struggle to keep the machine airborne on the return trip to base. It tells of the comradeship between the crew and conveys the sense of purpose that these men felt in doing one of the most dangerous jobs in the war. These truly epic stories are a fitting tribute to those who survived and the many thousands who died in the struggle against Hitler's dreadful ambitions in Europe, and are an appropriate epitaph to the men of RAF Bomber Command.

As Churchill said: 'Britain can never repay them as they should have been repaid for the huge sacrifice they made to ensure our freedom.'

Martin W. Bowman

1

FLIGHT LIEUTENANT RODERICK LEAROYD

The Germans worked hard to repair the damage to the Dortmund–Ems Canal after the raid on 19–20 June 1940 and they also defended the canal so well with searchlights and guns that they probably considered it impossible for any aircraft ever again to make a successful attack on the waterway. Nevertheless, the RAF went back from time to time to do their worst. On one occasion Acting Flight Lieutenant Roderick Alastair Brook 'Babe' Learoyd on 49 Squadron acted as a decoy to draw the fire of the defences while other bombers slid down to attack; another time he made a high-level attack. He was, thus, not unfamiliar with the Dortmund–Ems Canal when he started out to make his third attack upon it on 12–13 August, when two Hampden units, 49 and 83 Squadrons in 5 Group, carried out a low-level raid. It was a night of half moon, which gave sufficient light in which to see the target. The Hampdens carefully timed their attack so as to drop the special charge at intervals of exactly two minutes, beginning at 01.30. At one point the canal was especially vulnerable. North of Münster, two aqueducts, one on four arches, the other on two, carried the canal across the River Ems. The width of each channel was only 100ft at water level.

To destroy both aqueducts meant cutting the canal entirely, while the destruction of one would greatly reduce the volume of traffic passing through it. The aqueduct was heavily protected by anti-aircraft guns disposed so as to form a lane down which an attacking aircraft must fly if it was to reach the target, but it was decided to attack from a very low level in order to make certain the target would be hit. One by one, the eleven Hampdens went in from the north, the moon shining in the faces of their crews and throwing the objective into relief. The first aircraft was hit and the wireless operator on board wounded; the second was hit and destroyed. The third was set on fire, but before the aircraft became uncontrollable, the pilot succeeded in gaining enough height to enable the crew and himself to bail out. They did so and were made prisoners. The fourth Hampden was hit in three places but got back to base. The fifth and last Hampden, piloted by Flight Lieutenant Learoyd, went down the anti-aircraft lane at 200ft.

After a moment three big holes appeared in the starboard wing. They were firing at point-blank range. The navigator continued to direct me on to the target. I could not see it because I was blinded by the glare of the searchlights and had to keep my head below the level of the cockpit top. At last I heard the navigator say 'Bombs gone'; I immediately did a steep turn to the right and got away, being fired at heavily for five minutes. The carrier pigeon we carried laid an egg during the attack.

The attack achieved an element of surprise and the damage to the canal restricted barge traffic on this important waterway for a number of weeks. Learoyd was awarded Bomber Command's first Victoria Cross of the war. His VC citation read:

This officer, as first pilot of a Hampden aircraft, has repeatedly shown the highest conception of his duty and complete indifference to personal danger in making attacks at the lowest altitude objective on the Dortmund–Ems Canal. He had attacked this objective on a previous occasion and was well aware of personal danger in making attacks at the lowest altitude objective on the Dortmund–Ems Canal … To achieve success it was necessary to approach from a direction well known to the enemy, through a lane of especially disposed anti-aircraft defences and in the face of the most intense point blank fire from guns of all calibres. The reception of the preceding aircraft might well have deterred the stoutest heart, all being hit and two lost. Flight Lieutenant Learoyd nevertheless made his attack at 150ft, his aircraft being repeatedly hit and large pieces of the main planes torn away. He was almost blinded by the glare of many searchlights at close range but pressed home this attack with the greatest resolution and skill. He subsequently brought his wrecked aircraft home and, as the landing flaps were inoperative and the undercarriage indicators out of action, waited for dawn in the vicinity of his aerodrome before landing, which he accomplished without causing injury to his crew or further damage to the aircraft. The high courage, skill and determination, which this officer has invariably displayed on many occasions in the face of the enemy, sets an example which is unsurpassed.[1]

I joined the Royal Air Force on a Short Service Commission in March 1936, so by the time the war came along I had a fair bit of flying experience.

Ten days before the war started, when I was based at Scampton, Lincolnshire, I had been in the south of France. I wasn't supposed to be out of the country – nobody actually said so, but it was assumed. My father phoned and told me to get back quickly. I had to travel on a blacked-out and very crowded train. If the war had started during Chamberlain's 'Peace in our time' business, we'd have had biplanes and Rolls-Royce-engined Hawker Hinds as our front-line bombers with a twenty-pound bomb on each wing, a Browning front-gun and Lewis rear upper-gun. But luckily, the war was delayed and the next year we took over the first squadron of Bristol Pegasus-engined Handley Page Hampdens. Of course, the Hind was a much more nimble aircraft but we were very impressed with the Hampden. You could still play with a Hampden to a certain extent, much more, than say, a Wellington. In a Hampden you had a crew of four: the pilot; the navigator bomb aimer down in the nose – he didn't stay there all the time, because it was a pretty awful position. Then there was the upper gunner/radio operator and the lower-gunner who also didn't sit in that position unless he was preparing for action. The Hampden was a very pleasant aircraft to fly, but they did have one fault: they used to go into what is called a 'stabilised yaw'. If you got into a spin, the rudders were blanked off by the suitcase-like fuselage and it was difficult to correct the spin. I actually saw one spinning all the way down to a fatal crash – not a nice sight. Quite a number of aircrew (mainly in training) were killed in this manner. But we, who had a little more experience, had no real trouble.

That first day of war, I remember writing a letter to my mother and father, saying 'thank you' for everything – all that sort of stuff. One really thought something big was going to happen immediately and then of course it didn't. However, on the evening of that first day of World War II we did go out on a 'search' mission – to find the German Navy who were supposed to be en route from Kiel to Bremerhaven. And we were supposed to go and locate them. We soon lost our no. 3 in cloud and gathering darkness. My leader, George Lerwill and I found ourselves flying in and out of cloud and I had great difficulty keeping in touch with him. We didn't find the German Navy either!

There was a longish break after that and we enjoyed our off-duty hours as, in all the pubs of Lincoln and Nottingham, we were considered operational just because we'd been out and done a trip – so it was, 'Well done, come and have a drink!' The next stage was dropping propaganda leaflets over Germany. I'm not sure that I ever read one, but they said the equivalent of, 'Give up now!'

We did a lot of mine-laying in the Skagerrak and around that area and I can remember low-flying across Denmark once in broad morning daylight and seeing people waving to me. Denmark was not in the war at that time so nipping across that charming country in daylight at about two hundred feet was great fun. We then turned our attention to railway tunnels and marshalling yards. There was a lot of that, trying to disrupt rail transport. There was light opposition to those first raids, Bofors guns, etc. Then in August 1940 we started preparing for a low-level attack on the DortmundEms canal. Our target was an aqueduct carrying the canal over the Ems River.

We had had some practice in low-level night-bombing over water when mine-laying. However, a special exercise was devised for this mission – a small light was placed on a little fenland river and I had to drop my practice bomb – a small 81b smoke-bomb – on this target. Off I went on my run, flying solo (no crew). At first I couldn't see the light and then 'There it is!' As I approached it I suddenly realised there were houses going past my wing. I pulled up sharply, for obviously I wasn't in the right place at all. I never did find out what that light was! However, I did manage to find the right place later.

This was my first really low-level operation on the canal – I had carried out an earlier, higher, unsuccessful try. There were five aircraft, all from Scampton. We set off on 12 August and we were supposed to go in at 150 feet, drop the bombs, each with a ten-minute delay, at two-minute intervals and swing away. I was the last one in and so I had to be accurate with my timing, because the first bomb was due to go off very soon after I passed. I didn't want to be late!

Flight Lieutenant 'Jamie' Pitcairn-Hill on 83 Squadron led the way in and immediately came under fire. He levelled out at about 100ft, dropped his bomb and got away without any damage.[2] The next two to go were great pals, both from 83 Squadron – and both Australians. Pilot Officer E.H. Ross went first and he was hit and came down. The third to run the gauntlet was Flying Officer R. Mulligan. Before he reached his bomb-release point he was hit and one of his engines burst into flames. All four crew bailed out and survived as prisoners-of-war. The next one in was Pilot Officer Matthews who dropped his bombs – he got hit but made his way back.

Learoyd's VC was awarded in an investiture at Buckingham Palace on 9 September 1940, by which time he had been taken off operations and had been promoted to squadron leader. He was further honoured in November 1940 when he received the Freedom of the Borough of New Romney, Kent. Learoyd's navigator and bomb aimer was Pilot Officer John Lewis, the wireless operator and dorsal air gunner was Flight Sergeant Walter Ellis and the ventral air gunner was Leading Aircraftman William Rich. Ellis and Rich were each awarded the DFM. Rich's DFM was announced on 22 October 1940 and his citation stated:

> Leading Aircraftman Rich is an armourer and member of a ground crew who volunteered for training as a part-time air gunner. He has shown exceptional keenness and ability in his work, both in the air and on the ground, and by his enthusiasm, skill and courage very quickly became operationally fit as an air gunner. He has carried out a total of 8 operations against the enemy during the course of which he has completed 49 hours flying.
>
> He was the air gunner in the aircraft flown by Flight Lieutenant R.A.B. Learoyd VC, when a low level attack was carried out on the Dortmund-Ems Canal. In this and in all other operations in which he has taken part, LAC Rich has shown outstanding skill and courage in operating his guns against the enemy defences. By his enthusiasm, courage and devotion to duty, he has set an outstanding example to other airmen in this squadron.

Rich is believed to be the first leading aircraftman of the Second World War to be awarded the DFM. The recommendation for his award was endorsed by AVM Sir Arthur Harris, who wrote: 'Strongly recommended. A keen and efficient volunteer for dangerous duty without the pay and rank of regular crew.'

Ellis' DFM was announced on 22 November 1940 and his citation stated:

> This NCO has carried out a total of 39 operations against the enemy during the course of which he has completed 230 hours flying as a Wireless Operator/Air Gunner. Throughout these operations, Sergeant Ellis has shown outstanding ability, determination and devotion to duty, and has been of the greatest assistance to his Pilot, both as an air gunner and as a wireless operator.
>
> Amongst other notable and successful operations in which he has taken part, he was Wireless Operator/Air Gunner in Flight Lieutenant Learoyd's aircraft which carried out a successful low-level attack on the Dortmund-Ems Canal. His work has always been of the highest order and his efficiency and enthusiasm have been an inspiration to other Wireless Operator/Air Gunners in the squadron.

Learoyd resumed operational flying on 28 February 1941 when he was appointed commanding officer of 83 Squadron at RAF Scampton. In June that year, however, he took up a new post as Wing Commander Flying at 14 Operational Training Unit (OTU), RAF Cottesmore, Rutland. In December 1941, Learoyd succeeded to the command of 44 Squadron at RAF Waddington, Lincolnshire, and in May

1942 he was posted to 25 OTU, RAF Finningley, Yorkshire where he carried out more instructional duties. From then until the end of hostilities in Europe Learoyd remained non-operational, with postings to the Air Ministry and two further OTUs (109 and 107). In May 1945, he returned to flying when he joined 48 (Dakota) Squadron, which was posted to West Africa the following month. It was not until 14 October 1946 that Learoyd was finally demobilised. For three years he worked for the Malayan civil aviation department before returning to Britain in 1950 to accept a post with a tractor and road construction company. In 1953 he became the export sales manager to the Austin Motor Company. Learoyd died in Rustington, Sussex, on 24 January 1996, aged 82.

2

FRIGHTENED BY A DRAGON

GEOFFREY COLE

Geoffrey Cole joined the RAF Volunteer Reserve in early 1938 at Derby. He trained as a pilot and wanted to join Bomber Command with a view to becoming a civilian airline pilot. He was awarded his pilot's brevet in 1939 and joined 214 Squadron in July 1940, then 103 Squadron in 1943. Among other places, he was based in Lossiemouth, Stradishall, Elsham Wolds and Blyton. He flew Wellingtons with 3 Group and Lancasters with 1 Group, Bomber Command and, after completing fifty-four operations, he became an instructor on Lancasters and Halifaxes. For a short time he was seconded to the Royal Navy aircraft carrier, *Argus*. After the war he achieved his ambition of becoming an airline pilot with BOAC, Skyways and Court Line. He amassed a total flying time of more than 20,000 hours worldwide.[1]

I saw my first aircraft in 1926 when I was six years old. I was playing in the woods near my house with a friend when we heard a terrible roaring noise and something swooped above the trees. We were terrified. My friend identified it as a dragon then we fled in terror into the house. My mother allayed our fears and told us, 'It's an aeroplane, not a dragon. There's nothing to be frightened of. I think it's landed in the field just down the road. Go and have a look.'

Still somewhat apprehensive, we ventured forth but my courage grew as my brother and his friend joined us. Just as my mother had predicted there was the aeroplane. We watched from the edge of the field as instructed by the field owner. He went out in his car to talk to the man standing by its side. Eventually, the aeroplane was turned around, 'wound up' and came racing towards us. It took off and soared over our heads. The pilot waved to us and finally disappeared. We watched until it was nothing more than a speck in the distant sky then we raced back home.

'We saw it fly into the sky!' I told my mother excitedly. 'It just ran along the ground and then went right over us into the sky! But it never moved its wings – how can it fly if it doesn't flap its wings like a bird?'

'I don't know, dear. You'll have to ask your father when he comes in – he knows all about aeroplanes.'

When my father came in I told him the story and asked him how it flew.

'It's obvious, my boy. Sky-hooks, that's what keeps it up.'

'Sky-hooks?'

'Yes.' I puzzled over that for some time. Finally I said, 'Yes, dad, but what holds up the sky-hooks?' (I was a little boy with an enquiring mind.)

'Bigger sky-hooks.'

I realised then that if grown-ups didn't know the answer they told you a story! I finally learnt the truth about how aeroplanes fly from a Christmas present in 1931 – Every Boy's Hobby Annual had a chapter on how aeroplanes flew and an article about some fifteen-year-old apprentices at a place called RAF Halton who had actually built a real aeroplane. I did not realise it at the time but I was hooked on aeroplanes.

I was called up for regular service three days before war was declared in September 1939 having already attended various courses and clocked up solo flying hours as a pre-war Volunteer Reserve. I became a fully qualified pilot (twin-engined) in June 1940 at RAF Ternhill, Shropshire. From there I went to Lossiemouth – a new OTU flying Wellingtons with two newly commissioned pilot officers and Sergeant pilot Cattle (pronounced C'tell, not Cattle), who became a friend. It turned out that the aircraft were not dual controlled and we were to be instructors, which we didn't fancy at the time and so we went to see the newly arrived Wing Commander. We requested not to be instructors and said we wished to go to war.

'All right,' came the reply. 'Get yourself a crew!'

So we went round the hangar, talked to the chaps working there and acquired a crew. This consisted of LAC Flanagan, LAC Cook, LAC Hide and Sergeant Butcher, a direct entry sergeant navigator. We called ourselves

No. 1 Crew, No. 1 Course, Lossiemouth. There was one small snag: I had trouble with my take-offs and Cattle had trouble with his landings!

Our first flight together in a Wellington from Lossiemouth (now known as 20 OTU) was round the top of Scotland and lasted about four hours. A pilot, Sergeant Douglas, who had been on ops, accompanied us and 'knew all about it'. Towards the end of the flight he said, 'I'll show you how things are done on the squadron.' We were duly impressed when he got right down on the deck – really low – and for the last thirty miles or so came roaring back at minimum altitude.

Unfortunately, he had been used to flying the latest Wellington, the Mark Ic. This one was a Mark I and had a hydraulic system that had to be off-loaded by means of a power cock. Before putting wheels and flaps down it was necessary to turn on the power. Sergeant Douglas forgot all about this and we ended up in a heap in the middle of the field. It must have been the quickest evacuation on record!

I've said that Cattle was no good at landing and I was no good at taking off and so we swapped over when it was time to land or take-off. Obviously, this couldn't go on and so we put in some practice. One particular day returning from a cross-country flight we discovered there were two squadrons of Blenheims lined up on the far side of the field at Lossiemouth. Cattle was due to do the landing and, as often happened, he touched down well into the field; only this time it was worse than usual. However, he managed to turn the aircraft. We were now going sideways at a rate of knots but heading for a gap between the two squadrons. At that moment a Blenheim appeared in the gap from behind the other Blenheims.

'This is it. This is my lot,' I thought, 'I've had it.'

The Blenheim's propellers would slice right into us. I could see it coming. Cattle swung the aircraft again at the last minute and, instead of his propellers chopping us, ours chopped his nose off.

After a speedy evacuation from both aircraft it was discovered that the navigator of the Blenheim had been in the nose. We got him out. He was fully conscious but the propeller had chopped his arm off at the shoulder – clean as a whistle! We tried to staunch the bleeding with our shirts while the ambulance came – but it never did. We realised that no one on the airfield had seen the accident happen as they had all gone to the NAAFI for tea. The RAF was still operating under peace-time conditions.

Eventually, our navigator raced the full length of the field to get the ambulance. When it arrived the 'armless' navigator was sitting up smoking a cigarette. He got up casually, strolled into the ambulance, somebody put his arm in behind him – and off he went.

A year later he returned to Lossiemouth on a visit from Canada where he had been instructing navigators. Cattle and I were both back there as instructors having completed our first tour. He told us that the accident was the best thing that has happened to him as out of eighteen crews on 21 and 57 Squadrons (Blenheims) only four survived their fortnight at Lossiemouth.

Up to this time Cattle and I had taken turns to be captain but after this incident Cattle was made permanent second pilot by the CO.

We had been chronically short of equipment – so short that up to now we had had no guns and so, whenever we went out, the gunners just came along for the ride! Eventually, we actually got guns in our turrets and set off on a gunnery exercise. I was taxiing out in preparation for take-off when I felt a vibration from behind. I wondered if there was something wrong with the tail wheel or if it had collapsed. I asked the rear gunner, 'Tail wheel ok?' There was a slight pause then the rear gunner replied. 'It was me, skipper.'

'You?'

'I just fired my guns into the ground.'

'You did what? I asked incredulously.

'In the 1914–18 war gunners had to fire their guns into the ground just before take-off to test them. Standard practice,' he said.

'I see.' I had a suspicion that I had not heard the end of this.

We continued with the exercise and on return I wasn't in the least surprised to be summoned to see the Station Commander – on the double. I had to give my gunner all the support I could and explained exactly what had happened, praised his outstanding ability and keenness, proved when he said it was standard practice to test the guns by firing into the ground during the last war.

'Maybe it was then but it isn't now. Perhaps, Sergeant Cole, you'll be interested to know that the entire camp took to the air raid shelters, including me. In future, when you do things like this will you warn me first?' and I thought I detected a faint smile.

'Yes sir.'

'Dismissed.'

We had just completed our first raid. This was to Schiphol airport, Amsterdam and we were on our way back. I was now second pilot to Pilot Officer Filluel who had taken over my crew. Tension was high as there had been many rumours about German night fighters with lights on them. We had left the target about ten minutes when the rear gunner reported a light coming up behind. 'You sure?'

'Positive.'

Filluel dived and turned trying to lose the light but it remained steadfastly behind us. He ordered the navigator, 'Go take a look through the astrodome.'

'Definitely a light, skipper,' reported the navigator.

I then suggested, 'I'll go and look.'

Sure enough, there was the light. No matter what we did or where we went, it stayed with us.

'How about giving him a burst with our guns?' I suggested to Filluel, 'let him know we've seen him.'

'OK.'

The rear gunner blasted into the night sky. What a surprise – we had been trying to shoot down Venus – the morning star! In retrospect it was laughable but at the time, with nerves stretched to breaking point and an atmosphere of fear and tension, the slightest thing could spark imagination and defy reason. Shooting at Venus was just one of many similar incidents created, I suspect, by tension and anxiety. I believe other crews had also tried to shoot down Venus. It was, of course, the first year light bombers had operated and not many people had observed the early morning planet.

Two years into the war – 14 September 1941. It was the day the war could have ended if we could have found Hitler. We were to bomb a railway station at Ehrang in the Harz Mountains where, according to intelligence, Hitler was spending the night in a train. There was a lot of cloud but we let down through the cloud to about a couple of hundred feet and found the railway line and followed it but couldn't find the station.

We decided to drop a flare. We'd never dropped a flare before and the navigator went to do this. He came back, 'It's stuck, skipper.'

I went back to help him. It was wedged in the flare chute – not only that but the nose of the flare was already out. The flare's nose had a propeller and when the propeller came unscrewed the thing exploded. I was fiddling about with it when it started to fizz ominously. With an almighty shove I pushed it out. It fell into a field about 200 feet below us and killed a cow. By the light of the burning flare we found ourselves on the side of a hill, climbed to clear it and back into the clouds but they obscured our target and we never did bomb the station. Had we achieved our goal and killed Hitler instead of the hapless cow, maybe the war would have ended much sooner.

On 17 October 1940 my aircraft was one of three that took off thirty minutes before the main force of sixty aircraft detailed to light the target, Düsseldorf. On the way back we ran into a lot of cloud and so I decided to climb above it. We reached 14,000 ft when both engines stopped – iced up. I had had my aircraft fitted with a hand-operated, alcohol-pump that was supposed to de-ice both engines but they still would not start. There was nothing I could do as we steadily dropped. At 6,000 feet I ordered, 'Parachutes on. You know the drill.' The parachutes were separate from the harness and kept in a rack by the entrance door so that as you left you took your parachute and jumped out. At least, that was the theory. The drill was that the navigator would sort out the parachutes and hand them out. I looked round and was amazed to see the navigator on his knees praying. I also noticed my co-pilot had stopped pumping. Although I'm not a religious chap I offered up a prayer myself at the same time saying, 'Pump, you bastard, pump!'

Suddenly the starboard engine started but we were below 4,000 feet.

'We're OK. If she keeps going we can make England on one engine.' I tried not to sound too jubilant because our altitude was 2,000 feet and dropping – maybe we couldn't make it after all. On top of that we were attacked by ground defences. We were so low by this time that the searchlight beams looked almost horizontal and reflected on the sea; we realised we were heading over the North Sea at just 500 feet. We pressed on and rose to 1,000 feet. The port engine started and we made it back home.

The next day I was called into the parachute section.

'Where's your parachute, Sergeant Cole?'

'In the aircraft.'

'It isn't. There's one missing and it's yours.'

'I told them what had happened. In handing out the parachutes, the navigator had probably accidentally dropped one through the open door. If we had had to abandon the aircraft I would have been parachute-less. My mind went back to seeing the navigator praying – had he been praying for himself or me?

From then on I always wore a pilot-type parachute on which I sat. (Incidentally, of the three aircraft that led the raid, I was the only one to return. The main force of sixty all turned back due to bad weather.)

It was on my second tour on Lancasters on 103 Squadron, on a raid on Bochum in 1943, when we took a lot of flak. Even so, we came back relatively unscathed or so I thought. The next day the parachute section called for me.

'I can't have lost a parachute again,' I thought. I knew I couldn't because I had actually been sitting on it and it was attached to me. I went to see what the problem was. I was shown a black, sticky mess hanging from the rack.

'Your parachute, Flight Lieutenant Cole.'

I was handed a piece of shrapnel about four inches long.

'Where did that come from?'

'Your parachute.'

On inspection of my aircraft I discovered that this piece of shrapnel had gone through the bomb doors, through a can of incendiary bombs, through the floor of the aircraft, through the bottom of my seat and into my parachute. It had stopped there. Being red hot it had melted the artificial silk into a burnt, glutinous mess. Had I not been wearing this type of parachute I wouldn't be here to tell this story!

Pilot Officer (as he was now) Cattle and I were instructing on Wellingtons at Lossiemouth from 1941–42. There was also a New Zealander, Flight Sergeant Bagnall ('Baggy') and another chap whose name I've forgotten. On 22 August 1941 we were on night training exercises with pupils – circuits and bumps. I finished my shift and waited for the others. Cattle and the other fellow came in but there was no sign of Bagnall. We waited a while and presumed he must have gone home. The flare path was being cleared and the airfield closing down for the night.

'Wonder what's happened to Baggy? He's not signed in,' said Cattle. 'Let's check with the flight office.' The flight sergeant confirmed that the aircraft was still out. We called the Observer Corps.

'Nothing flying at all, sir. No aircraft airborne in Scotland at this time,' came the reply.

'He must have crashed.' We notified the CO and he raised the camp and a search party to search the cliff tops.

Cattle and I did a square search of the sea just off the coast. A Whitley from RAF Kinloss did the same thing and the lighthouse keeper also put on his light as a guide. In those days we didn't carry radio – just speaking tubes – so there was no contact with the ground once you were airborne. We started our search, combing the sea with our landing lights on at a height of 200 feet or so. Suddenly, we noticed air-to-air gunfire to port. An enemy intruder had joined us. I switched off the navigation lights immediately. The lighthouse did the same, so did the Whitley from Kinloss and the airfield. In the total darkness the three aircraft – two British and one German – flew round not knowing where the others were. I waited for the crash that I was sure would come ... Finally, as dawn broke we landed safely back at the base but no one had seen a sign of Flight Sergeant Bagnall.

'Poor old, Baggy, what a way to go – lost on circuits and bumps.' Cattle and I retired to bed having been up all night thinking we had lost a good friend.

In circuits and bumps the pupil, in effect, flies a square, four-legged circuit round the airfield and comes into land then takes off again, turns, goes round in 'legs', lands again and so on. It's easy to forget which 'leg' you're on and thus continue in a straight line. This happened to a pupil the morning after Baggy disappeared. The instructor let him carry on and waited for the pupil to realise his mistake but the pupil didn't. Eventually, after five miles or so downwind near the Spey estuary the instructor suggested it might be an idea to turn back to the airfield. The pupil, no doubt embarrassed at his lapse in concentration, did so. At that moment the instructor glanced out of the window and noticed a dinghy floating in the water with two people in it. It was Baggy and his pupil! (How lucky can you get?) The rescue people went out and the two were brought in and taken to hospital. We went to see him. 'What happened, Baggy?' was our first question.

'First take-off on the circuits and bumps the full flaps came on, the aircraft struck a hangar, damaged the propeller, knocked off the airspeed indicator, the engine caught fire and the next thing I remember was being in the sea. The aircraft sank but the dinghy floated to the surface. We scrambled in and sat there the rest of the night. We watched you searching and we waved like mad but you never saw us.'

Three weeks later he returned to circuits and bumps. (Sadly, Flight Sergeant Bagnall was later reporting missing in action while flying Stirlings on his second tour of operations.)[2]

I was a Squadron Leader on 1662 HCU Blyton near Gainsborough, Lincolnshire in October 1943. I was just twenty-three years old. One particular occasion [in all probability, the night of 7 March 1944] I was Officer-in-Charge of night flying and was about to go off duty as all the aircraft were back except one. He should be back any time, I told myself, but there was no news. I waited and waited then the telephone rang.

'RAF doctor here. There's been a mid-air collision between two aircraft about ten miles away. I think one of them is yours.'[3]

'We're expecting one back. What happened?'

'No survivors from one, I'm afraid. Not sure about the other. Would you mind going to the crash site where there were no survivors? My corporal will go with you and he'll bring the body bags.' The other RAF doctor was away on leave and it was an RAF requirement that there had to be an officer present at clearing up after such an accident.

The wreckage was still burning when I arrived at the scene. The corporal and I began our gruesome task and put bits and pieces in body bags. I saw a flying helmet on the ground not far away and picked it up. There was a head still in it and I looked into the face of a young lad I had been speaking to only four hours before.

We finished our grim task as dawn broke and returned to the airfield. Before going to bed I went over to the mess and ordered a late lunch for two o'clock. When I returned at two the mess was empty. As I was hanging up my coat the mess telephone rang. No one came to answer it and it continued to ring. It rang and rang. Suddenly I got the odd sensation that it was for me. What's more, I sensed it was the mother of the boy whose helmet and head I had found.

I forced myself to pick up the receiver. A gentle, woman's voice said, 'Is that RAF Blyton?'

'Yes,' I said.

'Who am I speaking to?'

'I had a strange feeling she knew without asking. I stalled for time. 'I'm afraid I can't say but can I help you?' She told me her name – it came as no surprise – and continued, 'My son's a bomb aimer in Squadron Leader Cole's flight. He's my only son – he's everything to me,' her voice trembled slightly, 'I'm a widow, you see.' There was a pause. 'I know this sounds silly but I woke suddenly at four o'clock this morning and I had a horrible feeling that something had happened to him – that he had been killed. I couldn't sleep after that and all morning I've been thinking about him. I just had to ring up and find out. I do hope you don't mind. I've been so worried,' she paused, 'has there been an accident?'

I couldn't tell her that I had been looking into the face of her beheaded son only a few hours ago. What does one say at a time like this? 'I believe there has,' was a much as I could say. 'I'll put you through to the adjutant. He'll be able to help you.' Thankfully I transferred the call. All the time I sensed she knew who she was speaking to – even though we had never spoken before. Four o'clock had been the exact time that the accident had happened.

I was on duty at RAF Lindholme and there were just three aircraft flying that night. It was winter with a slight mist over the hollows that would soon clear. The first aircraft took off and crashed shortly after take-off about two miles from the end of the runway. I sent the emergency vehicles – fire engines and ambulance – and notified the civilian people who sent their emergency staff and equipment. I put the other two aircraft on hold while all this was being sorted out. Very soon the telephone rang. It was the Air Commodore. I told him what had happened and that, until the emergency vehicles and staff were back on the airfield, I was holding the remaining aircraft which struck me as the most sensible and safe thing to do.

'Don't you know there's a war on? Get them airborne immediately!' came the angry reply.

'But, sir ...' I began.

'Get them airborne,' insisted the air commodore.

I was very reluctant to do this for what if they crashed too? It was unlikely but ...The next aircraft went off and it too crashed about five miles further on. Of course, there was nothing I could do about it. There were no emergency services – nothing. I told the duty clerk to tell the air commodore but I had to send off the third aircraft and this one also crashed about three miles beyond the second crash. I now had three burning aircraft – eighteen young men needlessly killed.

There was a sequel to this. About three years later I was a captain with BOAC and was flying out of Bordeaux one evening. Forest fires had been burning and smoke and mist was forming in the low-lying areas and drifting across the airfield. I told the crew to hurry up and take-off as quickly as possible before the fog came down.

We took off and at about 200 feet the first officer grabbed the controls. I looked up and was horrified to see that we were flying upside down! Above me was a perfect picture of the ground with moving vehicles, streetlights, house lights – everything. I snarled at him to check the instruments. Slowly he let go, checked the standby instruments and then mine. He relaxed slightly and sat back. The instruments were correct but we were apparently flying upside down. At 600 feet we flew clear. It was the strangest sensation I have ever experienced. My mind went back to the three aircraft that had crashed at RAF Lindholme. The meteorological conditions were almost the same. There was smoke and mist and I have often wondered how many aircraft crashes have been due to this phenomenon with the pilot ignoring his instruments and believing his visual sighting. To suddenly see the ground above you is unnerving, to say the least and to someone with relatively little experience of night flying, could prove fatal.

3

THE SERGEANT'S STORY
'A WING COMMANDER'

Every battle is an unrepeatable event and no one story can do duty for the sum of the experience of all the gunners of Bomber Command. But the story of a sergeant rear gunner – I have given him another name than his own – does at any rate show for what these men must have been ready. It happened on a night in February 1941; the gunner was in a Whitley, on its way to Bremen.

Sergeant Hunt, listening to what the crew had to say at intervals on the intercom, felt as much out of it as though he was hearing a play on the wireless. While the captain and the navigator watched the surface of the cloud for a hole in its moonlit expanse and a glimpse of something underneath, he himself was gazing backwards all the time, not looking for land or sea below him but searching the air. The cloud beneath was a level table-land at 7,000ft and above there was more cloud, cumulus cloud puffed upwards, but not enough of it to block the moonlight streaming down. So he was being taken backwards down a long, brilliantly lit passage. A perfect opportunity for fighters – a perfect night for them all round. So, after all, what the captain was saying now was very much Hunt's business. 'That exactor's still U/S,' he was saying and that meant one of the engines was groggy. They could not get above 9,000ft, as the captain was saying, and they would have to keep at that height all the way. It would make a lot of difference, Hunt said to himself, if they met any fighters. And with one engine running badly they wouldn't be able to manoeuvre well. Hunt searched the air even more intently, turning his turret from side to side; its rotation, at any rate, was smooth and easy.

One of the makers of these turrets used to make greenhouses before the war and, at the tail end of the bomber, shut up behind steel doors and so far away from the rest of the crew, Hunt sometimes felt as if he were sitting in a greenhouse at the bottom of the garden, with the rest of the family warm and comfortable inside the house. They had just about crossed the North Sea now and the captain was still trying to get above 9,000ft. The navigator was anxious about making landfall at the right place; he had seen something below the clouds and thought it might be Texel. But they were not yet over land when Hunt saw what he thought was a flare. It was a bright light, but it did not hang in the air or float gently downwards; it darted towards the bomber, like a shooting star, but more steady and with a more willed and intentional movement. Hunt waited. He braced himself, with his head against the headrest, his eyes about 6in from his gunsights. When he had first seen the light it seemed to be about half a mile away; now it was within 200yds. He was used to judging distances in the air and in the darkness. The light was getting still closer when Hunt fired. For eight or ten seconds he watched his bullets – one in ten was an incendiary and made a streak of light ahead of him – converging into the centre of the gunsight where the approaching circle of light was held. Then the light went out and in its place there was a dark fighter. Its nose was down and in a moment it had dived at a steep angle into the solid cloud below.

For a few seconds Hunt went on looking at the quickly receding patch of cloud where it had disappeared and then he spoke from his solitude along the wire that ran to the captain and the rest of the crew. They had seen nothing, neither the light nor its extinction. Hunt told them that he had seen no smoke or flame coming from the fighter. No claim. The bomber kept a level course, flying so for twenty minutes. They were over the enemy's country now and might be attacked from the ground as well as from the air. But Hunt had no time to think of this; the enemy for which he was watching was as powerful over the sea as over its own fields. There was still nothing of the ground to be seen below – or nothing, at least, on the few occasions when Hunt looked down at the clouds. The others were talking less than when they had been over the sea. There were long silences, but Hunt did not notice the change; he was too intent on his own work to think about the anxieties of the others.

He was very suddenly reminded that he was not alone. He heard the voice of the front gunner, loud and quick: 'Enemy passing overhead.' The front gunner hadn't finished speaking before a fighter was over Hunt's head, a black shadow only 20ft above. Hunt trained his guns upwards but there was just a perceptible interval before the fighter was far enough to the rear of the bomber to get into the gunsights. Hunt could see the white crosses on the wings, very clear in the moonlight, and the flames from the exhaust; though the moon was so bright, a flame close at hand was still lurid in the night. He fired as the enemy came into the sights and then lowered his guns and fired a longer burst when the fighter was farther away and, at less steep angle, could be more easily held in the sights. The combined speed of bomber and fighter took them apart before Hunt could see any more. He spoke again to the captain and learned that more of the crew, besides the front gunner, had seen the fighter. They told him that they had seen the white crosses; it was a Messerschmitt 109, of course; they could all see the square wing tips that belong to the 109. The pilot was talking about three reddish-orange lights ahead that stayed there for some time, drifting very slowly downwards. A signal, it was thought, and meant to show the bomber's course to the waiting defenders. The German observer corps was working.

For twenty minutes more Hunt was rushed backwards down the same moonlit corridor between clouds. They were getting near Germany itself when the captain spoke: 'Fighter attacking from the starboard beam.' The captain swung the bomber round so that Hunt could face the enemy. It was a quicker turn than Hunt had expected with one engine running badly, but it took long enough for the enemy to be able to rake the starboard side of the bomber before his target turned edgeways. 'This joker's got in first,' Hunt said to himself, but he couldn't tell what damage had been done behind his back. He turned his guns to starboard and waited for the fighter to come round the edge of the turret window and into the gunsights. His first burst was a long one, but the enemy went on firing. The tracer bullets – or were they, as Hunt wondered, cannon shells – were a vivid red.

They seemed to be coming from three guns, but everything was happening so quickly and the enemy was banking so fast that it was impossible to be sure. The fighter was banking to attack the bomber again from the beam; the red streams of light were coming at Hunt from the side again. The fighter was round now and just about to pass below the turret. Hunt fired again. The fighter went so close below the bomber that it must, as Hunt said to himself when he had time to think, have carried away the bomber's trailing aerial. It was still banking and now it was round to the port side of the bomber. In the second Hunt had lost sight of it, it had gone round the edge of the turret window and behind him as the last carriage of a faster train vanishes from the window of your carriage when you are sitting with your back to the engine. But the front gunner saw it again as it got ahead of the bomber. He had a glimpse of smoke and flame in front of him and then for five or six seconds there was a brighter, warmer glow on the cold white of the moonlit clouds underneath. The front gunner was excited; he was telling Hunt and everyone else about the smoke and flames. But Hunt found that he himself was merely annoyed; he didn't seem to feel any satisfaction at all.

Forty minutes more to the target, so the navigator was saying. It seemed that the second pilot had taken over the controls for a while; Hunt heard him say that the controls were very sluggish and the rest of them were discussing the damage that had probably been done to the bomber. But as the minutes passed and nothing happened it was a welcome rest for Hunt; five minutes, ten minutes and as his searching eyes found no more fighters and no sudden warning came down the intercom, he felt much easier.

They were running into Bremen now, or where the navigator thought Bremen must be and the navigator was usually right. One moment the moonlit path behind the bomber, in front of Hunt, was empty as before and the next moment, as Hunt methodically turned his head, there were three lights in front of him, dead astern of the bomber. He had the impression that they had been there all night, waiting for him, and their immobility now added to that impression. But then the lights, three searchlights in the noses of three fighters, began to go on and off. They were not swivelling to and fro, they were just being flicked on and off, like a sky sign that tries to attract your attention by movement as well as by light. The lights were certainly closer now, but as they were approaching the bomber from dead astern there was no impression of speed. Hunt thought very quickly. He would fire at the centre of the three and then perhaps a lucky bullet or two would spray out and hit the two on either side. He hardly knew who fired first, himself or the enemy, but the middle fighter was not firing. The red tracer was coming at him from either side. His own guns, he found, would not stop firing; two of them were definitely running away. It was rather odd, he found himself thinking, that this should happen then; it may happen when there has not been much firing beforehand, but it was not like that now. He didn't bother; he let them run on. The turret was getting filled with fumes from the guns; the smell of a rifle range is not unpleasant, but there can be too much of it in too small a space. Hunt was coughing and spluttering.

It seemed a long time while the guns ran on, but before they stopped the middle fighter was on fire. Impatiently, with a conviction that he would succeed at once, Hunt fired briefly to right and left at the other two fighters and they drove away into the night. The burning fighter had gone down below the turret and out of sight. Hunt was coughing so much and his heart was beating so fast with excitement that he could scarcely breathe. But he felt an immeasurable relief, a profound sense of gratitude, as he saw the helpless, undirected flaming object cut from his sight by the bottom edge of the window.

They met no more fighters on the way back from Bremen and for that Hunt was also grateful.

4

A TRIP OVER GERMANY

PILOT OFFICER ANDREW A. LAW

On 17–18 April 1941, 118 aircraft – fifty Wellingtons, thirty-nine Hampdens, twenty-eight Whitleys and a Stirling – were detailed to attack Berlin from two aiming points but haze prevented a concentrated bombing. Eight aircraft – five Whitleys, two Hampdens and a Wellington – failed to return. One of the aircraft that went missing on the return was Whitley V T4266 GE-O on 58 Squadron flown by Pilot Officer Andrew A. Law, who took off from Linton-on-Ouse at 20.41. Flak over Hamburg wrecked the port engine. At 03.50 the starboard motor seized and caught fire, followed ten minutes later by a ditching in the North Sea. Late in the evening of 20 April, a Hudson sighted the crew in their dinghy and a second Hudson later dropped Lindholme rescue gear in their vicinity. At 22.30 that same evening, one very exhausted bomber crew was rescued by an air-sea rescue (ASR) launch, sixty-four hours after coming down in the sea. Andrew Law suffered frostbite and was in hospital in Bristol, but returned to service soon afterwards. The rest of the crew consisted of Sergeant Alan Whewell; Pilot Officer McNeil; Sergeant Rose and Sergeant Charles Oliver Steggall.[1]

We set off from our aerodrome as it was approaching nightfall having been briefed to bomb Berlin. The trip over was uneventful. When we arrived over the target we ascertained that the target's appearance tallied with that which we had been given and then we came down lower to drop our stick of bombs. Big flares were seen to appear after we had made a circuit back over the target. That night we had also been briefed to take photographs of the damage caused. We therefore passed over the target once again to take a photograph. You have two photograph plates of which to use. All this time we were practically held constant with the searchlights and anti-aircraft fire or flak as it is known there. The barrage put up was terrific. We sustained one or two hits with shrapnel but nothing really serious. To escape this fire, we dived down low till the angle was so small that the guns and searchlights could not keep holding us in their range. I took a vote among the crew as to whether we should go back and take the other photograph plate left, but the crew decided it would not be advisable in the face of things.

On our return journey one of our engines begins to splutter and in my instruments, I could see that it was all up with that engine, it finally went on fire so I pressed the button for the fire extinguisher and switched off the petrol flow to that engine and the flames went out. We were still over Germany and now only had one engine to see us through. If a plane is flying on one engine the best height to fly at is about five thousand feet and I was nearly twice that height but height was, in the circumstances most precious to us, so I only lost height very gradually. The rudder of the plane had to be held very tightly at its extreme turning point to counterbalance the engine which was not in use. This was no easy job as it kept jumping back and forward. I asked the co-pilot to take some of the oxygen piping and tie it round the control levers of the rudder at the rear end of the plane. This was done but it still kept jumping back and forward and I could hardly hold it with my foot. I knew I would have to hold it like that for three or four hours.

We finally reached the coast line amidst sighs of relief from the crew, we were not out of the woods yet we had still the stretch of sea to cover. Heligoland was on our course borne and I hoped that their searchlights and flak would let us know when we were approaching it. By the time this happened we were getting fairly close to it and we had to take avoiding action very slowly owing to the one engine. We managed to keep well away from it and now with the very best of luck we had only to worry about the actual flying home. After a while the instruments showed that the remaining engine was about to seize up. The glycol cooling system gauge showed that the temperature was instead of 62°, 90°. The engine should last about five minutes flying. I thought I would give it a rest to let it cool down and try the other to see if it might go. While I was doing this I instructed the wireless operator to send out an SOS and give our position from time to time. He got in touch with the base and kept in touch. I switched on the other engine and it went for a few minutes, but finally stopped altogether. It was very disconcerting to see the propeller standing quite still when we were still in mid-air. I then went on to the other engine again, but it gave out also and I kept the plane skimming along the water gradually losing height. The wireless operator was instructed to say 'we were about to land and to give our position'. I had not time to press the extinguisher button to put the fire out on this engine because I was concentrating on the crash landing on the sea. I asked the co-pilot to strap me into my seat so that on impact with the sea I would not be thrown against the instrument panel.

The crew had been instructed to make ready the dinghy, wireless and provisions, Very light, pistol, etc. and to hack away the hatch door. This they did. When we hit the water, (I could not see till we were nearly on it because the light in the nose of plane could not show it up to me till fairly close), the tail hit the water first and tipped the nose up but the landing turned out perfect. Usually the glass at the nose of a plane should be smashed but it did not in this case and we were still perfectly dry. But the plane was becoming a raging inferno and the crew had thrown out the dinghy into the water. They were all out of the plane in a matter of seconds. Me and the wireless operator were still left, both being at the very front of the plane. I was tied in and was frantically trying to undo the straps. This took a matter of seconds, but even in that time the wireless operator was up and through the hatch (we were in such a hurry). He had jumped into the water and I went out with flames just at my back, in time to see him in the water. He apparently could not swim so I jumped in and caught him in the water by the scruff of the neck and made for the tail of the plane and hung on supporting us both. We had not had time to take the portable wireless, or provisions or anything else save two distress signals. The dinghy was hovering around near the tail and they picked us up. The crew behaved magnificently, there was no panic whatever. I said the sooner we put water between us and the plane the better because it would blow up because of the large petrol tanks.

We got away just in time, because it blew up and sank. At this point I take the opportunity to mention that when we knew we were going to have to come down in the sea, we got rid of everything we could to lighten the plane. Every few minutes the rear gunner would say over the intercom, 'Sir will I throw away the flares, the machine guns, etc, etc,' and I would answer, 'Yes'. 'Yes'. 'Yes'. This happened a few times. When I think of it now it was really very funny.

On the first day a plane like our own was flying straight for us but just as it was approaching it altered course. We took a vote among the crew as to whether we should use our second and last distress signal (we had fired off our first when the first plane passed near) when a Hudson of the Coastal Command came near, he was not as near as the first one had been, but to our amazement he saw us and circled round. This was on the third day. By this time we were pretty well exhausted. The dinghy was the wrong way up and the pockets at the sides which when the right way up filled with water, which stabilized the dinghy, were of no use as they were the wrong way up, so I cut them off and put them on top of the oar, which I stood up and held and waved. The rest of the crew lay on the bottom of the dinghy, so that the yellow sides would be shown. This must have helped him to see us. The pilot of this plane must have known just what to do. He dropped a bag with food, brandy and cigarettes about twenty yards from us, not in a zipped up bag as provided, but a bag sewn up at the opening with wool and razor blade fixed between two sheets of cardboard with 'Please find blade for opening bag.' Why a zip was not used was because in emersion in water the cloth behind shrinks and the zip will not open or close, as the case may be. Then as darkness came down this pilot dropped three flares which floated on the water, we kept in the middle the whole time. As soon as one went out or rather began to flicker he swooped down and dropped another at the same point. He signalled to us that he had wirelessed his base to send word for a plane to drop us another dinghy and also for a Naval Launch to come and pick us up.

A heavy bomber soon arrived and dropped the dinghy, which landed in the water only about twenty yards away from us. We paddled over to it and dragged ourselves into it. This dinghy was a much larger one and had buoys attached to it to keep it stationary and then not long afterwards the Naval cutter picked us up. We had lit matches to let them see exactly our position. They had to drag us up on board as we were powerless. On the way towards the shore the cutter had to go slow in case there were any floating mines, otherwise we would have been there in next to no time. It was about 08.00 when we moored alongside the pier. And so after three days and two nights in an open dinghy with no water, food, etc., we were rescued safe and comparatively sound to tell the tale.

Earlier on in the story I omitted to mention the fact that we entered a mine field to be in the direct shipping route in the hope of being picked up. One of the mines blew up and as we were about fifty yards away from it we still cannot understand what caused it to blow up. The whole time we were in the dinghy we were pitched up and down by the heavy seas. We used our gloves and pilots' helmets to bail out the water.

On the night of 6–7 August Andrew Law's crew survived a serious crash at Linton-on-Ouse when Whitley V Z6835 GE-Q overshot on return to base from the raid on Frankfurt at 05.57 and crashed into a hangar. No serious injuries were reported. On 3–4 September 1941 Law took off in Whitley V Z6869 GE-T from Linton at 19.21 for the raid on Brest but all aircraft of 1, 4 and 5 Groups were recalled at 20.30, probably because of worsening weather at bases[2] and he was ordered to divert to Acklington, where he hit trees landing in fog at Turnbull Farm, East Chevington, Morpeth. The Whitley burst into flames. Law was killed and Sergeant Wallace Howard Trewin RCAF; American Sergeant Robert Lawrence 'Larry' Ward RCAF and Sergeant Charles Oliver Steggall also died. Only Pilot Officer Edward Dmitri Comber-Higgs, the tail gunner, survived but he was lost with Sergeant Alan Whewell, who had been given his own crew, on 30 November when Whitley V Z6506 GE-V failed to return from a raid on Hamburg. All five crew were lost without trace.[3]

5

Twelve Lancasters Went for Augsburg

Squadron Leader J.D. Nettleton

In April 1942 Squadron Leader John Dering Nettleton, the South African CO of 44 Squadron, who had already completed two tours, was chosen to lead a special operation. Born in Nongoma, Natal, in South Africa on 28 June 1917, Nettleton went into the Merchant Marine for eighteen months after he left school in the 1930s and then decided that he wanted to be a civil engineer. During his engineering apprenticeship he worked in various parts of South Africa for three years and joined the Royal Naval Volunteer Reserve (RNVR). He was described as a tough 'Botha Boy' and served as a naval cadet on the same sail training ship, *General Botha*, as his fellow South African and future Spitfire ace 'Sailor' Malan.

Nettleton was commissioned into the RAF in 1938. Nettleton and Squadron Leader John Sherwood DFC★, the 97 Squadron CO, and selected officers were briefed that the objective on 17 April 1942 was the diesel engine manufacturing workshop at the Maschinenfabrik Augsburg-Nurnberg Aktiengesellschaft (MAN) factory at Augsburg. No one believed that the RAF would be so stupid as to send twelve of its newest four-engined Lancaster bombers all that distance inside Germany in daylight, but that is exactly what 5 Group did. The raid that followed was suicidal in the extreme; losses were high and damage to the factory was minimal but the official line in the following communiqué was that 'No life was lost in vain'.

Only to fly through cloud, through storm, through Night. Unerring and to keep their purpose bright, Nor turn until, their dreadful duty done, Westward they climb to race the awakened sun. (**Anon**)

✧ ✧ ✧

You'll want to hear something about the daylight raid on Augsburg that they gave me this VC for. The whole idea of the raid was surprise. That was why we simply flew straight at our objective, at under a hundred feet from the ground. In the case of the six Lancasters from the other squadron, surprise was completely achieved. Not one of them was attacked by fighters either on the way out or on the way back, though two were shot down over the target. But, very likely by sheer bad luck, the six Lancasters which I was leading ran into a patrol of 30 or so Jerry fighters six minutes after we had crossed the French coast. And it was then that four out of the six of us were shot down. I believe that we owe our survival to the fact that I took my aircraft down to no more than 25 feet above ground and my remaining companion followed me.

I wonder if you can imagine what it means for two of these huge four-engined machines to travel across Europe at that height? Of course we had to go up over every line of trees, to follow the contours of the ground, lifting over the hills, coming down in the valleys. Believe me, it's quite a strain to pilot a 30-ton Lancaster, fully loaded, hour after hour, doing that. But I think it was that that saved us. The fighters were going for us from directly behind. I had just seen the painful sight of the aircraft a few feet away to my left crash in flames. We flew with our wing tips almost touching for mutual protection. We saw the red roofs and white houses of a typical French village loom up in front of us. I couldn't see it from my position in the pilot's seat; but my bomb aimer, in the nose of the machine, told me that he could see the barrage of cannon shells from the German fighters, which had missed us, crashing into the roofs of the houses. The French village seemed to him to be going up in flames. Just think what it must have been like for its inhabitants, as the two vast black bombers, their twelve rear machine-guns firing all out, with a horde of fighters after them, spitting cannon shells, swept over them at rooftop height.

I couldn't help thinking it was a bit of a lesson as to what happens to countries which get knocked out and have the war fought all over them.

Well, as you know, eight out of the twelve of us got to the target and though three were shot down by the ground fire over it, all eight of us bombed it from rooftop height. I know that I for one had to pull up to clear the roof of that main assembly shed where they made the submarine engines.

There I saw the last of my six companions go down; his Lancaster was hit as he ran up, but though it was blazing he went straight on and planted his bombs on the sheds. The photographs taken since show that no submarine engines will come out of those sheds for a very long time. Thank goodness, I saw him make a perfect forced landing in a field and firmly believe that he and his crew are prisoners of war.

We suffered heavy losses and I lost good friends in that raid. But we got the target. And that is the main thing. I try not to think about my friends, but about the sailors who will be saved from the torpedoes of those submarines and the men, women and children who will eat the food that the ships which would have been sunk, but for our bombs, will now bring safely to them. I know that this is what my friends who went down would like us to think of.

The raid involved thirty-seven aircrew, of which twelve became PoWs and thirty-six returned. Nettleton, who landed his badly damaged Lancaster at Squires Gate, Blackpool, ten hours after leaving Waddington, was awarded the VC. On the night of 12–13 July 1943, on the raid on Turin, thirteen Lancasters, including 'Z-for Zebra' flown by Squadron Leader John Dering Nettleton VC, were lost. After a brief spell instructing with 1661 HCU and being promoted to Wing Commander, the South African had returned to command 44 Squadron at Dunholme Lodge in January 1943. Nettleton's Lancaster was shot down by a German night fighter over the English Channel on his return. All seven of the crew were lost without trace; their names added to those on the Runnymede Memorial.

6

'MILLENNIUM' – THE FIRST 1,000-BOMBER RAID

VICTOR ARTHUR MARTIN

Sir Arthur Harris had for some time nurtured the desire to send 1,000 bombers to a German city and reproduce the same results as those achieved at Rostock on 28–29 March 1942. The raids there had achieved total disruption. Whole areas of the city had been wiped out and 100,000 people had been forced to evacuate. The capacity of its workers to produce war materials had, therefore, been severely diminished. Harris wrote that, 'on the night of 28–29 March the first German city went up in flames'. His first choice for this new attack was Hamburg but he needed political support from Churchill. And so on the evening of Sunday 17 May Harris drove to Chequers to discuss his 1,000-bomber plan with the prime minister. The C-in-C outlined the plan, emphasising that the losses should not be greater than 5 per cent because the raid would be concentrated into ninety minutes and would, therefore, saturate the defences. Churchill listened intently and was enthusiastic. When Harris finally left at 03.00 he had Churchill's blessing and his statement that he was prepared for a loss of 100 aircraft, or 10 per cent. Driving back to his headquarters in his Bentley, Harris found himself humming *Malbrough s'en-va-t-en-guerre*, which always came into his head whenever he had just left the prime minister. The spirit of Marlborough going to war seemed appropriate.

On 20 May Harris wrote letters to his each of his five operational bomber groups, the two bomber training groups and to Coastal, Fighter and Army Co-Operation Commands, explaining the details for the 'Thousand Plan'. Sir Philip Joubert de la Ferté, C-in-C Coastal Command, offered Harris 250 aircraft, which on paper gave Harris 1,081 aircraft. However, before the transfer to east coast bases could go ahead the Admiralty, which controlled Coastal Command operationally, refused to allow them to take part in the raid. To help make up the disparity, 91 OTU Group was combed for training crews with at least an instructor pilot but forty-nine out of the 208 aircraft would have to take off with pupil pilots. On 25 May warning orders were issued for moving about 100 aircraft to southern and eastern England from their more distant training stations. These included the Isle of Man and 20 OTU at Lossiemouth in Scotland, where fourteen Wellington Ics were to fly more than 400 miles south to Stanton Harcourt, a satellite of Abingdon. At Harwell there were twenty worn-out Wellingtons and ten more at the 15 OTU satellite airfield at Hampstead Norris. All the crews were called to the briefing room and told 'there was something big on requiring a maximum effort'. The flight commander devised a scheme with playing cards to allocate aircraft and to create crews. When the final orders were ready on 26 May with the full moon approaching, Harris had only 940 aircraft. Even this figure was an optimistic one.

The next day Harris went down to the underground operations room at High Wycombe soon after 09.00 for his daily planning conference, which he liked to call 'morning prayers', with his deputy Commander-in-Chief Sir Robert Saundby and his air staff officers. Hamburg, the C-in-C's first choice of target, received a stay of execution as the weather over north-west Germany was especially unfavourable for three days running. On Saturday, 30 May, Harris decided to send the force to his second target choice, Cologne, where the cloud was expected to clear by midnight. The aircraft total rose to 980 and then to 1,000. He gave the order 'Operation Plan Cologne' to his group commanders just after midday so that 1,000 bombers would be unleashed on the 770,000 inhabitants.

On paper, the actual number of serviceable aircraft totalled 1,047 bombers – mostly Wellingtons (602) – almost 300 of which were clapped-out OTU aircraft. Forty-five Hampdens of 92 (OTU) Group were also detailed and even Whitleys had to be used. No Whitley squadrons were left in Bomber Command, partly because the last three had been transferred to Coastal Command. But twenty-one of these obsolete aircraft were found from 10 OTU at Abingdon and seven more at Driffield from the target-towing and gunnery flight and 1405 Blind Approach Training Flight. The raid would also include the first Lancaster operations of 106 Squadron at Coningsby, which was commanded by 24-year-old Wing Commander Guy Gibson DFC★, a leader who had already shown exceptional capabilities. All told, 5 Group detailed seventy-three Lancasters, forty-six Manchesters and thirty-four Hampdens for the operation.

Sergeant Victor Arthur Martin was the flight engineer on the Halifax crew on 1652 Conversion Unit at Marston Moor skippered by Flight Sergeant H.F. Spratt RCAF. He was the only Englishman on the otherwise all-Canadian crew:

Raid details are not yet known but aircraft reliability must be checked and routine armament testing carried out, all essential for a successful operation. Flying across the North Sea aircraft checks are carried out and over the water the gunners can concentrate on the efficiency of the guns by firing into the sea. All is well and return to base for refuelling and 'bombing up' with up to six tons high explosive or with a mixture of incendiaries.

Briefing is over and we are now aware of the target and the reason for the raid. On [30–31 May 1942] the industrial centre of Cologne is to be annihilated. Over 1,000 bombers will concentrate the attack from West to East with the aiming point of Neumarkt in the centre of the old town with all bombing to be completed in just ninety minutes. The first wave fully loaded with incendiaries and the final wave of four engined heavy bombers completing the raid with high explosives and incendiaries in the last assault of fifteen minutes.

As time for take-off approaches we are ferried to the aircraft. Engines running and all checks carried out we taxi to runway to await take-off signal, the green light flashes and with throttles opened to full power and boost the aircraft gather speed down the runway, a slight bounce and we are airborne. The lights of the flare path disappear below into the darkness and the raid begins as we trim for climb and set course.

In the dim glow of the cockpit all is well and with everyone in his place silence reigns until the navigator's voice comes over the intercom with words 'enemy coast ahead'. Shortly after crossing the coast we encounter the defensive line of searchlights and anti aircraft guns set up to protect entry into Germany.

The searchlights sweep the night sky and should an aircraft be caught the master searchlight immediately focuses on to it, then all others follow suit. The guns begin what is called a box, they fire above, below ahead and astern and gradually reduce the box until the aircraft is hit or can take violent evasive moves to extricate itself.

Silence reigned until the navigator's voice came over the intercom with the words 'enemy coast ahead'. Shortly after crossing the coast we encountered the defensive line of searchlights and anti-aircraft guns set up to protect entry into Germany. The searchlights swept the night sky and should an aircraft be caught, the master searchlight immediately focused onto it, then all others would follow suit. The guns began what was called a box; they fired above, below ahead and astern and gradually reduced the box until the aircraft was hit or could take violent evasive moves to extricate itself. Silence once again as we entered enemy territory with its defences now on alert following earlier waves, broken only by the gunners as they quietly checked with each other regarding the sighting of a night-fighter; we did not attack to give away our position but observed in case of a sudden turn for hostile action. The first wave had now attacked and in the distance a red glow was already visible in the sky. Above the fleecy lining of the clouds hiding the enemy below all seemed so peaceful; another aircraft appeared ahead and travelling at the same speed we were motionless. Suddenly the heavy anti-aircraft guns opened fire and the exploding shells shattered our world of peace. The aircraft ahead received a direct hit and with a blue flash was gone. Taking the immediate evasive action of undulating and banks to port and starboard, we continued our course.

Closing in on the target at Cologne, the intensity of the fire became more apparent to Victor Martin:

It was not the usual cluster of separate burnings; it appeared that the complete area below was ablaze in one large fire. A feeling of sorrow came but with a ferocious burst of anti-aircraft fire bouncing the aircraft about with explosions, concentration on the purpose of the mission became uppermost. With the most dangerous part now commencing, a level and steady course had to be maintained for accurate aiming, the navigator lying down over the bombsight giving instructions for lining up the target – 'left, left, steady, right, steady, bombs away'. As all bombs were released at once, the aircraft, relieved of its heavy load, rose like a lift and with so many bombers above this could cause a serious problem unless quickly controlled …

Course was set for home and the running of the gauntlet of ack-ack, searchlights and night-fighters once again. Dropping down to an altitude below the range of the heavy guns and above light fire, we were suddenly in a ring of searchlights giving a most eerie feeling, a ghostly light filling the darkness of the cockpit. The tracer shells from the guns seemed to be still as you looked at them, coming up and then flashing past the windscreen. A bank to starboard gave the gunners a better view to return fire; the aircraft filled with the sinister sound of machine guns firing at a rate of several thousand rounds a minute. Searchlights were hit and the tracer shells coming up, like water from a hose pipe moving around to cover an area, also ceased.

Dawn was breaking as we cross the coast and the number of aircraft in the sky is awe inspiring. Back at base it was discovered the navigator had cuts on each side of his neck, probably caused by shrapnel during the steady bombing run in course. If so a slight waver could have proved fatal. The raid was considered an outstanding success and smoke clouds at 15,000 feet delayed photographs being taken for several days. Some 915 tons of incendiaries and 540 tons of high explosives were dropped in ninety minutes causing awful devastation.[1] After de-briefing we were told: 'Have something to eat and get a rest; you are on again tonight'.

The second 1,000 plane raid, on Essen, on 1–2 June, proved to be one of those rare occasions where outside the usual and expected attacks by anti-aircraft guns etc everything went quite smoothly, tracer fire between night fighters and gunners seen in the distance. Briefing that day had the information that the target was Essen and Krupp works. Weather over target was quite clear and a direct hit on the works clearly visible.

Although the third 1,000-bomber raid was not as successful as the first to Cologne, large parts of Bremen, especially in the south and east districts, were destroyed. No.5 Group destroyed an assembly shop at the Focke-Wulf factory when a 4,000lb 'Cookie' scored a direct hit. Six other buildings were seriously damaged. The German high command was shaken but fifty-two bombers were claimed destroyed by the flak and night fighter defences for the loss of just two Bf 110s and four NCO crewmembers killed or missing. A total of 1,123 sorties (including 102 Hudsons and Wellingtons from Coastal Command) had been dispatched and fifty Bomber Command aircraft and four from Coastal Command were lost. This time the heaviest casualties were suffered by the OTUs of 91 Group, which lost twenty-three of the 198 Whitleys and Wellingtons provided by that group. All but one was manned by pupil crews.

'The day before the third 1,000 bomber raid, on Bremen on 25–26 June 1942,' continues Victor Martin:

'N-Nuts', our usual aircraft, suffered severe damage and was 'written off' and the only other plane available was an old one [Halifax IIV9993 GV-U] that had seen much service and better days. Briefing over and all preparations made, at approximately 2300 hours we were once again roaring down the runway on our way to Germany and the city of Bremen.[2]

Warning from navigator that the 'enemy coast ahead' coincided with one of the old engines deciding to give up the ghost. This was serious because on a 1,000 plane raid with all planes in and out in ninety minutes, timing was strictly essential with a wave given a ten minutes time range in which to arrive, bomb and leave, otherwise chaos would occur with the possibility of collisions. Shortly afterwards a second engine died, throwing behind our specified time and a secondary target has to be considered. Suddenly the sky was filled with cannon fire, exploding shells and tracers creating lines of light as they tore through and past the aircraft. Shells ricocheting off the steel door protecting the cockpit gave little lights as they were passing the small gap on the hinge side of the door. Without full power for evasive action the aircraft was immobilised within minutes and left no other alternative but to abandon. With the forward crew gone I dropped through the escape hatch and hurtled down through the darkness of the night into the pitch blackness of the unknown and enemy territory. Delaying pulling the rip cord to avoid any involvement in the action above I dropped several thousand feet. On opening the straps of the parachute, being a chest clip on type, it gave me a sharp blow to the head, but fortunately as I was still wearing a helmet this was considerably softened.[3]

Although well below the activity above the noise of the fighters seemed extremely near. Floating down a fighter circled as if checking my location. Strangely though my thoughts at this moment were not the usual associated with a dangerous situation but about missing a mess do arranged for that evening. Landing in a ditch without injury I was hiding my parachute when I heard the sound like a guard moving and shifting his gun. Quietly standing up the first thing I saw was a notice board with the word 'Verboten', apparently I was in some type of official establishment.

Crawling along the ditch for what seemed an interminable age I eventually felt safe and quickly made haste until finding cover under trees I sat down to consider the uncertainty of the situation and so lit a cigarette to help gather my thoughts. With dawn breaking, I took two buttons from my battle dress to make a compass and set course.

Eventually, well into Holland, I was captured while resting in a wheat field, surrounded by six men, each pointing a revolver at my head and saying stay still. So several weeks after being shot down, I found myself in August interned in Stalag Luft III. During the intervening weeks I was first taken to what appeared to be some type of official building for interrogation and then under heavy armed guard to a prison in Amsterdam. There in a small cell without daylight interrogation continued on a daily routine for several days. Then without warning I was taken under guard by train to Dulag Luft for further questioning and more solitary confinement and once again suddenly removed; to Luft III, to start life as a prisoner of war. A life that was to become strictly routine with its daily roll-call and counting and being locked into the hut at dusk, shutters closed on the windows and dogs let loose to roam the compound. The camp was built in a clearing among pine trees and surrounded by two high wire fences about six feet apart and containing barbed wire. Sentry boxes were situated about every 100 yards and being approximately twenty feet high could survey the perimeter clearly which was lit by boundary lights every forty yards. Each sentry box contained a machine gun and a searchlight. A wooden rail about two feet high was set in the camp about thirty feet from the main wire and the guards were under instruction to shoot at anyone who touched it.

The only relief from the monotony was to concentrate on escape methods. The camp was specially built for RAF PoWs and purposely sited on sandy ground to discourage and hopefully prevent escape by tunnel. The great escape however is very well known and illustrates the determination of those involved.

The huts were built on stilts to enable inspection by the 'goons' as the security guards were called for any evidence of escape. Several weeks later the Germans decided to reopen a camp called Stalag Luft to which, being smaller and situated near to the Baltic coast and seemly to offer greater opportunities, I volunteered to go and was transferred. Discovering that the stove in my room moved we found the opening of a previous attempt and so started the first of our tunnels. Working quickly we soon neared the distance to the wire fence when misfortune, as so often happens occurred and the roof collapsed leading to its discovery one night. Being called to check, when looking through a slit in the window shutter the guards threw sand into my eyes which took much washing to clear. After one occasion when I was overcome with fumes from the grease lamps I had to be dragged out by the feet; our tunnels were small, just enough to crawl into without ventilation normally. Other attempts followed and I was sent to Stalag Luft VI on the extremity of East Prussia near to the Russian border [situated at Heydekrug, near Tilsit, now in Russia].'

7

'THE STORY OF THE WATCH'
FLIGHT LIEUTENANT GEOFFREY HALL 'POP' PORTER

On 25–26 July 1942 my crew and I on Halifax II W1211 NP-J on 158 Squadron had been briefed to bomb a target at Duisburg, in the Ruhr. All went well until we had crossed the Dutch-German border at 18,000 feet, when Sergeant B. O. Collins my mid-upper gunner started firing his guns without warning. A few minutes later my front-gunner called up on the intercom that a night fighter was coming in from the starboard quarter. I immediately started a diving turn to starboard and at the same time felt the full wrath of the enemy's guns, which set fire to both starboard engines and killed my mid-upper gunner. My navigator went back to help, but it was useless because of the amount of damage. However, he informed me that my mid-upper gunner was dead. Sergeant C. Gissing my flight engineer was working on putting out the fires on the two starboard engines. I then feathered the props and re-trimming the aircraft, decided that we had better jettison the eight 1,000lb bombs (live, as we were now over Germany) and try to turn the aircraft to port. My navigator had given me a course to steer for England and we set course and tried to maintain height. Unfortunately, the bomb doors refused to close and we rapidly lost height. I informed my crew to prepare to bail out, but to await orders. When the aircraft was down to 3,000 feet the order was given to jump. At 1,000 feet I decided that it was time for me to go and

I left the controls to go forward to the escape hatch. As I got out, I somehow got caught up and was hanging out upside down. I spent a few terrifying moments hanging there, not knowing what to do. My first thoughts were, 'Well, that's it – I've had a good life – and that's it, God help me!' I then gave myself a good shake and suddenly I was free. I remember crashing through some trees and then everything went blank until I came to, hanging up in a tree six foot from the ground. I could see in the light from the fires of my burning aircraft that some people were shouting and milling around some distance away. After gathering my wits, I released my parachute harness and climbed down to the ground. I then made my way out of the wood, across a field and lay down in a small copse. As daylight was starting to break, I stayed there until nightfall.

I checked through my escape rations and escape money and when nightfall came, I decided to walk towards a hut I had seen, to look for water. This hut was empty so I proceeded on and eventually came to a farmyard, which I entered. But, as I was feeling my way into the barn, I felt a heavy hand on my shoulder and a man saying 'Politzei! Politzei! Kom mit!' I said 'Water, please!' He then called to his wife, who brought me a mug of water. He then took me along a lane towards a bungalow, where a man came towards me saying, in perfect English, 'Are you all right, old boy? I'll get you some milk, but I'm sorry I can't help you more – this man's a policeman and you will have to wait for the Burgomeister who will take you to the police station at Oplau.'

The Burgomeister eventually arrived and took me to the police station. I was greeted there by my bomb aimer, who had been captured earlier. I also met a young man, about twelve to fourteen, who was the Dutch policeman's son. He told me his name was John Freriks and he spoke English. I told him that I had some valuables and he said that the Germans would take them. 'They'll certainly take your watch and fountain pen and any cigarette lighter that you might have.' He then said that he would be happy to look after them for me until after the war was over. So I handed him a piece of paper on which I had written my name and the address of my parents. Now my parents' address (when I was shot down) was 'Dorchester', Dorset Avenue, Chelmsford, Essex.

About five minutes after getting to the police station, two fairly senior German Polizei turned up and took us to Eindhoven (previously a Dutch airfield now being used by the Germans). I was put into a single cell and left there for about an hour. The door suddenly opened and a German officer came in, said he was the Commanding Officer and asked me if there was anything that I needed. I said that I could do with a cigarette and he said 'That's all right. I'll get some for you and tell the guard outside that you can smoke while you are here.' He then told me in quite good English that he had been educated at Cambridge University! He said he was the station commander of a four engined aircraft unit. However, he said that the aircraft were quite different in configuration to the one I flew, as the engines were installed two-in-line on each side of the pilot. [The aircraft he was probably referring to was the Heinkel He 177A-0 Greif heavy bomber, powered by two Daimler Benz DB606 engines which were each made up from two DB601s, each pair driving a single propeller.]

He then said that he would have to go because he was going to bomb England that night. I told him that I hoped he didn't make it back and if he didn't, that he would be treated the same way that I'd been treated so far. (Take that any way you want to).

Soon after that a car arrived and took us off to another police station in Holland. I was given some eel soup to eat. I looked at it and said 'My God! This looks horrible!' and refused to eat it. They told me that this was some of the best food that you could get in Holland and considered to be quite a delicacy. However, I couldn't eat it and they took it away. We were then driven to the local railway station and put on a train. Don Hall and I were being escorted into a carriage full of German troops when a German officer came up to us and said, 'You are prisoners of war! You are British Officers and should not be transported along with other ranks, but should be put into a First Class carriage!' They then took us to another carriage, turned out the people that were in it and sat us down. After a few minutes, the man who had been sitting in the seat I was now occupying came back and shouted at the top of his voice, 'Wo Ist Meiner Schnitzel!' I gathered that he was looking for a meat sandwich that I had been sitting on and had actually started to eat. I had taken a mouthful just when he started complaining. Luckily, he was hustled out by the German officer, so I was able to finish it off without further trouble.

After we arrived in Amsterdam we were taken to the jail and I was put into a single cell until the next day, when a German 'Red Cross Official' came into my cell and wanted to know a few particulars. Per standard procedure and not really knowing if he was genuine, I gave him only my name, rank and serial number. He then asked me if there was anything that I needed and when I told him I could do with a shave he said that he would see what he could do. After about half an hour he turned up again and said, 'Kom mit!' I went with him to another cell and as they opened the door, there was poor old Linklater (my wireless operator) looking as white as a sheet. He turned to me and said, 'Christ, Skipper! I thought they were going to shoot me!' It turned out that he had travelled with a boy on bicycles all the way to the coast. The boy went on but Linklater had been caught by the police and taken to a place where he had been interrogated and threatened with his life. He said that they had eventually calmed down and he was then taken off to Dulag Luft with me and Don Hall. This was the main aircrew interrogation centre. We were again put into cells on our own and eventually given some soup and black bread.

I was in this cell for about three or four days. First of all they stripped me completely and then they threw in some old bits of a Russian uniform to put on. Soon after that a German interrogation officer came into the room to start a full interrogation. Just before he came in I had started to dismantle the heating system. It was mid-summer and they had the heat turned on! I'd got about half a dozen nuts and bolts in my hand when he came in but, fortunately, I was standing in front of the heater with my back to the door and he didn't notice anything. When he told me to sit down I was able to slip the loose nuts and bolts beneath me. I wouldn't answer his questions the way he thought I should and he became very livid and although he never actually touched me, it was quite apparent that he would have liked to knock me about a bit. However, he eventually calmed down and left me on my own once more.

I was then taken into the main area, where I met up with my two crew members once more. We were only in this area for a couple of hours before we were marched off to the station, put on a train and taken to Sagan. This was Stalag Luft III, the main German camp for air force officer PoWs. As I entered the camp I was met by a number of people that I knew. This actually helped quite a bit at the time, as we were getting quite worked up after all we had gone through. A few days later I started to look around to see how I was going to occupy myself from then on.

At the end of the war John decided that he would like to return the items, which he had hidden all those years in a tin in his garden. Although they were now really useless, the thing was that he really wanted to give them back as he had promised. However, he had lost the piece of paper with my name and address and all he could remember was 'Officer Porter, Dorset, Essex'. So, in December 1945 John Freriks wrote a letter to the Mayor of Dorchester, Dorchester being the capital of the county of Dorset. The Mayor traced my name to Gravesend, Kent, where I had owned a house before the war and sent the letter to the Chief Constable of that town. The police at Gravesend decided that the letter should be forwarded to the Chief Constable of Essex, as they thought that 'Dorset' might actually be 'Orsett', a town in that county. After some detective work, the Essex police found the name 'Porter' in the telephone directory under 'Porter, 'Dorchester', Dorset Avenue, Chelmsford, Essex' and put two-and-two together. On coming home one weekend, your mother told me that a policeman had called with the letter to see if it was really meant for me, which of course it was! After replying to John's letter, he came to stay with us and brought the items I had left with him in 1942. He spent a few days with us and we had a good old talk about times gone by. It appeared that soon after we had first met he had been taken off to Germany in a working party until the end of the war.

After the war he became an officer in the Dutch Air Force and in 1955 I was posted to Germany as second in command of RAF Wahn near Cologne. While stationed in Germany my wife and I went to Amsterdam and stayed with John and his wife, where he gave me the bomb aimer's compass from my crashed Halifax. It had been found by his father after the Germans had cleared the wreckage and exploded a 1,000lb bomb that had hung up and failed to leave the bomb bay when our bomb load had been dropped. In 1990 I also made contact with Charles Manders who had possession of my old flying helmet. After being found at the crash site, it had been buried again along with my parachute harness after the parachute silk had been 'rescued' to make undergarments for some of the local ladies.

8

THE FIRST FOUR LIBERATORS

Mr McKevitt was about to leave his home in Jenkinstown, 8 miles north-east of Dundalk in Ireland, at 07.45 on 16 March 1942 when he heard the engines of a large aircraft pass almost overhead, followed moments later by the terrible rending sounds of the crash and two dull explosions. McKevitt reported the crash, seeing two men setting off in the direction of the scene. These were Superintendent McDonagh and Detective Sergeant McCabe of the Gardia, who located the crash site. AL577, an LB-30 Liberator, had crashed in a mountain bog on Slei-na-Glogh, altitude 1,024ft, a difficult climb 2 miles up from Jenkinstown. The mist thickened into fog higher up until the visibility was only 20yds. After determining that there were survivors, McDonagh immediately left to bring medical aid. The Irish military search and rescue party had now assembled ready for the climb to the site. Commandant N.C. Harrington from HQ Eastern Command Dublin, who arrived to take charge, joined the climb.

AL577 was one of the first four Liberators allocated to 108 Squadron, which was reformed at Kabrit, Egypt, on the shore of the Great Bitter Lake, part of the Suez Canal system, on 1 August 1942.[1] 'We moved to Fayid on 12 September, a short distance north-west of Kabrit,' recalls Flight Sergeant Steve Challen, an air gunner on the squadron.

✧ ✧ ✧

The RAF station, next to the Royal Navy Aircraft Repair Yard, was set back from the lake, with the road from Suez to Ismailia passing the entrance. Some station buildings were still under construction so most aircrew again were given tents and directed to an area of sand. A week or so was spent trying to establish ourselves digging in our tents a foot or so below surface level using the spoil to fill sandbags, walling them up around the tent perimeter as additional protection against possible bomb blast. A wise precaution, the 'enemy' was within! There was a Canadian navigator who was apt to fire his .45 Colt automatic at random during the night at what he claimed were rats invading his tent which was NOT dug in! Slit trenches also had to be dug. Dodging this chore was sure to lead to another fatigue, unloading bombs from the rail wagons of a munition train on a rail siding not far distant. Our Wellington Ic's were being prepared for the first operation which took place 22/23 September, target Benghazi. The first casualty was also suffered at this time but not from enemy action but from a flare sticking and exploding in the chute injuring severely the hand of Ted Killen the wireless operator of Squadron Leader Bagnell's crew. The first casualty from enemy action was 25 September; Benghazi again. Two flak bursts which blew a hole in the tailplane, small holes in the turret and one in my neck lodging in my larynx and voice cords: Forever more the voice prompting the question, 'have you a cold?' The clever answer is 'no it's the German disease – FLAK', my stock reply! Operations continued when news filtered down the grapevine that 108 was selected to re-equip with the Consolidated B-24 Liberator. Excitement was at high pitch with the prospect, which was soon confirmed.

The US General George Brett, after a tour of inspection in the Middle East, requested without delay a delivery of sixteen Liberators (squadron strength) be delivered to the Middle East, the British to specify their destination. The Liberators were a French contract, some of which had been delivered to England. The French capitulation resulted in the British Aircraft Commission taking over the remainder under lend-lease. These sixteen Libs were to be fully armed ready for action complete with Sperry 'pickle barrel' bombsight, turrets and amidships .50 hand held machine guns (one Sperry sight was on the first Lib because it was used for taking drift sights – returned to the USA with the crews?). The Liberators were to be ferried by the USAAF Air Transport Command using an untried southern route only just beginning to be explored by the command and Pan American Airways. Countries on the proposed route, Venezuela and Brazil, were late with permission to allow armed North American military aircraft to land on their territory. Consequently the Libs were dispatched without arms and turrets fitted. However, there was some .30 and .50 calibre machine guns with damp proof wrappings stored in the rear of the aircraft.

The first Liberator took off from Lindbergh Field, San Diego, on the first stage to Borinquen, Puerto Rico, then on to Belem, Brazil. During this stage the high frequency Bendix radio failed. They continued to Natal a short flight on the 23 November, the departure point for the South Atlantic crossing. No technical services, weather or wireless information available. Refuelling was from 55 gallon barrels by hand pump. Because of the high priority of the mission they decided to 'press on regardless' a RAF catch phrase, not always a prudent decision. Take off at 2345 from Natal, they landed at Accra, Gold Coast (Ghana) 1300, 24 November. They were given a warm reception, the first USA plane to land there. Ignoring the advice of the Pan Am agent to start the next leg in darkness they took off at 0615, 25 November with the intention of bypassing Kano, Nigeria, as unnecessary. The next route stop El Fasher, Sudan. Due to heavy ground haze and blowing sand obliterating any sight of the ground they overflew some distance eastward. Dead reckoning navigation brought them back to El Obeid where they were able to make out a landing strip, with the help of alerted ground staff who organised their car headlights to indicate the direction. The Lib touched down but the pilot was unable to see a construction ditch and the spoil heap into which the aircraft plunged, writing off AL569. The crew suffered no injuries and were picked up by the next Liberator passing through. A detachment of maintenance staff from Fayid were sent to salvage everything usable for spares. The USAAF crews were to stay at Fayid for a maximum of one month to convert 108 crews to the new aircraft. The Libs were to be fitted in turn with makeshift gun mounting at 107 MU. The conversion of crews continued with the other Libs. Operations continued to be flown with the Wellingtons. The first to return was AL566 with two .50 calibre American Brownings mounted on a rolled pipe gimball ring mounted at each side, the gun barrels protruding through an aperture cut out of the blanking plate fitted where the rear turret was normally accommodated. The usual open beam positions had a framework mounted across the opening with a .30 USA Browning fixed on a universal mount. Perspex filled in around the spaces. The rear access hatch also had a .30 mounted in the same manner pointing downwards. There was no other defensive armament.

Wing Commander Richard John 'Kong' Wells, as he was affectionately known by his brother officers, Commanding Officer of 108 Squadron was eager to test the new aircraft in its role as a long range heavy bomber and promptly scheduled an operation with AL566. A mixed crew was made up of 'odd bods' not flying in Wellingtons for unserviceability or other reasons. The raid on Tripoli, Libya on 10–11 January 1942 was a success marred by three bomb hang-ups. Vibration had caused the safety switch for the roller bomb doors not to activate which ensured the doors were fully open before the bombs could be triggered. Joe Sunderland the wireless operator climbed down on to the catwalk between the bomb racks and as he described it 'kicked them off'. A very first for the Liberator as a bomber anywhere. Another first was made by Wing

Commander Wells DFC* using AL577/N for a Special Duties trip to Crete on 2–3 March dropping 44 heavy 'parcels' to the resistance force.

The 'Day of Infamy' precluded 108 receiving any more Liberators by the direct southern route. Reporting to Headquarters 205 Group Cairo Wing Commander Wells lobbied for permission to use one Liberator to fly to the UK with minimum crews as passengers to collect Liberators ferried to England by the northern route and modified to RAF requirements. Permission was granted. Turmoil ensued at Fayid. Who is going? How can we take something with us rationed or scarce in England, not too heavy but sure to be welcomed by ration plagued UK? Squadron Leader K.F. Vare the senior flight commander's crew 'B' flight was selected to fly the aircraft, probably because of our trouble-free trip to the Far East and return.

A message was received diverting us to Palembang, Sumatra, instead of our briefed destination, Singapore. The Bendix radio gave no trouble otherwise we may have met the Japanese at the island 'fortress'. Six pilots, three navigators, three wireless operators and a fitter made up the passenger list, six crew bringing the total to 19. The pilots, navigators, wireless operators – the nucleus of the crews who would be made up at OTU in the UK – collect Libs at the modification depot, flying them back to Fayid. All were converted and familiar with the Liberator. A scramble ensued to gather souvenirs and items rationed in Britain. My captain was replaced by Wing Commander Wells who decided to pilot the Lib himself. The evening before departure the gunnery officer, Flight Lieutenant Francis Charles 'Cocky' Barrett DFC told me he was going in my place (another escape for me). Liberator AL577/N was being prepared for the trip. 'Pat' Pattison WOp/AG, a passenger survivor comments that they were 'carrying reserve fuel tanks for a 14–15 hour flight'. Where these tanks were installed and how the fuel was transferred to the main tanks is not clear. The flight was under the control of OADU the Overseas Aircraft Dispatch Unit, Cairo, who supplied pre-flight information. On 14 March the loaded Liberator took off for ALG09 (Advanced Landing Ground) where they stayed overnight. The following day topped up with fuel they took off under the authority of OADU, 15 March for Southern England. Spirits were high until a recall signal was received because of worsening weather on their route. It was estimated they were approaching the point of no return. Coupled with this news the Bendix radio was reported unserviceable. Despite the efforts of all the wireless operators, who were unable to find and rectify the fault. Sergeant Gibbons had the most Bendix experience gained on the Sumatra trip. While these attempts to restore communication was in hand discussions took place on the flight deck whether to continue. The consensus, including the passengers was to fly on. The point of no return had been reached without a doubt. Much later they found themselves above 10/10's cloud which continued long past their ETA (estimated time of arrival) at Hurn, Dorset. Everyone was warned to prepare for a possible ditching. Descending slowly through the cloud a glow was seen which could only be the lights of a town or city in neutral Eire. The size and brightness of this illumination convinced Wing Commander Wells it was Dublin. Rather than risk internment in Eire he altered course for Aldergrove, Northern Ireland, failing to allow for high ground on their track. The fuel situation was now becoming serious. From his amidships' gun position Flying Officer James Robert Anderson DFC saw lights which the pilot decided must be Dublin. A new course was set. Anderson saw the ground flashing by – then oblivion.

Flying Officer Anderson was a New Zealander who had joined the RAF in 1939. He regained consciousness to find himself surrounded by puddles of burning petrol and discovered an unbroken bottle of whisky close by. This he continued to sip until the contents were exhausted! He asserts this contributed to his survival in those dismal cold conditions. His legs and hands were badly burned and he had an injured jaw. Reaching the crash site at 1330 hours, Commandant N.C. Harrington found it impossible to fully describe that scene. The whole area was strewn with bodies, baggage and debris. The flight deck nose section was completely burnt; the wings, midsection and tail were all very much damaged. Three survivors were sheltering as best they could in part of the shattered body fuselage. About twenty 4lb stick type incendiary bombs were scattered amongst the wreckage. These were the only bombs carried and must have been brought in case a target offered itself during the flight. Command Ordinance Officer Commandant Kelley disposed of the incendiaries, Very cartridges and flares at the site. Sergeant Thomas Edward Pattison had a severe spinal injury. Sergeant Cyril Rowland Amos, an Argentinean, had a fractured ankle, an injured right forearm and a wound below the knee.[2] Sergeant Sidney Frederick Hayden had compound fractures of the ankle and leg. He was attended by a civilian doctor where he lay. Pilot Officer Wilfred Bertrand Stephens had head injuries and was unconscious. One man was barely alive and he died on the way down the mountain. Commandant Harrington was able to form a list of passengers and crew by questioning the injured, now being prepared on stretchers for carrying down to the waiting ambulances. The five were taken to the Louth Hospital at Dundalk where they received the best of attention for their injuries.

Commandant Harrington visited them in the hospital speaking to the four who expressed their appreciation for all that had been done for them. Probably at this time mention was made of the wireless being u/s or some other slang expression misinterpreted as sabotage. Pat Pattison ridicules such a suggestion. Checking over the count of bodies which were in a temporary Dundalk store, it was discovered that one body had not been recovered. A search the next morning revealed the body of Sergeant Henry James Gibbons buried in the earth under a wing of the aircraft. The bodies were identified, sewn into sheets, labelled then taken to the border at 2245 on 16 March. All were handed over to the British Authorities at Newry. The body of Sergeant Gibbons was handed over the following day. Flying Officer Anderson and Sergeant Pattison were taken on 17 March by Irish Red Cross ambulance to Newry. When across the border the ambulance was pelted with stones and missiles. They were transferred to the British ambulance and taken to hospital in Newry. Pilot Officer Stephens died on 19 March: his body was taken to the border in an Irish military ambulance on the same day. When Flying Officer Anderson and Sergeant Pattison were deemed fit to travel they left Daisey Hill Hospital for other hospitals in England.[3] Amos and Hayden were taken to the border on 19 March in a civilian ambulance and transferred to the British authorities.

Wing Commander 'Kong' Wells fought to the end to bring the Liberator down safely. It was the opinion of the aircrew that he would not leave Sergeant Williams at the controls at its crucial and desperate time.

9

HOME ON A WING AND A PRAYER

LEONARD GRIBBLE[1]

Basil Vernon Robinson was a pre-war pilot, born in Gateshead in 1912 and initially commissioned in the RAF in 1933. He quickly distinguished himself playing rugby as a wing three-quarter for the RAF and his home county XVs, and by April 1938 had been promoted to flight lieutenant. By 1941 he had risen to squadron leader and been awarded a DFC in July of that year during an operational tour on 78 Squadron. An ebullient character, with a distinctly unorthodox approach to certain RAF customs and procedures, his trademark was a generously proportioned ginger bushy moustache. Wing Commander 'Robby' Robinson DSO DFC took command of 35 Squadron at Linton-on-Ouse in late 1941. On 18 December 1941, during a raid on Brest by forty-seven aircraft, he was forced to ditch 60 miles off the coast of England. The Halifax floated for twenty minutes and he twice re-entered the aircraft, the second time to look for his favourite pipe![2] The crew was picked up that same evening. Five other crews – four of them Stirlings – failed to return.

On the night of 18–19 November 1942, seventy-seven aircraft were sent to attack Turin. Wing Commander Robinson was captain of a Halifax, which unloaded flares and bombs over the city. Shortly afterwards, however, fire began spurting from the bomb bay. An extremely powerful flare, one designed to light up practically an entire city, had got hitched and ignited. The fire swept across the Halifax in gusts, spread to the port wing and it was not long before the whole aircraft was filled with smoke and noxious fumes. There was an explosion, which staggered the aircraft, and the bomb doors were opened quickly but the blazing flare did not drop through. The fire continued to take a stronger hold on the aircraft, which was now racing back towards the Alps, barely 1,000ft above ground level.

Robinson tried everything he knew to retain height but the aircraft sank slowly. It looked as though nothing could prevent the Halifax smashing into the granite sides of the Alpine peaks. There was only one thing to do and the captain did it. He ordered the crew to bail out. They did so. He saw the last man go down and was preparing to follow, when, inexorably, the fire went out. One moment flames were shooting up from the bomb bay, the next they were not. Robinson thought fast and took a chance. He stayed with his crew-less aircraft. He got it over the white-tipped peaks and continued the flight towards home, knowing that he had no flight engineer if anything went wrong mechanically, no navigator to plot a course for him past the heavily defended areas of France and no gunners to fight off any night fighters. He crash-landed at Colerne at 01.50 hours.

Low over the blacked-out expanse of the Italian city of Turin swept a Halifax bomber, with bomb doors gaping. Searchlights tried to pick up the dark shape of the British plane. Guns rumbled and flak filled the near-distance. Wing Commander Basil Vernon Robinson DSO DFC spoke into the intercom. 'OK,' he told the bomb aimer.

Seconds later the Halifax's load of bombs went down, followed by a load of flares.

'Bombs away,' the bomb aimer reported. Robinson circled Turin and set course for the frozen peaks of the Alps and home, but he had not flown beyond the outskirts of the city before an alarm was raised. The Halifax was on fire. The machine had not been set on fire by flak. One of the powerful flares had got lodged in the bomb bay and had ignited.

It was a bitterly cold night in mid-November and a high wind swept from across the Alpine peaks. Soon gusts of spreading flame were sweeping round the fuselage of the bomber and licking at the port wing. Robinson flew on, hoping against hope that the fire would either blow out or burn out but, while he battled to maintain height, smoke and noxious fumes began to invade the aircraft. He gave the word for the bomb doors to be opened again. With the doors open the bomber sailed through the Italian night sky like a blazing torch. Every gun in the district over which the aircraft passed was directed at it. But the flare did not shake loose and fall into the night. It remained hitched up in the bomb bay, burning fiercely and feeding the spreading fire.

The crew fought the flames, but could not extinguish them. Grimly they retreated farther into the aircraft while the fire took stronger hold. Robinson, fighting at the controls, was heading for the Alps at barely 1,000ft above the ground. He tried every flying trick he knew to gain height, but despite all his efforts the aircraft continued to sink. It was not long before every man in the blazing bomber knew what they faced, the prospect of crashing headlong into a granite shoulder of one of the Alpine peaks. Or, should they be lucky enough to clear the serrated ridge of the mountain mass, there lay the prospect of being burned alive.

There was only one thing for the captain of the Halifax to do in the circumstances. Robinson did it. He ordered the crew to bail out and, one by one, while he continued at the controls, he saw them step up to the escape hatch and pitch into the darkness below.

For a few moments he sat there, alone in the aircraft, his thoughts very mixed. A trick of fate had determined that he and his crew should spend the rest of the war in an Italian prison camp. He rose reluctantly, steadied the controls for the last time and made to move towards the gaping escape hatch. As he did so, as though the hand he had extended to steady himself held a magic wand, the fire suddenly and unaccountably went out. One instant the flames were hissing up from the bomb bay, the next moment they had gone.

For some seconds Robinson stayed there, inclined to doubt the evidence of his senses. But the fire was out. There could be no mistaking that. The aircraft was flying on towards the Alps, dangerously low, but no longer menaced by the hungry flames. Robinson decided to take a chance; a very long chance. He went back to the controls and began to battle the Halifax higher in the sky.

It was a grim, rather frightening tussle, with the odds very much against him. He was alone in the fire-damaged aircraft. If anything went wrong he could look for no assistance and something might go very much wrong at any instant. He had no flight engineer to turn to, no navigator to plot a course for him. Before him were the Alps and beyond them hundreds of miles of enemy-occupied country. He would have to fly through the enemy's flak lanes, push on through belts of night fighters, weave over cones of probing searchlights after hostile radio location stations had picked him up. He had no gunners to fight off an attack. He had – only himself.

By brilliant work at the controls he lifted the labouring bomber over the glaciers and snow-clad tips of the Alps, buffeted his way through streams of icy cloud and headwinds and continued northwards over France. That he got back, alone, in his badly charred aircraft, tired and cold and hungry, seems little short of a miracle, but he did. He wormed his way through the sprawling expanse of the

German defence system, headed over the Channel and finally managed to make a safe landing on an English airfield not far from the coast. When he touched down, the last of the night's bombers had returned from their long flight across Europe and Bomber Command had chalked up another of its famous 'White Gloves' raids.

In getting back Robinson completely fooled the enemy, who announced over the Rome radio: 'The British Air Ministry communiqué today says that all the British aircraft which bombed Turin last night came back to their bases. The British have been misinformed, because some of the members of the crews in the British planes which bombed Turin last night have been made prisoner after their planes were brought down.'

The Italians had some prisoners, the members of Robinson's crew, but the wing commander's determination to struggle on despite all hazards spoiled their claim.[3]

10

MINE LAYING IN DANZIG BAY

SERGEANT 'NICK' CARTER

'Jarmany calling; Jarmany calling.' William Joyce, or Lord Haw-Haw, as he was unpopularly known, allegedly announced on the wireless at Apen near Hamburg on the night of 13–14 March 1943, when there was no main force activity, that a Lancaster had been shot down over Denmark. Fifty-one Wellingtons and seventeen Lancasters carried out 'gardening' operations at Lorient and the Kattegat respectively and two Wimpys failed to return. A Lancaster (W4201 on 57 Squadron at Scampton), piloted by Flying Officer W.E. 'Bill' Jeavons, was intercepted by an unidentified fighter when about 20 to 30 miles off the west coast of Denmark on the return journey. Extensive damage was caused to the aircraft but the first casualty of war is truth, which was exploited at every opportunity by Joyce, who was an Irish-American fascist politician and Nazi propaganda broadcaster.

The odious propagandist was born on Herkimer Street in Brooklyn, New York, on 24 April 1906 to an Anglican mother and an Irish Catholic father who had taken United States citizenship.[1] His broadcasts initially came from studios in Berlin, later transferring (due to heavy Allied bombing) to Luxembourg and finally to and were relayed over a network of German-controlled radio stations that included Hamburg, Bremen, Luxembourg, Hilversum, Calais, Oslo and Zeese. In 1940 Joyce had an estimated 6 million regular and 18 million occasional

59

listeners in Britain. The broadcasts always began with the announcer's words 'Germany calling, Germany calling, Germany calling'. These broadcasts urged the British people to surrender and were well known for their jeering, sarcastic and menacing tone. There was also a desire by civilian listeners to hear what the other side was saying, since information during wartime was strictly censored and at the start of the war it was possible for German broadcasts to be more informative than those of the BBC.[2]

The true story of Bill Jeavons' crew is told in the words of Sergeant B.G. 'Nick' Carter, the flight engineer.

Once again we were detailed for mine-laying. The Main Force was going to the Ruhr again but that was cancelled because of weather conditions over their target, just before their take off time. We had departed three hours earlier. It must have been a last minute cancellation for them because when we arrived back we found a number of them in line on the perimeter track, but more of this later. This time we were going to Danzig Bay carrying only four mines because of the distance involved. We flew over Denmark and over the southern end of Sweden, which of course was a neutral country and we could see all the towns' street lighting, it looked so nice after our British blackout. We arrived without any problems at Danzig and commenced our level flight to drop the mines when a dense curtain of flak burst around us. We had never experienced this before; it was the German Navy taking exception to our presence. It took under a minute to drop the mines but it was a very long minute. However, we were not hit and then started back on the return journey, once again over Sweden and then at 7,000 feet over Denmark. We had left the Danish coast about fifteen minutes earlier and Sergeant J.B. 'Paddy' Hughes the rear gunner had just said that it wouldn't be too long before we were having our eggs and bacon, when it happened.

A Junkers 88 night fighter fired at us from slightly below and behind. 'Paddy', nor Sergeant George Cooper the mid-upper-gunner, spotted it until we were hit. The aircraft went into a steep dive; the cabin was full of smoke and flames and the side windows had been blown out. Our cabin lights were flashing on and off, mainly on and the wing tip lights were on. 'Bill' Jeavons seemed to be having a hard time pulling out of the dive and I tried to assist. She finally came out at what I thought was 700 feet (Bill said years after that he thought it was 500 feet). We both agreed we could see the waves far too clearly. Flying level we then had to worry about the fighter. We concluded some days later that after seeing all the flames and lights he had decided we were finished.

Meanwhile, Pilot Officer D.W.W. 'Dougie' Warwick, navigator, had been dealing with the flames which turned out to be signal cartridges which had been hit by a cannon shell, so we had a wonderful, but very unappreciated, firework display of all colours. Dougie tried various methods to get rid of the burning cartridges and finally ended up putting on several pairs of gloves, picking up the cartridges and throwing them through the now windowless side of the cabin. I had to do something about the flashing lights and having quickly opened the fuse panel taking out what fuses I could, smashed others which I couldn't remove which were giving trouble. We worked out later that the 20mm cannon shells which had set fire to the cartridges and blown out the windows must have missed Dougie and me by about 24 inches. [The two other members of the crew were Sergeant Robert 'Bob' E.H. Hood-Morris, bomb aimer and Pilot Officer R.E. Gibbons, wireless operator.]

Now it was time to see what other damage had been done, the intercom was dead – which was not a good start but not too much of a problem. It was when I went down the rear of the fuselage with my flashlight that I found the problem: The elevator and rudder controls were square sectioned tubes passing down the port side and located in supports made from a material called Tufnol. Between two of these supports the elevator control had been completely severed with about a ten-inch gap, the supports had been blown 40 or 50 degrees out of line and had jammed the rudder control. Then I went forward into the bomb aimer's compartment. From there I could check the aileron controls – more problems, the chains had formed a loop and severely restricted the movement. No wonder Bill was complaining that the aircraft was difficult to handle. I reported back to Bill and suggested that I could try to do something with the rudder control but he said to leave it alone, he was coping and didn't want to take any chances that might make it worse. Dougie by this time had collected his 'Gee' maps which had blown down the back because of the wind coming through the missing windows and was trying to find out where we were. Luckily the 'Gee' equipment was still working. I thought perhaps we could do something to prevent the wind from giving us so much trouble. The lower part of the cabin below the windows had some fairly stiff panels so I unscrewed them and to my great surprise (and Bill's) managed to jam them into the blank spaces, where they stayed for the rest of the flight.

The next problem to overcome was communication. Dougie had to give Bill changes of course, but this was solved when I suggested that I would be standing next to Bill and Doug could tap me behind either my right or left knee using one tap for each degree of turn. I would then change the needle of the directional compass as required. This worked very well and when I changed the reading Bill would give me an OK nod. By very careful engine control Bill managed to fly the aircraft quite well. It was a case of decrease power to lose height, increase to climb, to turn port, open up the starboard engines and the opposite to turn starboard.

After what seemed like ages we crossed the Lincolnshire coast. I flashed out an SOS message on the downward identification lights. Although we didn't know at the time, the signal was seen by the Observer Corps, who phoned the local RAF stations to ask if they had a Lancaster missing. There were only eleven Lancs in action that night and so Scampton were standing by when we approached. Then Bill, having decided that a landing with no flying controls would be very tricky, decided that we should bail out. It was then that I had to tell him that I couldn't because my parachute had been used by Dougie to smother some of the burning signal cartridges. Bill then wanted the other five crew members to bail out while he and I attempted to land. This they refused to do saying that they would stick with us but would, of course, take up crash positions between the front and rear wing spars where they passed through the fuselage.

We prepared for landing as soon as we could see the airfield. By now it was 0630 and fairly light. On Bill's instructions I selected flaps down and that was OK. The next thing was to get the wheels down. Nothing happened so I moved back to the wireless operator's position to where the emergency hydraulic hand pump was on his left hand side. All I found was a hole in the side of the fuselage where the pump should have been. There was one more thing to try, a last resort, a compressed air system that if used would blow all the oil out of the hydraulic system and hopefully lower the wheels. However, this meant that they could not be retracted. It worked, they came down but the starboard tyre had been slashed by the cannon shells which didn't help the situation.

Now it was more or less up to Bill. As we came closer to the airfield, losing height for touchdown, we found we were making directly for the line of aircraft left in situ when ops were scrubbed for that same night. All Bill could do was to use the engine power to gently make a 360 degree turn to make another approach, it was probably a ten mile radius and we were not happy to find that we were still lined up with the Lancs on the perimeter track. It was then that Bill took drastic action. We were at about 1,000 plus feet and he suddenly opened the engines up to nearly full power. The aircraft banked to port in the required direction in what was a twenty or thirty degree bank. Now we had to straighten up and so at Bill's nod I put the port engines at nearly full power, reducing the power on the other side. Nothing happened; we just slid sideways straight into the ground. I had tried to jam myself between the back of the pilot's seat and the navigator's table watching the ground come close and thinking 'Bloody Hell, this is it'. The next thing I knew I was laying full length on my back in the bomb aimer's compartment feet facing forward, with the front gun turret which had come off its mounting sitting on my legs.

I looked over my head towards the back of the aircraft and there was Dougie trying to open his escape hatch but turning the handle the wrong way. I yelled to him to turn it the other way, which he did and promptly left. I then found I was the only one left in the aircraft and could see that there was some smoke coming out of the starboard wing. I tried to free my trapped foot, the left one, but without success and then had a sudden brainwave, I unzipped the flying boot and out came the foot unharmed. Then it was a simple matter to exit via the pilot's escape hatch and slide down the side of the fuselage; except that I hadn't unplugged my intercom from the socket and found myself suspended about a foot above the ground by my leather flying helmet! At that moment 'Paddy' and George ran back and while Paddy held me up George removed the helmet. It really is very strange but we had come to rest in a field next to our own dispersal point and there was our own ground crew coming through the hedge to help us, plus an ambulance crew who had been waiting at the control tower with the fire engine and another truck with cutting equipment. I learned afterwards that my little RAF friend Twinkle was also with the spectators.

Although I felt fine and I am sure we were all glad to be alive, in my travels from behind the pilot's seat to the nose of the aircraft my face must have come into contact with the four throttle levers and also the four propeller pitch levers; cutting me over the left eye and eyelid and also across the mouth. It looked much worse than it proved to be but the medics insisted on stretchering me back to the ambulance. All the crew were with me and on arrival at the medical centre I was taken into the operating room and though Bill stayed with me the others went for debriefing and then to the officers' or sergeants' mess. I was placed on a flat padded table to allow the very young doctor to see what he could do. I remember Bill gripping my right arm above the elbow and me feeling embarrassed because I had a hole in the sock on my left foot. The doctor said he would have to put some stitches in but couldn't give me an anaesthetic because of shock. I think Bill felt it worse than I did. After that I was given a large morphine tablet and woke up 24 hours later in a hospital bed. One of my earlier thoughts was that this episode should be worth a few beers.

I hadn't been awake very long when there was a huge explosion from somewhere on the airfield and later we found that a 'cookie' – a 4,000lb bomb – had blown up one of the aircraft destroying, I believe, three other Lancasters.

I soon had visitors, first Twinkle and another waitress and then the crew. My head was bandaged so that just my eyes and mouth were visible. I did get to look when the doctor was checking progress. After he'd left I nipped out of bed and viewed my reflection in the brass finger plate on the door. Later I heard during breakfast of the morning of the crash that Paddy had complained that his legs were a bit painful. He ended up in a local hospital where he had small pieces of his rear turret removed from the knee area. A cannon shell had passed under his seat and exploded. One foot higher and Paddy would have been killed. I often wondered why the heck he should volunteer when he came from Southern Ireland. I believe he survived the war, he was a great chap. He and George had carried me from the aircraft to and through the hedge before the medics took over.

I was then given some sick leave and ordered to report at the end of my leave to Emmanuel College, Cambridge, to have the stitches removed. The college was being used as an initial training wing for aircrew cadets. With my small suitcase I stood at the bus stop by the Scampton gate when a large Rover car pulled up and the driver asked if I would like a lift? This, of course, was very welcome and he started a conversation by stating that a Lancaster had crashed into one of his fields a few days before. I said I knew; I was in it. 'Well I'm darned,' he said, or something like that; 'If you've got time before your train I'm going to buy you a lunch,' which he did. How nice it was of him. The day before, I had walked over to the site of the crash. I could see where the wing had first hit the ground and could work out what had probably happened. On first contact the reaction had righted the plane to level attitude. It had torn across a field and then knocked down a derelict cottage and passed through a small orchard. Then it had reached the road past the airfield which being higher than the field took the undercarriage off allowing us to pass over the road like a flying boat. We then knocked down a telegraph pole and went through the barbed wire boundary fence which was about fifteen feet high. This wrapped itself around the two outboard engines and tore them off, the fuselage ending up in the field next to our dispersal area. I went into what was left of the aircraft and found a ground engineer writing a report and sitting in the pilot's seat. Now the funny thing was just prior to the trip I had got an empty dope can and painted it in blue and white stripes so that any of us at the front end could use it if we were taken short. We had used it and I had wedged it behind Bill's seat. It was still there and I remarked about it as I took it away. The officer said he had been puzzled by the awful smell. Why it stayed in place while I didn't was, I suppose, a matter of weight![3]

Lord Haw-Haw recorded his final broadcast on 30 April 1945, during the Battle of Berlin. Rambling and audibly drunk, he chided Britain for pursuing the war beyond mere containment of Germany and warned repeatedly of the 'menace'

of the Soviet Union. He signed off with a final defiant 'Heil Hitler and farewell'. There are conflicting accounts as to whether this last programme was actually transmitted, despite a recording being found in the Apen studios. The next day Radio Hamburg was seized by British forces, who on 4 May used it to make a mock 'Germany calling' broadcast denouncing Joyce, as spoken by Wynford Vaughan-Thomas:

This is Germany calling. Calling for the last time from Station Hamburg, and tonight you will not hear views on the news by William Joyce, for Mr Joyce – Lord Haw-Haw to most of us in Britain – has been most unfortunately interrupted in his broadcasting career, and at present has left rather hurriedly for a vacation, an extremely short vacation if the Second British Army has anything to do with it, maybe to Denmark and other points north. And in his place this is the BBC calling all the long-suffering listeners in Britain who for six years have had to put up with the acid tones of Mr Joyce speaking over the same wavelength that I'm using to talk to you now.

I'm seated in front of Lord Haw-Haw's own microphone, or rather the microphone he used in the last three weeks of his somewhat chequered career; and I wonder what Lord Haw-Haw's views on the news are now? For Hamburg, the city he made notorious, is this evening under the control of the British Forces, and we found a completely and utterly bomb-ruined city.

We thought Bremen was bad, but Hamburg is devastated. Whole quarters have disintegrated under air attacks. There are miles upon miles of blackened walls and utterly burnt-out streets, and in the ruins there are still nearly a million people and 50,000 foreign workers living in the cellars and air-raid shelters. Today you don't see a single civilian on the streets; as soon as we came in we imposed a forty-eight hour curfew, and there's a Sunday quiet over the whole city; all that stirs in the streets is a British jeep or an armoured car, or a patrol of British Tommies watching that the curfew is strictly enforced.

The docks are even more devastated than the town, the great shipyards of Blohm and Voss are a wilderness of tangled girders, and in the middle of this chaos fourteen unfinished U-boats still stand rusting on the slipways. Work on them finally stopped two months ago; after that date Hamburg was a dead city.

Rummaging through Lord Haw-Haw's desk we found a revealing timetable he drew up for his work, for 10 April 1945 and at the end of it is the glorious item: '1450–1510 hours. A pause to collect my wits.' Well – he and the citizens of Hamburg have now got plenty of time to collect their wits, for tonight the sturdy soldiers of the Devons, the famous Desert Rats, are on guard over Haw-Haw's studios, the Allied military authorities are now running his programme, and instead of 'Germany Calling', the colonel in charge gives you now the new call-sign of 'Station Hamburg'. This is Radio Hamburg, a station of the Allied Military Government. [Same announcement in German.] And from Hamburg we take you back to London.[4]

On 28 May Joyce was captured by British forces at Flensburg, near the German border with Denmark. Joyce was taken to London and tried at the Old Bailey on three counts of high treason. He was sentenced to death on 19 September 1945. He went to his death unrepentant and defiant: 'In death as in life, I defy the Jews who caused this last war and I defy the power of darkness which they represent. I warn the British people against the crushing imperialism of the Soviet Union. May Britain be great once again and in the hour of the greatest danger in the West may the standard be raised from the dust, crowned with the words "You have conquered nevertheless". I am proud to die for my ideals and I am sorry for the sons of Britain who have died without knowing why.'

Joyce was hanged by Albert Pierrepoint on 3 January 1946 at Wandsworth Prison, aged 39.

11

'F FOR FIRKIN'

Nineteen bombers were lost on the Duisburg raid of 8–9 April 1943 from a force of 392 aircraft, only one of which was shot down by a night fighter. Another eight Lancasters failed to return from a force of 104 Lancasters and five Mosquitoes that went to Duisburg again the following night. Thick cloud again caused a scattered attack and bombs fell over a wide area of the Ruhr. On the night of the 10th–11th a force of 502 Lancasters, Halifaxes, Stirlings and 144 Wellingtons took off for a raid on Frankfurt. At Linton-on-Ouse, twenty-one Halifaxes of 76 and 78 Squadrons were detailed for the operation. Group Captain John Rene Whitley AFC commanding RAF Linton-on-Ouse wanted to get an updated view of the problems of his crews but normally station commanders were not allowed to go on ops – it was considered that they were privy to too many secrets – but he had managed to get 4 Group's permission to go on the raid. He shaved off his moustache, bundled up a set of civilian clothes that he had always carried with him on operations and went on V-Victor[1] with Flight Lieutenant Arthur Horace Hull; one of 76 Squadron's more experienced pilots.

Twenty-one-year-old Sergeant H.J. 'Jack' Adams and his crew, who had recently joined 78 Squadron, on 28 March, were another of the crews that went. Adams was a tall, athletically-built married man from Wimbledon, south London, who had worked in the accounts department of the London Fire Brigade. He had trained in Southern Rhodesia and was known for his sense of humour and broad grin. Twenty-one-year-old Pilot Officer Philip Hyden, the navigator, had the looks, charm, manners and accent expected from someone educated at public school. He came from a military family in Aldershot, joining the RAF straight from school. He was thrown off his pilot's course in Canada just before getting his wings after gleefully flying a single-seat trainer aircraft beneath a railway bridge that crossed a river. Nevertheless, Hyden had since managed to pilot an old lumbering Whitley and the much larger Halifax. A press-on character, he was the only commissioned officer in a bomber otherwise full of sergeants.

The bomb aimer, Stan Hurrell, lived with his widowed mother in Totnes, Devon. Quiet and studious, he had been a Post Office counter clerk before training as a bomb aimer. Aged 22, he was a dead-keen type, who had brought back the squadron's best bombing photographs of the operation on 2 April that attacked the U-boat pens at the French port of St Nazaire. Nineteen-year-old Clifford Price, known to his crewmates as 'Junior', had worked at a solicitor's office in his home town of Woking, Surrey. Now he was a wireless operator, quiet, small and very boyish, providing his crewmates with good music on the aircraft radio during long cross-country exercises. The flight engineer, Matthew 'Nobby' Clarke, 21, joined the RAF at the outbreak of war and trained at Halton as an aero engine fitter. From Bury St Edmunds, Suffolk, he was a silent type, living almost exclusively for his beloved Rolls-Royce aero engines. Jethro Nathaniel Enwright, the mid-upper gunner, was pleased to be known as 'Joe'. Twenty-nine, taciturn and married to Mavis, with a small daughter of the same name, he came from Easington, County Durham. This was his first sortie. Stan Reed, the rear gunner, 21, also married, was from Purfleet, Essex, where he worked in a cardboard mill. He considered himself to be a country lad and a conscientious plodder, but was proud to be in the crew. The trip to Frankfurt was the second operation for Clarke, Hurrell, Price and Reed.[2]

Halifax 'F-Freddie' had been christened 'F for Firkin' by the crew. Sergeant 'Stan' Reed recalls.

'F-Firkin' was a fairly new kite and hadn't done too many operations. It was a Mark II Series 1 (Special) of which, the nose and mid-upper gun turrets had been removed to help improve the rather poor operational performance leaving only the rear turret for defence. The mid-upper gunner now manned a ventral position when on operations, looking downwards through a small Perspex blister fitted to the floor of the aircraft just aft of the rear door. Not a well sought after position as it entailed lying flat out on the floor for hours with one's head in the perspex blister. This position had been brought in to reduce the heavy losses caused by the deadly attacks from below, which were so favoured by Jerry night fighters. Alas, the position was not armed until later with a .5 calibre Browning machine gun. An intercom point, oxygen outlet together with a signal light and switch were installed alongside the blister but no form of heating was provided and a cold, draughty and noisy position it was indeed.

On the night in question our take off time was 23.34 hours. It was a very dark night with no moon and 10/10ths cloud cover. After leaving base we did not see another aircraft although on several occasions we became aware of their unseen presence as we flew through their slipstreams. I flew from Yorkshire to the south coast sitting up front alongside our Skipper on the second pilot's seat whilst 'Joe' Enwright manned the rear turret until it was time for me to take over; somewhere over the English Channel. I very much enjoyed riding up front in the utter dark of the night, watching avidly all that went on about me with great interest. It was all so different to my normal lonely vigil in the rear turret. I studied Jack at the controls, clad in his leather Irvin flying jacket and helmet with his face half hidden behind his oxygen mask, in the dim red glow from the instruments on the panels before him. Being at the very heart of this huge powerful bomber made me feel privileged to be aboard. An enormous and deafening constant roar from the four big Rolls-Royce Merlins dominated everything up front. I was conscious of 'Nobby' Clarke behind me, busy as always at his engineer's panel. Flying Officer Phil Hyden, navigator, Sergeant Cliff Price and Sergeant 'Stan' Hurrell were at their respective stations on the lower deck of the Halifax, beneath and in front of me.

My job during this part of the outward flight was to maintain a constant lookout for other aircraft in case one should come just a little too close for comfort. Flying blind on the aircraft's instruments alone in a night bomber stream with no radar could, to put it mildly; be disconcerting at times. Hopefully all the bombers were not at the same height even though we were all flying in the same direction or at least, should be doing so. Imagine if you can a corridor of air space one hundred miles long, ten or more miles wide and about a mile and a half high with the lowest strata being at least at 12,000 feet. In this corridor in the sky were at least 500–600 bombers all heavily laden with petrol and a large bomb load and all were heading in the same direction in the pitch darkness. Each wave kept to a specified height. The poor old Stirlings with their rather poor maximum operational ceiling were always at the lowest level. Behind and above them at 15,000–16,000 feet would come the Wellingtons and then the Halifaxes at about 18,000 feet, with the Lancasters bringing up the rear in the last wave at 20,000 feet or more. With all these unseen heavy aircraft around us collisions in mid air were known to occur but officially the percentage was less than half of one per cent of the total force. It had to be for morale purposes did it not? Many more aircraft were lost through enemy action!

Having left the English coast we were soon well out over the Channel. I prepared to go aft and take up my normal station in the rear turret for the remainder of the operation. I gathered up my parachute pack and the rest of my gear including a big thermos flask of hot coffee. Then I discovered that my microphone in my face mask had gone unserviceable and no one could hear what I was saying. No amount of banging would clear the fault, although I could hear perfectly well through my flying helmet earphones. We didn't have a spare headset on board and I made a mental note to remind Cliff Price to draw a spare set from stores come the morrow. Jack decided that Joe Enwright would now remain in the rear turret for the rest of the trip whilst I would take the ventral position in his place. It was essential that the rear gunner was able to communicate with the pilot. Joe was our sole means of defence. Even if the intercom system became unserviceable, communication was still possible between crew members and their pilot by means of small lights fitted at all crew positions. Any trouble would be flashed immediately to the pilot using the appropriate letter in Morse code like 'F for Fighter'! The pilot would then take immediate avoiding action by frantically weaving and corkscrewing the aircraft until hopefully clear of danger.

I settled down in the blister position aft, laying on some none-too-clean canvas engine covers, which were stowed in the aircraft adjacent to the ventral blister position. I had done one operation with my head in the perspex blister, which did not suit me at all but I could only try to make the best of the situation. After all it was my mike that had gone U/S wasn't it? I always felt very much at home behind four Browning machine guns in the rear turret with a little armour plate beneath my seat. Now I felt rather naked and very vulnerable lying flat out on the thin metal floor. I flashed Jack up on my signal light to let him know that I was in place and received a reassuring acknowledgement in return before settling down to gaze upon the awful nothingness below. We were flying around the 18,000 feet mark. Normally, with a full petrol and bomb load on board we couldn't get the old Mark II Halifaxes, even with all their recent modifications, much higher than this. I could see nothing below, just total blackness. It was damn cold too with no heating available. I could hear the rest of the crew going about their duties with Jack quietly in command and not saying much. Phil our navigator was trying to work wonders from his 'Gee' set, which was being 'bent' by 'Jerry'. Phil was telling Jack that the set was practically U/S and he would have to rely on his D/R plot from now on.[3] Stan Hurrell in his bomb aimer's position was busying himself looking out for PFF flares and markers, which should be showing up soon as we approached our next turning point, a little to the north of Dieppe. Cliff Price was conscientiously searching his allotted wave bands hoping to pick up Jerry night fighter controllers nattering to their airborne charges so that he could give them a blasting from a microphone positioned alongside one of our Merlin engines and thus interrupt their broadcasts with some beautiful aero engine noise. 'Nobby' Clarke was checking his petrol tank gauges and effecting changeovers from one tank to another to maintain our centre of gravity in flight as petrol was used. We used an awful amount of petrol per hour when airborne. Joe Enwright in the tail obtained permission from Jack to test his guns. I then heard the familiar rattle as Joe fired off a short test burst from the four .303 Brownings. That very morning he and I had harmonised those guns down to one hundred yards.

Jack warned us that we were approaching the French coast just north of Dieppe per Phil Hyden's calculations. It was always a gut tightening occasion and put everybody on their mettle. Jack then commenced a gentle weave (a winding course on a general heading of intended flight with variations of height) to distract enemy night fighters and predicted radar controlled flak. I could see no flak near us. No one mentioned seeing any close to us up front either. Stan Hurrell counted the yellow PFF flares aloud. We were heading towards Metz in eastern France where there was to be another change of course on PFF markers. Jack warned us that we were now in the Jerry night fighter belt. Nothing keeps you on your toes than the prospect of being caught by a Jerry night fighter. It concentrated the mind wonderfully. However, all was going well. 'F-Firkin's four aero engines were all roaring on. All was quiet up front with just the occasional word from Phil warning Jack of a slight alteration of course. The golden rule was that no one spoke on the intercom over enemy territory unless one had to. Jack however did speak individually to us from time to time with quiet words of encouragement, which always went down well. All was completely black below. It must have been 10/10ths cloud cover all over northern Europe. We duly turned onto our new heading over Metz amid a sprinkling of yellow PFF markers but other than that I saw nothing of the French city beneath me at all. We flew on, weaving more vigorously now with everybody on the 'qui vive' maintaining a close vigil of the black sky all about us.

Suddenly from out of the utter nothingness below and a little astern, came several blinding lines of very bright green lights. Tracer and lots of it! 'Christ!' I cried out loud. A bloody night fighter had caught us from below. The lines of tracer tore into us at a terrible speed. Our 'Hally' was raked from tail to nose in just one long savage burst, which could not have lasted for more than three seconds. The noise was considerable and above the roar of the engines too. It was as if a giant was tearing up sheets of corrugated iron by hand and doing it very fast indeed. It was 20mm cannon fire that was hitting us and some of the cannon shells were exploding on impact in bright little splashes of light. How I

71

was not hit I just do not know for the tracer appeared to go all around me lying there on the engine covers on the floor of the Hally, as if frozen stiff. I was just 2° from being absolutely petrified. Faintly, over the intercom I heard that someone up front had been hit. Fire must have broken out immediately from amidships where the main petrol tanks and our bomb load, mainly incendiary bombs in metal containers, were and flames streamed back underneath the aircraft.

I saw nothing of the Jerry night fighter that had caught us. He obviously knew his profession very well, creeping up quite unseen, entirely on his airborne radar no doubt and then hitting us plumb amidships just where he could do the most damage. And all in the one short burst too. He must have then stood off and watched our demise. I was told after my capture that a Bf 110 night fighter had shot us down and that we were one of twenty bombers brought down that night.[4] Cliff had been hit in the leg. I could now hear over the intercom and Nobby was saying that he had badly burnt hands. Fortunately, no one else appeared to have been hit in the attack, which was miraculous considering what had gone by me and struck up front. There was some shouting and a bit of a flap but no real panic. I heard nothing from Joe in the rear turret but that wasn't unusual as Joe never did say much nor had I heard his guns firing. He couldn't have seen the fighter either. I gathered quickly that we were now well alight and that it was impossible to control the fire, let alone put it out. All this had happened within seconds although it appeared to last for an age. In fact less than twenty seconds only were to pass from the moment of attack to the time Jack and the last to leave our doomed Halifax bailed out. Time certainly seemed to stand still. I still couldn't believe that it was all happening to us. It was all so unreal. Was this a nightmare? I kept telling myself that this is what befell other crews; it just couldn't happen to us. I came back to reality rather abruptly when I heard Jack on intercom say very calmly, 'this is it chaps. Better get out quickly. We've had it.'

'Phil then shouted something about Switzerland but by then I had pulled my intercom plug out and was making my way to the rear door on the port side of the Halifax, having grabbed my parachute pack. I opened the door inwards up to the roof of the aircraft and saw fully for the first time the whole mass of flames tearing past underneath me. 'Christ' I said. It was damn noisy too. We had really had it all right. I had to get out fast before the kite exploded. I paused looking down into all that blackness I was about to jump into. Beyond the tearing flames I saw two bodies flash by so I knew that at least two members of the crew had managed to get out OK and wondered which two it might be. I sat down on the floor with my legs out of the doorway and prepared myself to abandon the 'Hally'. I must have been sucked out or drawn out by the roaring rushing slipstream tearing past and in the mere seconds of receiving Jack's 'bail out' call I found myself out in the cold night air with the huge tail of the Halifax shooting past over my head. She was certainly well on fire amidships and diving away obviously out of control.

Was I the last one out, I wondered?[5]

Complete cloud cover in the target area again led to failure. At Linton-on-Ouse there was no sign of V-Victor and Flight Lieutenant Hull's crew. Ron Read was OC flying for 78 Squadron that night. He remembered the 'long weary wait as it became apparent that Hull was not coming back'.

'The group captain was missing. A little shiver ran through us in the control tower; if they could get "Groupie" Whitley we felt that they could get anybody.'

12

ONE OF THE DAMBUSTERS

Flying Officer Joseph Charles 'Big Joe' McCarthy DFC RCAF, a burly 23-year-old, 6ft 3in Irish-American from New York City, had just beaten the odds by completing his first tour with 97 Squadron at Woodhall Spa, on 11 March 1943. A few days later he received a telephone call from Guy Gibson. The 24-year-old wing commander told him, 'I'm forming a new squadron. I can't tell you much about it except to say that we may only be doing one trip. I'd like you and your crew to join us.'

It was on 17 March 1943 that 'Squadron X' was formed, at Scampton in Lincolnshire. McCarthy, who was fascinated by all things aeronautical, was a favourite of his fellow pilots and was known on the squadrons as 'the big blond American'. On his uniform he wore dual shoulder flashes, 'USA' and 'Canada'. Born in St James, Long Island, on 31 August 1919, McCarthy was raised in Brooklyn. His family had a summer home on Long Island where one of his summer jobs was as a life guard at Coney Island, the money helping to pay for private flying lessons at Roosevelt Field where, in 1927, Charles Lindbergh had taken off on his epic solo New York to Paris flight. In 1940–1941 McCarthy tried three times to join the US Army Air Corps but he never heard back from them! One of his neighbourhood lifelong friends was Donald Joseph Curtin, who suggested that they enlist in the Royal Canadian Air Force. Because of the war, Curtin had been laid off from his job as a cruise director with the Holland America Steamship Company. McCarthy and Curtin boarded a bus and headed north for Ontario. They crossed the St Lawrence River by ferry and Canadian customs helped them get a connecting bus to Ottawa. They spent the night at the

YMCA and the following morning, 5 May 1941, they proceeded to the recruiting office. However, they were told to come back in six weeks. The two Yanks told the officials that they did not have the money to return again so if the RCAF wanted them they had better decide that day! The warrant officer in charge took a second look at the two American volunteers, changed his mind and had them sign enlistment papers.

Pilot Officer Curtin went on to fly Lancasters at Syerston on 106 Squadron. His 'B' Flight commander, John Searby, remembered him years later as 'a crisp, curly-haired individual who always looked as if he had just stepped out of a bath'.[1] He was awarded the DFC after his first sortie in July 1942 and a further award of a bar to his DFC was approved in January 1943. During the period Curtin was on 106 Squadron, Guy Gibson was his commanding officer. It was during a visit to see Curtin at Syerston that McCarthy first met Gibson. He remembered him as one of those men to whom leadership came as naturally as breathing; autocratic and impatient at times, yet commanding instant respect. It was a foregone conclusion that Curtin would certainly have been invited to join 'Squadron X' if he and his crew had not been lost over Nuremberg on the night of 25–26 February.[2] Don was 25 years old. He and his crew were buried in the War Graves Cemetery in Dumbach, Germany.

All but one of Joe McCarthy's crew of six eventually decided to follow their aircraft captain to 'Squadron X'. Sergeant George L. Johnson, his bomb aimer, almost did not make it as he was due to get married on 3 April and his bride-to-be had warned him that if he was not there on that date then he needn't 'bother to come at all'. McCarthy, with his customary directness, told Gibson that they had finished their tour and were entitled to leave. They got four days' leave and Johnson made it to the church on time.

Of the 133 men who would crew the Lancasters on the secret operation, only twenty of them were decorated. Gibson selected many of these, such as McCarthy, Hopgood, Burpee and Shannon, personally. He chose Squadron Leader Henry Melvin 'Dinghy' Young DFC★, who came from 57 Squadron at Scampton, as his 'A' Flight commander. Young, whose father was a solicitor and a second lieutenant in the Queen's Royal West Surrey Regiment and his mother, Fannie Forrester Young, formerly Rowan, an American from a socially prominent Los Angeles family, was born in Belgravia, London on 20 May 1915. Educated in England and in California and Connecticut, he attended Trinity College, Oxford, where he studied law and was an Oxford rowing Blue. The first of his ditchings, which earned him his nickname, was in a Whitley in October 1940 when he spent twenty-two hours in a dinghy in the Atlantic before being rescued, and again in November following a raid on Turin. In May 1941 he was awarded the DFC for his service with 102 Squadron and a bar followed in September 1942 when he completed a tour with 104 Squadron.[3] The following summer he married his 33-year-old American fiancée.[4] Young has been described as 'a large, calm man' and 'a very efficient organiser'. His favourite trick was to swallow a pint of beer without drawing breath. By mid-1943 he had completed sixty-five ops.

Before take-off, the crews went through a variety of rituals. 'Dinghy' Young tidied his room, several played cards, rolled dice and/or dozed. Many wrote letters home. Joe McCarthy, commander of the second wave assigned to attack the Sorpe dam, and his crew climbed into 'Q for Queenie'. A bouncing bomb attack would be ineffective against this target because an earthen wall surrounded the dam's concrete core, so McCarthy would have to make a conventional bomb drop. However, during the pre-flight check 'Q for Queenie' was found to have a coolant leak in the starboard outer engine and the aircraft had to go unserviceable. The only reserve Lancaster was ED825 AJ-T, which had been flown from Boscombe Down that afternoon by a ferry pilot. Although 'T-Tommy' was bombed up, there had been no time to fit a VHF radio or Aldis lamps. McCarthy and his crew jumped out of 'Q-Queenie', the big American snagging his parachute on a hook in the process, and finally they got all moveable equipment out of the aircraft and rushed over to 'T-Tommy'. There they found that the compass deviation card vital for flying the carefully charted route accurately was not in the cockpit. The chances of flying the Lancaster at low level (between 75 and 120ft) through the myriad of flak emplacements and around night fighter bases, which lay between them and their target, were zero without it.

Joe McCarthy climbed down from the cockpit for the second time that evening and, with his 'Irish temper' near boiling point, jumped into a truck and headed for the hangar, where he ran into Flight Sergeant G.E. 'Chiefy' Powell, 617's Senior NCO. After a very short, expletive-filled, one-sided conversation, Powell took off at the double to the squadron's instrument section. He was unsure of what exactly he was looking for but he managed somehow to locate a blank card. He thrust another parachute into the impatient pilot's lap and McCarthy headed off to the hard stand, where the compass was swung with Upkeep in position. He finally got airborne at 22.01, thirty-four minutes behind his section. By the time 'T-Tommy' reached Vlieland, at 23.13, McCarthy had reduced the deficit to twenty-one-and-a-half minutes. He received a 'hot reception from the natives' when 'T-Tommy' crossed the coastline. 'They knew the track we were coming in on, so their guns were pretty well trained when they heard my motors. But, thank God, there were two large sand dunes right on the coast which I sank in between.'

The Lancasters took off in three waves. The first nine aircraft were to target the Möhne and then carry on to the Eder dam, followed by other targets as directed by wireless from 5 Group Headquarters. The second wave of five was to act as a diversionary force and to attack the Sorpe and the final five were detailed as back-up aircraft with alternative targets at Achwelm, Ennerpe and Diemi dams if they were not needed in the main attacks. The first wave would fly in three sections of three aircraft about ten minutes apart. After crossing the north-west coast of The Wash about 5 miles north-east of Boston, their route was across Norfolk past East Dereham and Wymondham near Norwich to Bungay in Suffolk and on to Southwold before heading out across the North Sea to Holland and on to the Möhne. The second wave would fly to the Sorpe dam via a different route to confuse enemy defences. This route was slightly further via the Friesian Islands, so the second wave actually took off first. The third wave of five Lancasters was to set off later and act as a mobile reserve to be used against such dams as were still unbroken.

The fourth and fifth hits on the Möhne dam by Squadron Leader 'Dinghy' Young DFC* and Squadron Leader David J.H. Maltby finally breached the structure at 00.56 hours. Melvin Young's nickname 'Dinghy' was transmitted back to 5 Group Headquarters, to be received with yet more celebration, but his Lancaster was hit by flak at Castricum-aan-Zee, Holland and crashed into the sea with the loss of all the crew. Young was 27 years old.

The Lancasters flown by Flight Sergeant Ken Brown and Flight Lieutenant Joe McCarthy headed for the 226ft-high Sorpe dam at the northern end of the Sorpe River. It had been realised quite late in the day that this was effective if the dam was built of concrete but no good for an earth dam, as the Sorpe was. Their instructions, therefore, were to fly over and along the line of the dam at 60ft, releasing the bomb as near the centre of the dam as they could.

Arriving over the valley at fifteen minutes after midnight, McCarthy initiated a diving attack on the dam nestled at the bottom of two steep hills. As the Lancaster circled over Langscheid, McCarthy exploded; 'Jeez! How do we get down there?' He decided that he must go round the church steeple of the village to line up his run. Coming over the top of one hill, using full flaps to keep the speed of his 30-ton Lancaster under control, McCarthy dived down the slope toward the 765yd-long dam. To escape, he had to apply full power to his four Packard-built Rolls-Royce Merlins and climb at a steep angle up the side of the second hill. And if that wasn't difficult enough, a thick mist was filling the valley as he arrived. The blinding moonlight turned the mist into a writhing phosphorescent pall, which made it extremely difficult to judge the bomber's height above the lake. On the third attempt to locate the target, McCarthy almost flew 'T-Tommy' into the water. It was not until the tenth run that bomb aimer, Sergeant George 'Johnny' Johnson, was satisfied and released the bomb from a height of just 90ft. The weapon exploded squarely on top of the parapet, damaging and crumbling for more than 50yds the crown of the earthen wall.

Shortly thereafter, Flight Sergeant Ken Brown attacked the dam and then they transmitted 'goner', indicating that they had attacked but not breached the dam.

The 'last resort' targets, the Lister (Schweim) and Dieml dams, were not attacked. However, the damage inflicted in the first two attacks proved the operation's success. The surge of water from the Möhne and Eder dams knocked out power stations and damaged factories, and cut water, gas and electricity supplies. As many as 1,300 civilians, including about 500 Ukrainian women slave labourers, died. Eight Lancasters were lost, fifty-three men were killed and three were captured. Joe McCarthy, David Maltby, Mick Martin, Dave Shannon and Les Knight were awarded the DSO.

It was decided to keep the Dambusters in being as an 'old lags' squadron (Harris' affectionate and respectful name for experienced men who only wanted to fly ops) and to use it for independent precision raids on small targets. These would be carried out using the Stabilising Automatic Bomb Sight (SABS), which had been invented at Farnbrough in 1941 and incorporated a bulky gyro. In perfect conditions SABS could aim a bomb very accurately but a bomber using it had to run perfectly straight and level up to the target for 10 miles. Harris said this would result in too many bomber losses but the argument was that SABS could be used economically by a small force operating at a fraction under 20,000ft over a well-marked target.

At 5 Group the Air Officer Commanding (AOC), Air Vice Marshal The Honourable Sir Ralph A. Cochrane KBE CB AFC, intended that 617 be trained to use SABS and deliver Barnes Wallis' new 10-ton bombs coming off the drawing board. In the meantime, the targets on the night of 15–16 July were two power and transformer stations in northern Italy. The intention was to disrupt the supply of electricity to the railways carrying German troops and supplies to the battle front in Sicily using twelve Lancasters of 617 Squadron, with a dozen more from 5 Group. Six of the Dambusters were led by Holden to Aquata Scrivia, near Genoa, and the other six to San Pola D'Enza, near Bologna, were led by Dams' veteran Squadron Leader David J.H. Maltby DSO DFC. The raids were not successful. No flares or markers were carried and the targets were partially hidden by haze. After bombing, the Lancasters flew on to Blida in North Africa. There was little opposition and two Lancasters of the supporting force were lost.

All the Dambusters landed safely at Blida, where Flight Lieutenant Joe McCarthy DSO DFC threw his parachute down digustedly and said, 'If we'd only carried flares we could've seen what we were doing.'

In North Africa, bad weather grounded the Lancasters for ten days and they finally flew home via Leghorn, where bombs were dropped through the persistant haze into the harbour below. Back at Scampton the crews unloaded the Lancasters. In spite of everything, they could hardly regard it as a fruitless trip as they struggled to the mess with crates of figs, dates, oranges, bottles of red wine and Benedictine.

It was exactly four months after the famous Ruhr dams raid on the night of 15–16 September when 617 Squadron, which had moved to Coningsby with its asphalt runway on 30 August, was tasked to carry out a raid on the banks of the Dortmund–Ems Canal at Ladbergen. This time the delayed-fuse mines were even bigger. The first attempt the night before had been aborted.[5] Squadron Leader David J.H. Maltby DSO DFC and crew, all of whom had flown on the dams raid, were lost on the way home 8 miles north-east of Cromer when their Lancaster hit someone's slipstream and cartwheeled into the North Sea.[6] With little sleep, eight of the crews were ordered back into the air the very next night to try again with the 12,000lb light-case bombs. Ray Grayston, the recently commissioned flight engineer on N-Nan captained by Pilot Officer Les Knight DSO Royal Australian Air Force (RAAF), says, 'We didn't think it was a very good idea and we were right.' The attack on the Dortmund–Ems Canal was led by Squadron Leader George Holden DSO DFC★ MiD in S-Sugar. In the control tower at Coningsby Joe McCarthy, now a squadron leader with a DSO for the Dams raid and a bar to his DFC added at the beginning of his third tour, watched as the eight Lancasters took off and headed east for the Dortmund–Ems Canal at around midnight. Outwardly McCarthy had a personality that matched his physique. His colourful American expletives were freely lavished on all who crossed his path. This was in marked contrast to the more austere profanity of the British pilots. Also watching was a 'languid' WAAF (Women's Auxiliary Air Force), who said as the Lancasters merged with the darkness, 'My God, I only hope they get there tonight! The trouble the AOC's gone to over this …' McCarthy turned on her and snarled, 'The hell with you and all the AOCs. What about the seven lives in every kite!' The building vibrated as the door slammed behind him.[7]

Near the end of the war, Big Joe McCarthy adapted to the British way, being seen with a pipe, a walking stick and a dog on a lead. 'If I'm going to be an officer and a gentleman, I'm going to have a crack at looking the part,' he said.

13

NEARER MY GOD TO THEE
FREDERICK JOHN COLE

During Christmas 1938 I was sixteen and waiting for the results of my examinations. When they came through I was lucky to have passed the 'Matric' that was the level necessary before taking any University Degree course. With the help of my father I found myself with a job almost immediately working in the Registrar's office at the Technical College on Normanton Road in Derby. I remember it well. There I discovered that I was also entitled to a day off a week for part time studies; so after considerable discussion I opted to go for the 'Bachelor of Commerce Degree', largely because my father was adamantly against me going into engineering (I won't tell you what he said about all the engineering apprentices – that would be another story altogether!).

The college year didn't start until the September of that year. The intermediate degree was three years and a further two years to complete the final degree. So, in the meantime I was offered 'fill in' courses and lectures whilst waiting for the September to come around. When September finally arrived, two things happened. The first was my seventeenth birthday; the second was the commencement of World War II! This left serious question marks on my planned training and what the future held. I opted to continue working and spent one day and two nights a week studying. During the course of the war time years I had all sorts of experiences from fire watching to walks home through smoke screens and all the various happenings that went with hiding Derby from any visual contact from the air. I remember hearing the planes going over the top of Derby en route to Coventry the night of the big blitz. Putting aside these, which were rather traumatic experiences in themselves, I continued studying until my nineteenth birthday. On my eighteenth birthday I immediately volunteered for the RAF for flying duties and sure enough, I was called to go to Birmingham where I was interviewed. All sorts of tests were carried out including a full medical and before I knew it had received a letter from the air force saying that I was to keep in contact. In the meantime I continued working for my degree. When the results came through in May 1941, I passed the 'Intermediate Degree' and almost immediately got a call to report to the RAF. This signalled a complete change in my life and introduced me to all that went with the military service.

I remember having my case packed and travelling down to London to stay in a big hotel that was not far from London Zoo. I booked in and met all my fellow travellers. We shared four to a room and after introductions were paced through all the 'spit and polish' of RAF routine. We were kitted out, had dental inspections, medicals and were given a series of 'jabs'. It was not too bad. We would march to London Zoo for our meals and dined in the Zoo dining room that was opposite the monkey house! Well, the monkeys must have had a 'ball' every day seeing these idiots queuing up to get some 'grog'!

Before I know it we are sent to Newquay in Cornwall and once again it proved to be a complete change of lifestyle. On arrival in Newquay we found ourselves in a fairly large guest house, right on the front by the sea overlooking a small island. We had a room each and ate our meals in the apartment block – we ate well! There were pilchards from the local fishing fleet for breakfast and lunch – even dinner was punctuated with pilchards! In fact, getting the bones out became the art of perfection.

During this time we had lectures on flying and learning about all the aspects of the RAF, etc, further medicals and also reported to the dentist. Much to my horror when the dentist saw my teeth and all the 'holes' that had been patched up and filled, he decided in the interests of being able to fly and withstand all possible pressures I should have them removed! So right from that point on I had a small dental plate that fitted to the back of my lower jaw. I always think back on that because that set of teeth lasted me right through until I was fifty odd years of age!

We did the training and our square-bashing, marching up and down the front. This continued for quite a number of weeks, I think eight in all. During the course of that time we were in and out of the sea, bathing and enjoying the beach. The bathing was great and needless to say we naturally bumped into several ladies during the course of our time there. The one lady I met that I can remember clearly was the daughter of a London stockbroker. I remember her being very bright and intelligent but a bit 'toffee-nosed'. The only other occasion was when I met dear Dot and that was in itself an interesting first encounter!

One day I was walking with a chap called Jack Davies I had got to know well in the Air Force. As we were walking past two ladies, well they were girls rather than 'ladies' I suppose; one of them shouted 'Jack!' It turned out they were both from Hereford and knew Jack. That evening we went to a dance in the village school hall and to my surprise found myself dancing with Dot; the other lady who had been with Stella. We had a wonderful dance and a wonderful evening and I remember so clearly that our last dance was the Anniversary Waltz.

After that meeting, I saw Stella and Dot going down to the beach and enjoying themselves. It was coming towards the end of the week and Jack had been moaning to me that he had had dates with Dot and she kept letting him down. As it happened I was out for a walk one day and saw her coming along the front and decided to talk to her. After we had been chatting for a while Dot said, 'Oh but I don't want to date Jack, I don't even like him.' Anyway it ended up that we went out together that evening and had a wonderful time! I can't quite recall now whether it was walking back that evening or the following day, but before Dot and Stella left to return home Dot and I walked along the beach and past a bookshop. As Dot passed the shop she said she had forgotten to pick up the book she had asked them to keep on one side. Unfortunately for Dot the shop was closed – so of course I immediately stepped in and said, 'Don't worry about that, I'll get the book for you and post it on to you.' The effect of which, of course, was an exchange of addresses and, if I remember correctly, a photograph at the same time!

After our training in Newquay had finished I was posted to 16 EFTS (Elementary Flying Training School) that happened to be based at Burnaston near Derby (my home town). Arriving there I discovered that we had been billeted in the chapel at Repton College where we were allocated bunks in the hall. The time spent there was quite enjoyable, except for the one night that I remember being the only time I was ever put on a charge. I was due to take over guard duties at about three o'clock in the morning, but the man who I was relieving failed to wake me up and so I didn't report for duty and found myself on 'jankers' and got a 'rollicking' for it, but that was all. However, it was quite an experience.

Flying was based at Barton, just the other side of Burnaston, and we flew the Tiger Moths. When I started flying my instructor was quite an old Flight Lieutenant but, as it happened, a very nice chap. The first lesson was on learning the general controls of the aeroplane and what happens and so forth. We strapped ourselves in – you had to double yourself up to put the belt on because it was an open cockpit with no protection at all. So, we took off and I really enjoyed it. I got a great thrill out of spinning the aircraft down and pulling out and was doing very well. However you can get a bit relaxed after flying a bit and I must have not tied my belt as tight as I should have done because my instructor said, 'You did tighten your belt up didn't you?' and I said 'Oh yes' and then he turned the darned thing right upside down and I must have pulled the joystick out of the floor! Anyway, that was a lesson!

After seven hours of flying I was given the controls of the aeroplane and told to go and do a circuit – well what a wonderful exhilarating experience! I was in control and out there flying! Then, before I knew it, I was coming in to land and did the most perfect landing (although I say it myself!). I reckon that I had a smooth landing and stopped within about twenty yards! Having stopped at twenty yards and right at the beginning of the runway, I instinctively looked at the length ahead and thought, 'What the hell's the point in going all the way down there, lets turn off!' and so, without a further thought, I turned and went straight in. Much to my surprise I received the biggest 'rollicking' I've ever had! That was because I had forgotten the golden rule – once on the runway you must always go to the end. In retrospect I guess I momentarily, in my excitement and thrill of feelings of success forgot the 'golden rule' and that proved to be my downfall. I think that momentary lapse cost me any chance of becoming a pilot as I had wanted but the consequence of that will evolve later in my story.

Shortly after this I have three weeks leave. This was easy to sort because Derby was where I lived anyway. While in Derby I had been in contact with Dot in Hereford but was still quite surprised when I received a letter from her saying 'Why not come and spend a few days in Hereford?' I read the invite to my father who, much to my astonishment said, 'Well why don't you go!' Some of the things you do on the spur of the moment can give you some of the greatest pleasures in life.

I remember getting off the train at Hereford station just hoping that I would recognise her and of course I did. She took me to her home that was near the SAS headquarters just outside Hereford. I met her family and was instantly made to feel at home and thought what a lovely family. The first shock though was when she took me upstairs and said, 'Now this is my bedroom and you're sleeping here'. I confess I was a bit 'taken aback' for a minute, but then realised that she was sleeping somewhere else – so that was a relief in a sense! We had a great time and I got to know her youngest brother Alan really well. His arm may have been in a sling but he religiously followed the instructions that had been detailed by their mother to accompany us wherever we went – talk about a gooseberry! Anyway it resulted in the start of a friendship with Alan that has lasted from that time to this.

At the time I was non-commissioned, an LAC. We walked out one evening and called in at a pub where Dot's father used to drink. When we went into the lounge we were told 'Officers only' so we had to leave and walked into town. I forget the time, there was a dance on at the Odeon Theatre but I said, 'Let's have a drink' so we went to the Garrick Hotel and asked Dot, 'would you like a drink?' and to my surprise she said, 'Yes please, a beer.' Well in those days women never drank beer, it was gin and orange or something similar. Anyway she insisted, so I went to the bar and got two pints and she drank a pint just the same as I did! By then it was nearly closing time so I went and got two more beers. Well that was quite an experience to me because I had never bought a girl a drink before (a beer at that!), and certainly never been to a pub with a girl on my own. It was no surprise that we then had a wonderfully enjoyable dance at the Odeon!

Inevitably the time came to report back to Derby and from Derby onward to Ludlow where the RAF had recently started a campsite holding area. We camped in bell tents and had to dig our own latrines. There was a house at the top on the main road going towards Shrewsbury that was used as a medical centre. However, we did not stay long. I remember one night when four of us went into Ludlow and went to a pub called The Feathers where we decided to try some of the local cider. I had drunk cider before so I knew how strong it was, but the other lads were novices and got quite tipsy – it was their heads that suffered the next morning, not mine!

From there we were sent to Heaton Park just outside Manchester. This was the final reception point for aircrew under training who were likely to be sent on for further training elsewhere. In Heaton we were called in one day to be given a full briefing and names were called out and the selection of what you were to be announced. In some ways I was bitterly disappointed to hear that my task was that of bomb aimer. I recalled my previous performance on the runway and thought that that was that, but in any case it was said that the need for bomb aimers was important because of the increasing number of Heavy Bombers coming into service that required a specialised and broad basis of training. We were also told that our training would ensure that we were sufficiently capable of taking over if ever an emergency arose (i.e. the Bomb Aimer took over the controls should the necessity arise).

In my case, I was sent to Canada and went on a journey that ended up in Gourock, not far from Glasgow, where we were then ferried out to a large vessel at anchor. Everything was dark but once we were aboard found ourselves on the Queen Elizabeth, that, at the time had not actually been commissioned for cruise duties and was being used by the RAF for its speed to transit large numbers to and from Canada or wherever. It was a very unexpected, pleasant surprise.

The one thing I remember about the train journey were the dear ladies of the Salvation Army who always seemed to produce a sausage or something when you were having a 'nap'. Apart from that I remember little about the journey, we always seemed to be in the dark and it wasn't long before we were out at sea. At some point we were told that we were destined for Halifax or Nova Scotia and that from there we would then be transferred to Monkton, a large reception camp. After finally arriving in Monkton we decided on the first evening to go for a walk to the nearby town and there found a cinema and a shop selling bananas. We bought a couple of bananas each and went to the cinema. After the movie ended we went to the British Legion club where the only beer was bottled Pilsner ale and it was served to you at the table. Curiously, on each table was a salt pot that I think was made of pewter, rather like the ones that we used in our local fish and chip shops in England, but we had no idea what they were for until we spotted some 'locals' using them. Every time they opened a bottle of Pilsner and poured it into a glass they added salt! We rumbled in the end after talking to some of the locals that it was to take the gas out of their drink. However, it was quite novel to us at the time.

After a brief stay in Monkton we were put on a train to Lethbridge, which was not too far from Winnipeg. I remember the train being quite luxurious with a full bunk to each compartment and being well looked after by a coloured gentleman. It was a very exciting and absorbing journey that seemed to go on for ages. We finally arrived in Lethbridge; it resembled a town created to serve some of the old cowboy films and flat as a pancake to walk around. Anyway we were transported by bus from there to a camp that had a small airfield. It was all very well planned and thought out.

When training started it was split into two sections; navigation and the other was bombing and gunnery and we flew in Ansons, a British-made aircraft that did invaluable service throughout the war in all sorts of roles. Flights and navigation training was done at night and then we did some gunnery shooting and also dropping practice bombs. There was a warning that not far from the camp itself was an Indian Reservation and that on no account should practice bombs be dropped in that vicinity. Occasionally bombs did go astray but no questions were asked!

Whilst there we tried our hand at ice hockey – that was great fun and there were also dances every so often when some of the ladies from Winnipeg came in a coach. On one occasion we met up with three young ladies from the same family and were invited back to Winnipeg to meet their mother. They were a lovely family and we thoroughly enjoyed the day when we were showed around Winnipeg.

Then came the day when we were briefed what the 'score' was. We were called up one by one, photographed and presented with our wings. When the presentations were over there was a silence. An announcement then came that the following men had been awarded a commission. The first person called out was the name Bennett and then, much to my surprise, the name Cole, F.J. To be honest I just couldn't believe it! It had never been my ambition to achieve officer rank. Anyway there it was, so a new pattern of life started to evolve because from then on I was placed into different quarters and had the services of a batman. We were then sent to Winnipeg with some money for uniform allowance to be measured up for our uniforms. Later, when I went back to collect my uniform and tried it on – well I can assure you it was quite an experience getting into a uniform for the first time.

We were next sent to Lake Dolphin, further north and an advanced 'gunnery' training establishment. Before going there we were in contact with an organisation that arranged meetings with American families who wanted to entertain members of the RAF for a few days in the States, in Minneapolis. So, as a result I found myself in Minneapolis and met by Mrs Reynolds. She took me to meet her family and was shown around the house. I remember being taken to a luncheon one day that was attended by mainly businessmen and there was this huge table rather like King Arthur's with rotating discs on the table loaded with everything you could imagine! The second thing I remember was that on the back of every butter pack was stamped 'Remember Pearl Harbor'. (That was the nearest I got to any sense of being in a war at that time).

The family was lovely and I got on extremely well with her daughter Ginnie. She was a great conversationalist and we spent many a time talking and also with her brother who was learning to be a fighter pilot. It included a day when we visited the lake and went out in a speedboat for most of the afternoon. It was a most enjoyable and memorable time.

After that I was back up at Lake Dolphin and started training in the Fairey Battle, which was a different type of flying machine altogether. The training consisted of flying and having moving targets in the air to fire at, very intensive and absorbing. Shortly after we were assigned back to Moncton and then back home.

Another memory I recall was a Sergeant based on the camp. I happened to bump into her in Lethbridge one evening whilst having a drink on my own. We talked and it was a pleasant conversation. There was a bus that ran from the camp to town but when it was time to leave we decided to walk back as it was a beautiful moonlit night in the snow. We hadn't walked very far when a car pulled up and the driver asked, 'Where are you going?' and when we replied he said, 'Oh yes, I'm going past there.' This driver was totally inebriated but we failed to realise until after we had got into the car – it was the most hair-raising drive back to camp! I suppose that formed a friendship between us and I enjoyed the acquaintance. I think her name was Miriam Campbell.

On our return to Monkton and coming home we were assigned to a vessel that was called the Louis Pasteur, an old French liner, we boarded and sailed unescorted back to Liverpool. We slept in hammocks that proved to be great fun, both getting in and out of them! We did have one or two rough nights though. The ship had a gun on the back and one night they fired it and thank god it was only a test! I thought the whole vessel was going to fall to bits. Anyway we made it back and docked at Liverpool.

Returning from training in Canada and arriving at Liverpool we were transferred to another holding camp based at Harrogate. It was not long before some of us were sent to Jurby in the Isle of Man. This was a base camp for an advanced training course that did not involve any flying and to some extent I found rather boring. After that I proceeded up north, but this time via Liverpool and was sent straight up to Thurso at the tip of Scotland, en route to Skivray in the Orkneys. It was a long trip. We were put on a ferry that had a concrete bottom because it was such a rough sea to cross the water to Skivray. Believe it or not there was a theatrical group called ENSA to entertain the troops on board as well. Eventually we got there and it was a really outlandish outpost but needless to say the orchestra accommodation was excellent! We were also very well catered for.

The purpose of the training at Skivray was for us to become familiar with and get used to, bombing moving targets. There was this young New Zealander pilot who loved flying in and out of the cables holding the balloons over Scapa. It was either that or we were low flying, and by low flying I mean you could have put your hand out and almost touched the grass! It was an exhilarating experience but he was 'mad as a hatter'. One day we were up flying and he put the Anson into a dive and a whole sheet of metal came off the side of the aircraft!

While there, as already mentioned, we were bombing moving targets and often flew over the fleet. I recall seeing the American aircraft carrier Wasp and think that at the time it was leading out a convoy destined for Narvik. Also visible was the battleship Royal Oak lying in the water alongside the dock, the entire ship was clearly in view just as the German Submarine had left it. Interestingly, the Navy often entertained us! We were picked up and taken out to one of their ships at anchor and it became a well-known fact that none of us ever came back with two legs on the ground! Maybe it was fortunate that these excursions were called off, I think due to the pending expedition I referred to, going over to Norway.

I had a dreadful cold at the time and remember phoning my Father for advice and he told me to have a rum and blackcurrant with hot water – it worked! Apart from that I forget how many weeks we were there, but before long we were back on the move and this time were sent down to Wigtown on the Scottish coast.

As an interesting aside story, Dot was by that time in the Wrens and based down at Falmouth in Cornwall. She applied for what was then called a compassionate posting so she could be close to where I was at that time. Unfortunately in practice, I was sent up to the Orkney Isles while she, at short notice, was sent to the Scilly Isles – that was about the furthest we could be away from each other! It took about two days (I think) to work out how we could meet together when we both had leave from our various posts. We did manage it though and when we met again, (my memory is a bit rusty), I am sure it was in Derby.

We were next sent to Upper Heyford. This was the place where we were all assembled, discussions ensued and we talked to each other to decide on choices to form a crew. I opted for Phil Ainley as pilot, joined by Les Bradbeer, a Canadian navigator, and a 'happy-go-lucky' wireless operator by the name of Alf Fishburn. Later, Harry Evans joined us as flight engineer. This was the formation for our crew, a basic crew who would then fly as a team in a Lancaster.[1]

We went to Upper Heyford at the beginning of November 1943 and continued until the end of March 1944. Dot and I had managed to see each other many times after my return from Canada and she came up to Derby once to see me and I was in Hereford once with her. Well the bond of friendship continued to grow from strength to strength and from this point on whatever I did, wherever I went, whatever happened was in the name of two and no longer just me.

Back to the flying, we were crewed-up and flew in the Wellington bombers, still training, exercising and getting to know each other. We were operating from Barford St John, a satellite to Upper Heyford. Every so often we had a bus to transport us into Banbury for an evening out on the town. It was during one such time that Dot had somehow or other got herself from Falmouth to

Banbury by train by fooling the system! We only spent the day together, but a wonderful occasion and it was at this point we decided to get engaged.

When the RAF flying training was completed at Upper Heyford we were transferred to a heavy bomber conversion unit to fly, of all things, Stirling bombers! These aircraft were all based in the East coast area. In the meantime Dot was in the Wrens and at that time waiting for a posting to train as a 'Visual Signaller' at Lowton St. Mary's not far from where some of her relatives lived in Leigh, Lancashire. Then came the memorable meeting when she said that she had heard that she could be posted to India if successful in her exams and, needless to say, she was successful. Full of apprehension I chanced to say, 'They can't make you go, not if you are a married woman they can't'. Well that was all I said! About four days later I get a letter back from Dot to say that not only 'was it on' but that the date was already fixed, the calling of the bans sorted — the whole lot! It was fine by me and I left Dot to do all the 'fussing' and sort everything out. The date of our wedding was fixed for 10 April. I managed to arrange a week's leave for myself and day's leave for my mates Phil and Brad so they could come along and attend the wedding in Hereford. Phil acted as my best man. All went extremely well and within days of having become man and wife once more Dot, through some mystic way, managed to arrange a couple of further days leave to come up and stay not far from the airfield where I was based.

During this time we were going up and down in a Stirling bomber, getting used to the handling of a 'big kite' and the Stirling was a big kite! It felt like you were about fifty feet off the ground when you were in the cockpit but gradually you became attuned to it. The aircraft itself was like a flying tank with armour plating inside and surprisingly comfortable but the manoeuvrability was not of the same standard that we had become accustomed to when flying the Lancaster.

At Wigsley we collected our air gunners. The mid-upper gunner was Arnold McTrowe, a Canadian lad; and the tail gunner was Doug Salisbury, who came from up North somewhere. We were moved to Swinderby, a conversion unit to Lancaster bombers and spent some time there completing flying exercises, dummy runs, etc, until we were finally posted to 57 Squadron at East Kirkby on 15 May. Initially we did a variety of further training with the squadron and made our first bombing run on 24 May to Antwerp. It was not too bad an experience. In those areas the density of the gunnery from the ground was always intense but for us it was our first insight as to what the war was all about. Three days later we were sent on our second operation to St. Valéry in Northern France, a time when flying bombs were becoming a major threat.

On 1 June we were involved in a moonlight mission flying to the south of Paris to bomb a bridge at Saumur. We were not flying at a particularly high level as we approached the target area. The night sky was beautiful and the target quite clear. As we started on the bombing run there were suddenly 'tracers' going all around from attacking enemy aircraft. I was down in the bomb bay that provided forward vision only (i.e. not sideways or below). We kept going despite several continued fighter attacks until we were in fact over the target. Like I said it was clear as a 'bell' and you could see exactly what was going on. We beat a hasty exit as quickly as we could, 'corkscrewing' nearly all the way home. 'Corkscrewing' is a flying tactic where you flew like a corkscrew through the sky to make it more difficult for any fighter aircraft that might be following to beam on to you and fire.

All was fine until we got back to the airfield and got out. What a shock awaited us! Across the fuselage and under the middle of the aircraft were twenty-nine holes and after inspection the aircraft itself was written off. We were damned lucky but we didn't know it at the time, by that I mean it wasn't until we landed that we realised, so were damned lucky. Anyway, that was quite an experience and an eye opener for us all. Following that night and throughout July and into August we were flying roughly every second or third night or a bit longer all depending on the weather conditions.

Most of the early flights were based around northern France attacking the flying bomb sites and rocket areas, things of that kind. There were also long sorties in support of the D-Day landings and the subsequent problems such as Falaise Gap after the landing had taken place. However, I am going to concentrate on talking about the trips we did that were somewhat different and what one might call of a 'non-routine' character.

During this period, Dot had been transferred to the harbour office at Grimsby as a Visual Signaller. Her duties involved monitoring vessels coming in and out of ports and very often they were carrying airmen who had been shot down on missions, etc. It was not a very pleasant job for her to do, but somehow or other, and I can't remember doing this, we managed to locate a place where we could stay in the village of Stickney in Norfolk that was just the other side of the airfield.

The place was called 'Woodbine Cottage', a delightful little dwelling with a big windmill at the bottom of the garden, and the owner was called Peggy Donna. She had a young daughter who was then four or five years old. Dot, with her usual determination, had found a way that she could, with the help of one or more of her friends, arrange to have pillows placed under the covers of her bed during her absence so that she could sneak off all night every so often, sometimes even two nights! She would go to the train station, change into 'civvies' so as not to be identified and then buy a ticket to Stickney on the train that in those days was a restricted area for travel, quite a risky thing to do at the time! There was no Station Master or ticket collector to question her arrival, so she used to get off at Stickney to meet me – an arrangement that went on for a long time. So that is how we managed to get together every so often. The times we were not together she always knew when I was on a 'mission' because I would write to her and sign the letter 'I'll see you again'. That was our way of saying I am doing something I can't talk about tonight.

One of the most significant operations I flew on was during the middle of August [on Wednesday the 16th] when we were called upon as a squadron to do some special low-level 'Gardening', (that is dropping mines.) This was in a channel between Danzig ('as was') and Stettin. Now at the same time a large raid was taking place at Stettin that could be seen in the distance from my position with everything going off. [2]

We were on our own and came in the back way so to speak. The marker had been 'plonked' right on the little island that we used as a start for our run-in. We hadn't gone very far when a voice came over the intercom saying: 'This is Wing Commander Porter, we've been hit; we're going in,' or some words to that effect. That was very unnerving. [3]

Anyway, I placed my parachute under my belly as we were descending; we were going down to 250 feet. The target was a waterway that, at that level, was illuminated with lights that you could see on the approach but couldn't see if you were directly overhead. There were three 'eggs' to be dropped and I recall that we had to count to five between each 'egg' drop. These bombs were special; some were timed to explode as the first vessel went over them, some after the second or third and so on.

Battle stations had started and we found the channel; all hell was let loose with 'tracers' left, right and centre that fortunately seemed to be going too high above us to make a target as we were underneath them. Somehow we managed to get through it and every member of the crew was shouting to each other, 'Come on Mike, you can do it!' We shot up into the night sky like a rocket, up and away. That was quite a thrilling experience for us and thankfully we had a safe journey back home. This was the occasion when Phil the pilot was awarded the Distinguished Flying Cross.

Another trip I should mention was to Königsberg in Russia. [4] We were airborne for thirteen hours. It was an uneventful trip and I have always thought it was more of a gesture of support than a serious bombing operation. I say this because the weight factor was fuel and not bomb load.

One time we were sent on a daylight bombing raid in Belgium, the target was a large airfield and I remember that as we approached there was formidable attack fire with shells exploding all around us. We were flying not too far behind another Lancaster, the crew of which I knew very well – all of a sudden they just disappeared. A shell had caught the bomb load and the only evidence we had were bits and pieces in the leading edge of our wings. On the same raid I witnessed a bomb go straight through the wing of another Lancaster but it just kept on flying.

There were some unusual trips. We had a few 'boffins' about with theoretical ideas on how to improve bombings and so forth. On one trip [27–28 September] we were sent to Kaiserslautern on the French–German border. Based there was a big circular of railway sheds and in a brief we were told that each bomber would have a coloured flare attached to the pins of the bombs to be dropped so that it could be clearly identified where the bombs were going. Well, this was fine and the target was as clear as a 'bell' and everything was great until the first bombs were dropped. Now you need to know that when you are 'pumping' an aircraft through a narrow gap in a comparatively short time and start dropping bombs it does not take much of the imagination to realise that the bombs were not only missing the tail but also just missing the side of the aeroplane! Actually the gunners and everyone in the aircraft were all shouting at once – I won't tell you what a colourful language came out! Nevertheless we succeeded in completing the bombing run but there was one thing I am certain of – that demoralising exercise was never to be repeated again. I hope that the person or whoever thought up the idea was told it didn't work![5]

On another occasion we were asked to try out a new 'pilot' type parachute that was strapped to the back as opposed to the traditional chute that was separate and clipped on to two 'D' rings at the front. Well, strap the parachute on and you could hardly move in the aircraft – that was the end of that idea! After that, someone came up with the idea of using electric jackets that could be plugged into the aircraft electrics to keep you warm – like toast! That idea didn't last long either.

There was this one time when we spotted the exhaust of another Lancaster that seemed to be very close and so dropped the nose down sharply. In doing so the 'astrodome' flew off the machine, our navigator's 'curtain' went through the hole and it was 'bedlam' – What the navigator was saying was completely unrepeatable at this scary moment but it didn't affect us as he decided to take some of the pressure off by reducing height.

We didn't always fly at maximum height. Once on a trip when we were flying at 20,000 feet at maximum speed I do recall the time when I needed to go to the Elsan toilet and to do this you had to unplug your oxygen mask from the socket you were using and remember where the other sockets were along the aircraft for the return journey as the 'loo' itself was halfway down the fuselage – well could I find the socket at the Elsan end? I ended up feeling giddy. Eventually I found it but I never tried to do the same thing again. Nothing like learning from experience I guess.

Towards the end of flying duties, I was sleeping 'out' one night at Woodbine cottage. Dot and I were awakened in the early hours by a car hooting outside. It was some of the crew yelling that we had been called for 'Ops'! In the rush I had no alternative but to dress over my pyjamas! We returned in time for the briefing but shortly after the operation had been called it was, fortunately, cancelled.

On operations it was a wonderful experience in itself because you and the aircraft were identified together, you spoke to the aircraft and the aircraft was a part of you. You may have been apprehensive at times but never afraid and it always struck me, after the event, what a wonderful companionship we had as a crew and a weird sort of feeling of safety. I can't find the words to explain it.

There we are, I had completed my operations, thirty-three in all, and finished flying on 5 October 1944 when we did a last daylight trip to Wilhelmshaven. As a crew we had finished flying and I must have had some leave and Dot had leave, so we had arranged to meet in Skegness. We were to rendezvous at a railway station en route at a certain time. I cycled to the Station but no train arrived, so I cycled back and on my return there was a message that Dot got through on lines that were not supposed to be used (I still don't know how the devil she did it!), but it was a message to say that she was already in Skegness. Right, that was it, I quickly went to my billet to get my bike but it wasn't there – the flipping batman had borrowed it! There I was hanging around and in the end he rolled up. I quickly retrieved the bike and started cycling from the camp towards Skegness. I hadn't gone too far when a petrol bowser pulled up and asked me where I was going, so I told him. 'Well,' he said. 'I'm not supposed to do this,' but nevertheless he fixed the bike on the back of the petrol bowser and took me nearly all the way to Skegness. He dropped me off at a nearby village and I cycled from there.

On arrival the first port of call was the railway station because I knew that if you got stuck for the night you could always sleep in a railway carriage. I started asking folk if they knew of or had seen Dot. I think it was the local butcher who was able to tell me where she was! The following morning we decided to go for a walk, it was a lovely day although a cold wind was blowing. Some people we passed commented, 'Oh you found him, we're so glad' etc, etc. Well it wasn't long before we got on a train and went down to London and decided to spend a couple of days there. We stayed at the Great Russell Hotel (or was it the hotel in Great Russell Street?). It was great and on the second night we went to see My Fair Lady – we got seats right up in the gods! I never felt so uncomfortable in my life because I can't stand such heights when my seat is attached to the ground! Flying is a different feeling altogether. (Many years later we went to Toronto and stood at the top of the tower over Niagara Falls and I could hardly move! – 'Nearer my God to thee,' came a voice. 'Jump you silly b ...!')

Dot left London to return directly to Grimsby and I went back to Skegness – I'd left a bike somewhere there! Eventually I made it back to camp. Having completed all our operations the crew was split up and everything changed.[6]

14

THE VALLEY OF DEATH

Warrant Officer Angus Robb completed two tours of ops as rear gunner on
Pilot Officer Van Metre's crew on Wellingtons on 431 'Iroquois' and 432 'Leaside'
Squadrons RCAF, and 405 'Vancouver' PFF Squadron RCAF on Lancasters
between December 1942 and April 1945. His crew's (uneventful) baptism on
operational flying began with a 'gardening' trip to the Frisian Islands on the night
of 2–3 March 1943 when sixty aircraft were detailed to sow mines in coastal areas
between Texel and the River Gironde. Two Wellingtons and a Lancaster were lost.

Every one in ten sorties undertaken by Bomber Command during the war
was devoted to mine-laying, or 'gardening'. At the end of the war 'gardening'
became seen as one of the most effective campaigns in which Bomber Command
had participated. Apart from impeding U-boat training in the Baltic it put an
enormous strain on the vitally important coastal convoy lanes and caused hundreds
of German and German-controlled ships to be damaged and sunk through mine
explosions. By 1944 it also forced the Kriegsmarine to engage 40 per cent of its
forces in minesweeping. Bomber Command crews usually regarded the gardening
trips as something of a 'rest trip' from the more demanding bombing raids over
the mainland of the Third Reich. Casualties on mining operations, however,
could be heavy on a percentage basis for the following reasons: a few isolated
aircraft in a particular dropping zone were more easily detected; the mines had
to be dropped after an accurate fix had been obtained, requiring an area search; a
low-level timed run of three to five minutes from this fix to the dropping point
had to be straight and level; at the dropping height of 600ft, the 'gardening' aircraft
were highly vulnerable to enemy flak defences, both from shore batteries and
from flak ships guarding the convoy lanes.

Angus Robb and his 431 'Iroquois' Squadron RCAF Wellington crew were detailed to bomb Essen in the Ruhr Valley three nights later, on 5–6 March. They were part of a raid that heralded the beginning of what went into history as the Battle of the Ruhr. The ever increasing numbers of four-engined Stirlings, Halifaxes and Lancasters were led by the new target-marking Pathfinder Force and guided by the newly introduced blind-bombing device Oboe. After the long and painful struggle in its pioneering years, Bomber Command was finally capable of inflicting enormous damage on the industrial heartland of Nazi Germany. Although the Battle of the Ruhr was the first major successful wartime campaign for the command, it was achieved at a terrible price. No fewer than 1,000 aircraft were lost from the 23,401 night sorties despatched between 5 March and 24 July 1943, in a grim battle of attrition with the German night defences. Sergeant Angus Robb expands on his experiences:

The Battle of the Ruhr was an attempt by 'Bomber' Harris to demolish all the cities and towns in the Ruhr Valley and therefore cripple the production of war materials, it being the centre of the heavy industries in the Third Reich. This being the case, it was also the most heavily defended area, with the exception of Berlin, in Germany. It was considered, that to attack any city or town in the Happy Valley, as we called it, you had to fly through twenty miles of concentrated flak. Some of this was box-barrage stuff, in other words the shells were fused to go off at certain different heights which never varied but just filled the sky with shrapnel. It was no use trying to weave or dodge this type of fire. A straight and fast run was the only answer to it. The other type of fire was known as 'predicted'. This was controlled by radar and singled out one particular aircraft for attention. Very difficult to escape from if encountered over the target and mixed in with the box-barrage. Searchlights were another hazard we had to cope with. Although, by themselves, no danger, it was the feeling of being visible for miles that made the heart race. Usually used in conjunction with night fighters, but over the target they were used in collusion with the flak guns and could make life very uncomfortable.

On 5 March we were detailed to participate in a raid on Essen in the Ruhr Valley. And here I should say that very seldom did we, amongst ourselves, say we were 'on operations'. It was either 'dicing with death', 'juggling with Jesus' or 'gambling with God', reduced, in most cases, to 'dicing', 'juggling' or 'gambling'. I suppose you could say 'this was the night that changed my life'. We took off at 1815 and for the first hour or so we flew happily over the North Sea, with, it seemed, no one but ourselves in the sky. It was strange, flying on night operations; the sky, for most of the time, seemed completely empty, although you knew for a fact that there were hundreds of your compatriots all over the place.

It was when we reached the coast of Holland things started to happen. Searchlights were much in evidence and flak, although not close, was very active. It was as we approached the Ruhr Valley for the first time that I realized I had made a mistake in volunteering for aircrew and should have accepted their offer of being a member of an air-sea rescue launch. I have never been so frightened in my life and in fact I would better describe it as terror-stricken! There was no way, in my opinion, that any aircraft could fly into that amount of flak and come out the other side and that was without taking into account the German night fighters that were patrolling the skies just looking for me! It really is impossible, for anyone who was not there, to fully comprehend the sheer weight of metal that was thrown into the sky over those German cities. What with that and the fiery red glow, intermixed with explosions of all colours, from the ground, it was a scene from Dante's 'Inferno' brought into reality. There was also the spectacle of bombers exploding in a shower of red-hot debris when they received a direct hit from a flak shell, or had come off worst from an encounter with a German night fighter. It was a terrifying experience and if there had been some way I could have got out of ever flying on operations again, without losing face or being graded LMF [Lack of Moral Fibre]; in other words a coward, after that second trip I would have taken it. That may seem a cowardly admission to make, but I never really believed that there were many heroes among my contemporaries, only people that had got into a situation they could not get out of without dire consequences to themselves and just kept going on and on, with the fond hope that their God, whoever He was, would see them safely to the end. Of the 125,000 Bomber Command aircrew, 55,000 were killed and another 25,000 wounded, so if you survived, your God did look after you.

Operational aircrew had a leave entitlement of a week every six weeks; double that of other members of the RAF. The system employed split the crews into lists of six and when a crew reached the top of the list, off you went on leave. If, however, a crew went missing from your list and they were above you on that list, then you automatically reduced your waiting time by one week. The losses were such during this period that we were on leave about every three or four weeks. It was the case that if you survived, your chances of survival increased. New crews were the ones at risk. You needed luck to remain alive and by keeping alive learned the skills that perhaps, but only perhaps, would keep you ahead of the game. I should add, however, that I thoroughly enjoyed flying. There was nothing better than flying around the countryside, in fine weather, with the towns and villages set out beneath you and a view that stretched for miles in all directions. It was the operational flying that scared the hell out of me!

At no time in my RAF career can I ever recall any discussion taking place of the reason why we were dropping high explosive and incendiary devices on to German towns and cities. Neither was there any hatred for the Germans. In a strange way it was as if there was no one underneath our aircraft when we unloaded our bomb-racks and even the defences that were trying their best to destroy you were in fact not controlled by people, but were simply machines doing these things by their own volition. So I cannot say it was with any great desire to make the world a better place to live in that I volunteered for the RAF. It was simply an ardent wish to become a pilot – and fly.

One of the statistical facts of the Bomber Command offensive that is easily overlooked is that an estimated one in every six bomber losses occurred over the United Kingdom and not over enemy territory, due to crashes on take-off or landing, or aircraft limping back from the Continent with heavy battle damage and crash-landing on British soil. Sergeant Angus Robb, rear gunner on 431 Squadron 'Iroquois' RCAF, recounts such episodes:

There was the occasion when a 51 Squadron Halifax, stationed at close-by Snaith, landed at Burn for some reason and on take-off back to base developed a fire in one of the engines, which spread rapidly. The rear gunner must have seen the flames passing his turret and decided to get out. At the height he jumped his parachute did not open before he hit the ground, killing him instantly. The irony was, the pilot made an emergency landing with the wheels up, the Halifax split into two pieces and the rest of the crew scrambled out, unhurt.

Another Halifax from the same squadron, coming back from 'ops' badly damaged, attempted a landing at Burn but did not make a landing on his first approach so tried to go round again. Unfortunately, he did not have the power to gain enough height and in doing a banking turn hit a small brick-built hut at the end of the runway with his wing tip. This caused the Halifax to start cartwheeling from wing tip to wing tip, coming to rest a good two miles across the fields. When the medics got to the wreck, the crew were smashed to pulp with being thrown about so violently during the last few moments of their existence.

It was a strange time, with injury and death ever present and yet a few hours after the incident I have just described, we would be drinking with gusto and making plans as if the war did not intrude into our lives at all. Do not get the impression that it was all doom and gloom, rather the reverse. Losses were accepted as part of the game and in many ways it was a game to us; it would happen to that crew over there but not you.

On 3 June 1943 we made, for a Wellington, the long trip to St. Nazaire to drop our two sea-mines in the harbour. Mining was not an easy option for bombers. The Royal Navy was most explicit as to the exact spot they wanted the 'vegetables', as they were code-named, dropped. To achieve the accuracy required, on most occasions 'time and distance' were made. This meant flying from an identifiable point on the coast to the dropping point using a stop-watch and a careful monitoring of the air-speed. It seems a simple enough task, but bomber crews did not like the restriction of having to fly straight and level at low altitudes into heavily defended harbours. There were many anxious airmen, I can tell you, until the navigator with the stopwatch said 'NOW!' and the bomb aimer said 'mines gone'.

The dropping of sea-mines was done from a fairly low altitude and to ascertain the exact height, someone had come up with the idea of fixing a Very cartridge into the base of a cocoa tin, with a lead weight in the bottom and a nail sticking into the base of the cartridge. The rear gunner dropped the contraption out of the turret and told the navigator, who started his stopwatch. When the gunner saw the light from the can appear, he passed the message on, whereupon the navigator stopped the watch. From the time taken for the can to reach the surface of the water, he could work out the height of the aircraft above the sea. And they say today is the age of the technocrat.

On 5–6 July [when 34 aircraft carried out mine laying off the French ports and in the Friesians] we did another 'Gardening' trip to St. Nazaire, our only operational sortie of the month. At the end of the month we were on our way to another Canadian Squadron, 432, which was still flying Wellingtons, stationed at Skipton-on-Swale. We did six mining trips and one bombing trip in August. Four of the 'gardening' exploits were to the Dutch coast, the other two to Brest. The trips to Brest became very hazardous indeed. The channel to the mouth of the harbour was marked by normal light buoys, which we followed to the inner harbour where we dropped our mines. One night the Germans replaced the buoys with flak ships, displaying the same light pattern. We lost a number of aircraft that evening from that ploy and it made it, from then on, a very dangerous place indeed.

During 1943 and early 1944 Bomber Command had been transformed into a mighty four-engined force equipped with a wide range of technical aids for navigating, target-marking, blind-bombing and electronic warfare. Combined with major tactical developments such as diversionary and 'spoof' raiding, the introduction of the master bomber and the use of high-flying, Oboe-equipped, target-marking Mosquitoes, these enabled the bomber crews to deliver devastating blows to the Third Reich.

Angus Robb joined 405 'Vancouver' PFF Squadron RCAF as a second-tour air gunner in September 1944. He compares the operational conditions on bombing raids at this stage with his experiences during 1943, when he completed a tour on 431 and 432 Squadrons.

Our crew were Blind Illuminators and it was our job to get to the target a few minutes before the 'H' Hour of the raid and along with usually five other Blind Illuminator crews, drop a stick of ten illuminating flares over the target. These flares were 'hooded' from above, which made it possible to look 'through' them and so allow the other crews involved in the early part of the raid, the Master Bomber and the Primary Visual Markers, to ensure that the RAF were in the right place before allowing the raid to proceed. The dropping of the flares required the aircraft to fly in a straight line for 100 seconds, they were dropped at ten-second intervals and you can believe me when I tell you that 100 seconds is an eternity when you are flying over a heavily defended target and cannot take evasive action no matter what happens.

When it was decided that the RAF were in the right place, the raid was allowed to go ahead, the rest of the marking was done and the Main Force dropped their bombs on the PFF markers, whose official name was Target Indicators, or TIs to us.

The Master Bomber was a new arrangement as far as I was concerned. In 1943 the individual crews made their own arrangements and dropped their bomb load when they felt the moment was opportune. Now the Master Bomber could stop the bombing, tell the attacking aeroplanes to go higher or lower before bombing, instruct them to ignore certain markers if he felt they were in the wrong place and generally act as a real 'busybody'. That is unfair – they were brave men, the crews of the Master Bombers, doing a highly dangerous job. They had to stay in the target area for the whole raid, twenty or so minutes, sometimes longer, whilst the rest of us got the hell out of it as soon as we possibly could.

The other thing that was different was the numbers of aeroplanes involved. As an illustration: on 8 April 1943 392 aircraft attacked Duisburg in the Ruhr. On 14 October 1944 the RAF attacked Duisburg with 1,013 planes, but were able to attack the same city on the following evening with 1,005 bombers. The logistics of putting this number of planes in the air on successive nights is quite staggering and illustrates the strides made in the planning aspects of aerial warfare in such a short time.

It should also be noted that the raids we were a part of were, in most cases, not the only large-scale operations that were taking place on the same night, or day, as on my second tour we did several daylight raids.

With a view to achieving further improvements in Bomber Command's effectiveness, plans were made during 1941 and the first half of 1942 to establish a specialised Target Finding Force. Group Captain Donald Bennett was put in command of what was called the Pathfinder Force (PFF) on 15 August 1942, with five squadrons, Nos. 7, 35, 83, 109 and 156, forming PFF's backbone. Their main task was accurate target-marking, which was slowly but steadily brought about over the coming months, mainly with the aid of 'Oboe' and H$_2$S, the world's first radar ground-mapping bombing aid. Warrant Officer Angus Robb, who did a second tour of ops as air gunner on 405 'Vancouver' PFF Squadron RCAF between August 1944 and April 1945, recalls:

> The atmosphere on a PFF squadron was vastly different from what I had encountered during my time with 431 and 432 Squadrons, which were both Main Force squadrons. The majority of PFF aircrew were very experienced, with at least one tour of ops behind them, and the pilots and navigators particularly were exceptionally good at their craft; they had to be as the degree of accurate flying required for the job of marking the targets for the rest of Bomber Command was very high indeed. To assist in achieving this accuracy, PFF aircraft were given their own operational height, usually 16,000 feet, in which to operate. No other planes were supposed to be within 500 feet of this altitude, so there was less turbulence to fly through.
>
> Though it was never openly stated, it soon became clear that to belong to a PFF squadron put you a 'cut above' the normal run of aircrew in Bomber Command; just the idea 'Bomber' Harris had been against when the suggestion of a Pathfinder Force had been mooted originally. Firstly, on arrival at a PFF squadron you were given an immediate one-rank promotion; I was made a Warrant Officer on my first day at Gransden Lodge, and secondly was the award of the Pathfinder badge. This was the RAF eagle, which you were allowed to wear on the flap of your left breast pocket, and highly prized they were. This was not given automatically, you had to do six 'marker trips' and then you were given a temporary award of the badge. Only when you had completed your 'tour-time' with the PFF group were you given a certificate stating that you had now been awarded the badge permanently.

On 7–8 March 1945 Bomber Command mounted three major raids on Dessau, Hemmingstedt and Harburg. Among the 526 Lancaster and five Mosquitoes of 1, 3, 6 and 8 Groups that were detailed to attack Dessau in eastern Germany were sixteen Lancaster IIIs from 405 'Vancouver' Pathfinder Squadron RCAF. The bomb load of the Blind Illuminator Pathfinder aircraft consisted of a Wanganui Flare, to achieve accurate target-marking in cloud-cover conditions, along with four 1,000lb and one 500lb bombs. Warrant Officer Angus Robb, veteran mid-upper gunner in Flying Officer 'Bud' Larson's crew, took off from Gransden Lodge in Lancaster PA965 'D' for his forty-eighth operational sortie.

The trip to Dessau was a disaster, as far as we were concerned, as it was on this trip that we lost Warrant Officer Ronnie Hainsworth, our rear gunner. We had been detailed to get to the target about two to three minutes after the raid had officially finished to mark for any stragglers who had been delayed and were therefore over the town virtually on our own. We bombed at 22,000 using an airfield as our aiming point. The bombs had just left the aircraft when we were attacked by the first of three Ju 88s. The first one was shot down by Ronnie in the rear turret as it came into attack, but the second set the rear turret alight before I managed to get a short burst of gunfire into it, setting it on fire. It was then we heard Ronnie say 'For Christ's sake get me out of here.' The last words I suppose he ever said.

The third Junkers also hit us, putting my turret out of action, a cannon shell moving the whole turret, with me in it, about a foot sideways, severing all the vital links: electricity, oxygen, oil and the intercom and generally causing damage to the rest of our Lancaster. The fire in the rear turret had been caused by the severing of the hydraulic pipes and the ignition of the fluid. The fluid was being pumped into the turret by the engine-driven generator, fuelling the blaze, and the cut oxygen lines were making it burn with a terrifying intensity. The bottom of the turret appeared as a white-hot ball of fire and the slipstream through the aircraft was blowing the flames behind us like a blow-torch.

Due to the attention of the remaining Ju 88, holes kept appearing in various parts of the airframe and at frequent intervals the supply of ammunition for the rear turret kept exploding as they were hit by the gunfire. At one time I thought I had had my leg shot off as it suddenly gave way under me, but to my relief I had merely put my leg through a hole which had suddenly been blown in the floor of the Lancaster. Eventually, however, the wireless operator Pilot Officer Van Metre and I managed to get the fire in the rear turret under control, but by that time it was obvious to us there was little we could do for Ronnie. He was hanging half-in and half-out of the turret and the metal had melted due to the heat of the flames. We took the decision, unspoken, and got him out of the aircraft, pulling his parachute ripcord as he went. It seemed that the sooner he got medical attention the better and we were a long way from home.

The remaining enemy fighter had, whilst all this was going on, continued his attacks, scoring hits on us at will, but it says much for the construction of the Lancaster that, despite it all, no fatal damage was done. We could only assume that he ran out of ammunition, as after about ten to fifteen minutes he drew alongside, waggled his wings and peeled off.

During our running battle with the remaining night fighter, Sergeant B.A. Potter, our engineer, had been having his own hair-raising moments. In the nose of the Lancaster, aft of the bomb aimer's position, a hole had been cut in the floor which allowed one of the crew to put his head out of the plane, looking underneath to spot any fighters coming up; a blind spot on all bombers, with the exception of those equipped with ball-turrets. This was the task generally assigned to the flight engineer during fighter attacks. The hole was protected by a bubble of perspex to disperse the slipstream. Our engineer was doing his duty and had his head out of the hole when some of the fire from the attacker took the perspex bubble cleanly away from the nose, leaving him to the mercy of the night air. Naturally, he got up rather quickly and in the process managed to open his parachute, which he had put on earlier in the attack, leaving himself with an armful of parachute silk. He apparently asked the pilot, with just a hint of pleading in his voice that we were not going to evacuate the aircraft.

We had sustained a tremendous amount of damage. One engine was out of action, another had no cowling left and was running very roughly (this was due, we discovered on landing back at base, to the propeller blades being bent at right angles about a foot from each tip). The intercom was out of action, so it was a case of passing notes to each other or shouting in one another's ear. One rudder was waving freely in the breeze and as we did not know how much damage had been done to the other, violent movement of the aeroplane was out of the question. The mid-upper and rear turrets were both out of action and there were large holes in the side and floor of the plane. Generally speaking, we were in a mess.

We had a discussion as to the merits of trying for the nearest emergency drome in England, but decided that 'Home is where the heart is' so we set our course back to Gransden Lodge. I can honestly say that at no time during the nine hours we spent airborne was there any real panic amongst the crew. At no time can I recall thinking that we were not going to come out of the situation other than in one piece. When we had taken the decision, by writing notes to each other, that we would try to make it back to Gransden Lodge, it seemed as if we all accepted the fact that we would make it.

Our troubles though, were not yet over. We were steadily losing height due to the damage we had received and decided to lighten the aircraft where we could. We had got rid of most of the loose stuff lying around when the bomb aimer remembered that we had some of our bomb load still aboard. He opened the bomb doors and pressed the 'tit' to release the remainder. Unfortunately, it slipped his mind that our markers were barometric pressure-fused to go off at 3,000 feet. By this time we were quite a bit lower than that, so as soon as he let them go they exploded, filling the floor above the bomb bay full of pyrotechnics! It took the wireless operator and a lot of kicking and stamping to eventually get rid of them.

So the long night wore on and we continued our way across Europe, slowly but surely, and you can imagine how much of a relief it was to arrive back over our base at Gransden Lodge and take up our crash-landing positions – just in case – but we landed safely after just over nine hours in the air. It was then a case of being debriefed and spending the night in the sickbay, at the insistence of the MO, before being sent on survivors' leave for seven days.

As far as I can recall, our Lancaster 'D for Dog' never flew again, but we must have had a replacement, as after one trip in 'K for King' my log book shows I did my remaining eight in 'D for Dog'.

Ronnie, sad to say, was dead when he reached the ground, being buried near the town of Dessau, but since the end of the war his body has been removed to the War Cemetery in Berlin where over 3,000 British servicemen lie, the majority of them aircrew.

I have often asked myself the question 'Did we do the right thing? Should we have done it any differently?' and to be honest I don't know. At the time it certainly seemed the right thing, in fact the only thing to do and I suppose one has to live with that. I only know I lost a man who was the closest thing to a brother I ever had. To add further irony to the affair, the 7th of March 1945 was his twenty-third birthday and the day previously he had become engaged to be married.

For their valiant efforts that night, Pilot Officer Van Metre was awarded the DFC, while Warrant Officer Angus Robb received the CGM (Flying) on 16 December 1946. In fact, their Lancaster PA965 was repaired and relegated to 1660 CU and later to 1656 CU, 12 and 9 Squadrons before being struck off charge on 15 November 1946. From the 531 aircraft attacking Dessau on 7/8 March 1945, eighteen Lancasters were lost, but the raid was devastatingly successful, with the town centre, residential, industrial and railway areas all being hit.[1]

I often wondered, through the tears, if the sacrifice of so many young lives was worth it all. I made a visit a few years ago to the British War Cemetery in Berlin, where my friend Ronnie is now buried, along with about 3,000 others, the majority of them aircrew in their twenties. I wondered, again, was it worth this? On the same trip we were taken to Dachau, the site of the infamous concentration camp which is now a memorial to the millions who died in the camps. It was in that, still sorrowful place, I thought to myself; if it stops anything like this ever happening again, yes, their sacrifice was worthwhile. But I would make this plea to the ones this was really written for, my grandchildren: Try to ensure it never happens again. Forgive, yes, but never, ever forget.[2]

15

HORSES FOR COURSES
ARTHUR TAYLOR

War is bloody – it always has been.

On 16 June 1943 I finally made the grade and became a sergeant wireless operator/air gunner and headed off home on leave to await posting to an advanced flying unit (AFU) at Wigton, when I started cross-country training with another WOp/AG and two navigators (we used to take turns at the wireless set and the navigators shared the plotting, etc). The aircraft we flew in then was the Avro Anson – an amazing old aircraft. My next stop was Abingdon where they were flying Whitleys, but I had only been there for a few days when a request for an exchange posting to Wellesborne Mountford came through – just what I had always wanted – to fly on Wellingtons. However on 20 September 1943 we had our first crash. We were practising one engine flying overshoots when the starboard engine failed to start again, cutting out at a crucial moment that we needed more power. The pilot instructor grabbed the controls off our trainee skipper and managed a wheels-up 'pancake' in a nearby field, where we all scrambled out with our gear, got away from the smoking aircraft and were picked up within thirty minutes and got airborne on another aircraft.

On 24 October we were taking off at night when the port engine cut on take-off, swinging us violently around and heading towards the control tower.

We were going too fast to brake without causing more danger so in the few seconds he had our skipper made the decision to pull the undercarriage up, which had the desired result, saving both us and the people in the control tower. Alas, he got a red endorsement for his efforts.

On 15 October my CO very reluctantly gave me a 48-hour pass so I could get married on 16 October. The trains were running late and I didn't get home until the early hours. We were married at St. Thomas in the afternoon and parted company Sunday afternoon to go our separate ways (my wife was serving in the WAAFs then).

Oh dear – here we go again; on 2 November we were flying on night circuits and bumps (landings) when we had trouble with the starboard engine, so we called in on the radio and got permission to land (which we did). The sergeant flight mechanic came over and checked the engine out but couldn't find anything wrong with it so we got airborne again. We pulled away from the airfield to do a circuit and again the starboard engine played up and started to overheat and the skipper [Sergeant W. M. Bowyer], who was an American from Boston who had joined the RAF, had to shut the engine down. With only one engine we started to lose height and radioed in for an emergency landing and had just turned into an downwind leg when the port engine started to overheat and the bomb aimer came back to try and pump more oil up into it, but to no avail. We were just over 600 feet then and knew we were going to crash so I fired off all the red Very cartridges and the bomb aimer and myself jettisoned the escape hatches and prepared for the worst and got into our crash-position. The port engine gave out about halfway along our downwind leg and we crashed [into the side of Loxley Hill on the south side of Wellesbourne Mountford airfield] and caught fire. I didn't know this at the time but the near turret broke off and was thrown clear of the fire but the gunner [Sergeant G. W. Milne] broke his back. I was very dazed and with blood running down my face and into my right eye I found it very difficult to open the bulkhead door that I had propped myself against. This door opened inwards so I had to take my gloves off (bad mistake) to prise it open and when I did eventually get to the front escape hatch the metalwork was red hot and I had to ball myself up out of this and on to the nose of the aircraft and jump off.

The trees and bushes and the poor old Wellington were now well alight and then when I got clear I started hurting (didn't feel it before). I called all my crew's names but got no reply. I knew the skipper was out because I used the same exit. The aircraft was completely burnt out in a very short time. I saw a torch light up in the woods and shouted for help. It was the RAF blood wagon who had followed us as soon as they realised we wouldn't make it back to the drone and safety. I was extremely lucky, although seriously injured and with burns to my face and hands I was the only one to fly again. Our skipper was sent to a special burns unit. The bomb aimer [Sergeant L. E. Hance] was very badly burned and injured and died next day in hospital. He was in the bed next to me and I could hear his wife, who was pregnant, crying pitifully but they wouldn't tell me at first what the score was. Some things you can never forget! There I was in hospital at Stratford on Avon without a stitch of clothing to my name but as all the little hurts started (you only feel the burns at first) I acquired a few extra bandages and supports here and there. A couple of weeks later an American Red Cross nurse came round and gave me some pyjamas and some cigarettes. In a few weeks I had healed up very well, although at one time skin grafting on two of my fingers was considered a possibility and as usual the new skin on my hands kept cracking at first.

Originally, I was awarded 28 days' survivors leave but this was cut to three weeks because new crews were needed on squadrons quite urgently. I was soon pestered again and requested a return to a Whitley OTU and that's where I crewed-up again at 24 OTU Long Marsden, where nearly all the aircrew were Canadian. My new skipper was Flying Officer Murray Marshall. I was a bit edgy when I first started flying again but Murray said he did not think the odds would be against me any more and was glad to have me aboard. We soon trained on and converted to 'heavies' and were then posted to my first operational unit – 427 'Lion' Squadron RCAF stationed at Leeming in Yorkshire in 6 Group RCAF.

They figured that after forty operations my skipper needed a break. All the rest of the crew and myself had completed 39 operations, eleven of them daylight attacks, sometimes with fighter escort when possible. One of the operations was a moonlight raid on Hamburg and after bombing we had that choice of either climbing up to our ceiling or flying back at minimum height. Our skipper decided to climb and with the booster on we got up to well over 25,000 feet, which was a new thrill to us then. We were then flying in Halifax Mk.IIIs and they were very good on climbing and with good speed.

Another outstanding operation we did was to Brunswick. There was solid cloud up to 12,000 feet, then a gap and then solid cloud again from 16,000 feet up. We flew all the way to Brunswick between the two layers of cloud (quite eerie) using navigation and H_2S. This operation was deemed to be over 60% successful but was never repeated as (so we were told) it was morally wrong!

Come D-Day we went to Conde sur Loire, a ridge of hills just the other side of Caen, to do a low level attack on a German Panzer division tucked in and waiting for our lads to move forward. We had never done a night attack that low before and the repercussion from the bombs going off just below was scary.[1]

Our last trip on 427 Squadron was a daylight attack on Emden [on 6 September 1944]; a little place about the size of Woodbridge. We were given the centre of the town as our aiming point followed by the remark, 'Don't worry if you overshoot, you'll hit the docks.'[2]

After the celebrations of our survival we went off on leave and I was posted to Kinloss but got so fed up being in 91 Group training I pulled all the strings I could and after further training got posted to 90 Squadron and back on 'ops' again – this time on Lancasters. Then along came VE Day and we were told we would be training hard for Far East duties and it was estimated at that time it would take us another ten years to conquer the 'Japs'. We all knew then that a lot of us would not survive. The atom bomb on Japan most probably saved my life. War is bloody – it always has been.

16

Joining the Caterpillar Club

George Cash was the oldest of two sons born to George and Lylie Cash, who lived in a cramped Victorian back-to-back terraced house in West Ham in London's poverty-ridden East End before the war. They realised that education would be their sons' salvation and they scrimped and saved to give their two sons the opportunities they never had. George matriculated in July 1938 and was working as a junior in a chartered accountant's office, studying for exams, when some of his former schoolmates returned from Dunkirk.

The evacuation brought a new sense of urgency and Cash decided to abandon his ambitions in the world of accountancy. When the Blitz destroyed the family home and they fled to Dagenham, Essex, he decided that he would become a fighter pilot. He enrolled in the RAF in July 1941 at Oxford with the intention of becoming a pilot, for which he had already grown a bristling moustache to go with his pilot's wings. His outstanding ability at mathematics, however, made him realise that he would be more use to the war effort as a navigator. In May 1943 he was posted to 1655 Mosquito Conversion Unit at Finmere and he became equally adept as an advanced navigator, a wireless operator, bomb aimer and gunner, and he went on to serve on 139 Squadron, 1409 Meteorological Flight and 571 Squadron in 8 Group (Pathfinder Force).

I had been on ops for nearly a year and Tuesday, 18 July 1944 began like any other day – but little did I know what lay in store! That evening, when we went into briefing, I had no undue feelings of trepidation – certainly not like the 'butterflies' that I had when I first flew on ops. During training and flying time, I had formed quite firm friendships with various fellows. Friends had gone on different postings from mine and we'd parted. Crews on ops had gone missing or had been killed. One was saddened for a short time but life went on and they went out of mind; that was the way of things. Like many others, I suppose, I thought that nothing would ever happen to me and that I would just go on until the end of the war, or until such time that I felt like packing up. Experience and the knowledge of what to expect helped to allay one's fears although, however much experience a man had, I don't think that any airman could truthfully say that he did not feel some apprehension before setting off on an operation. This time, I saw that 'A' Flight – ours – was to go to Cologne and 'B' Flight to Berlin. Accordingly, I began to get out maps and charts of the Ruhr in readiness when I noticed that our names were not on the A Flight list. I pointed this out to my pilot, who was always known as 'Doddy' (Squadron Leader Terence Edgar Dodwell RAFVR DFC*, twenty-nine years old, whose wife, Olive, lived in Thorpe Bay, Essex, had completed part of a Mosquito tour with 1409 Met Flight before joining 571 Squadron. Before this he had completed a tour with Squadron Leader Peter Ashley on 110 Hyderabad Squadron, flying Mk IV Blenheims). He nodded and remarked that we were going to Berlin instead. 'There's a sprog crew in "B" Flight,' he said, 'so I offered to take their place – they can go on a short trip, some time to break them in gently.' In the Services, one was always told never to volunteer for anything. A dangerous job in the line of duty was one thing but you did not stick your neck out needlessly and go looking for trouble! Somehow, deep inside me, I had an uncomfortable feeling that this was 'It'.

We had the usual briefing: target, routes into and away from 'The Big City', deployment of defences along these routes, met report and so on. During the briefing, the Intelligence Officer warned us of the Germans using experimental jet-propelled night fighters over Berlin. I didn't pay much heed to this for I had heard it all before. (Big head!) After preparing my flight plan and marking my maps and charts with information that I would need, I packed my things and 'Doddy' and I walked across to the crew room to get our Mae Wests, 'chutes and dinghies. We were unusually silent and I wondered if he sensed what I was thinking.

It was time to go. The crew bus arrived, we clambered on and soon we were dropped off at our dispersal. We climbed into the aircraft, stowed our gear and while I fixed my charts and flight plan, Doddy carried out his pre-flight check.

When he came to run up the engines he found that the port engine had a mag drop and consequently was u/s. We collected our things, climbed out of the aircraft and sent one of the ground crew to get a van to take us over to the reserve aircraft ['V for Victor' MM136]. By now, the rest of the squadron had taken off and were on their way. We raced round the drome to the reserve aircraft, climbed aboard and after hurried checks all round, took off well behind the rest. All this rush and frenzy had been most unsettling – it was a very bad start. We were more than fifteen minutes behind and could never make up that time which meant that we would be 'Tail-end Charlies' out behind the mainstream. This would make us very vulnerable – an easy target for flak or fighters as we knew from experience – and yet, strangely, I remember that I wasn't particularly perturbed by the prospect.

As we climbed to our operational height – 28,000 feet – we began to settle down and by the time we levelled out, we were quite calm and I was too busy with my navigation to worry about anything else. We were approaching the enemy coast and, as normal, we began to siphon fuel from our overload tanks to the outer tanks in the wings to replace fuel that we had used.

We had just crossed the Dutch coast when near Arnhem a stream of tracers from below indicated that enemy fighters were on to us. 'Doddy' immediately took vigorous evasive action – always difficult with a 'cookie' on board. For a few hectic minutes that seemed like an age, we ran the gauntlet of what we thought were a couple of Ju 88s. We felt a few thuds in the fuselage but there did not appear to be any serious damage. We shook them off eventually and resumed our course, each of us in our own way breathing a sigh of relief. I suddenly realised that, in the heat of the moment, we had forgotten to turn off the petrol siphons. The outer tanks had filled and we had been discharging precious fuel into the slipstream. We must have lost a considerable amount and it crossed my mind that we might not have enough to get us home. This must have occurred to 'Doddy' too, as he gave vent to a few choice phrases but, once again, I wasn't particularly bothered. It seems, in retrospect, that I was subconsciously preparing for the worst – that we wouldn't be coming back anyway. This had put us further behind and, although the next part of the route was a dog-leg round a heavily defended area near Wittingen, we decided to take a chance and fly straight across. I worked out the new course and just as we were thinking that we had got away with it, all hell broke loose. Shells burst round us too close for comfort. 'Doddy' put up the nose, opened the throttles and climbed as fast as we could go. It seemed ages before we got away but not before a huge lump of shrapnel had smashed through the back window into the 'Gee' box by my side – another few inches and I wouldn't be telling this tale!

At the turning point in our route which was to take us on a dog-leg to Stendal – our last turning point – in the distance I saw that the target indicators had already gone down over the railway marshalling yards north-west of Berlin – the target. Ahead of us were searchlights and bursting flak. The raid had begun. We decided to fly straight there to make up for all the lost time. I worked out a course to steer and then began to 'Window' 'like mad'. Unfortunately the route took us over the flak at Wittingen, which immediately opened up on us. Suddenly we found ourselves in a box of heavy predicted flak with shells bursting all around. Shrapnel rattled down on to the cockpit of the aircraft and we could smell the cordite. 'Doddy' put the aircraft into a steep dive; a chunk of flak smashed through the fuselage and hit the 'Gee' set, putting it out of action. The evasive action finally took us clear of the flak and on an ETA for Stendal we climbed back to 32,000 feet. 'Doddy' decided to skirt round the defences and come in from another direction but, just then, we were coned. We were blinded by the glare. 'Doddy', once more threw the kite around, diving and banking, turning and climbing, in an effort to get away but to no avail. Then, suddenly the searchlights dipped – we had shaken them off – but we ought to have known better!

We were now in sight of the target indicators and I noted in my log: 0200 hours. Target sighted, preparing to bomb. I stowed my equipment and knelt down ready to crawl into the nose to the bombsight. I had hardly moved when we felt a quick succession of thumps as cannon shells smashed into the fuselage. A tremendous whoof and the port petrol tanks exploded. The port engine burst into blames. I realised, all too late, why the searchlights had left us. A night fighter had homed on to us and had flown up beneath us to deliver the coup de grace – we had been a sitting duck. With the cockpit now well ablaze, 'Doddy' said, 'Come on, we've got to get out of here!' I pulled up the cover of the escape hatch and threw it into the nose. When I got up, I found that I was on my own. Doddy had exited smartly through the top hatch. I couldn't blame him – his seat was on fire! (In dry runs on the ground, we had practised getting out in a hurry through the conventional exit below the navigator's position. We had to aim at getting out in ten seconds. With all our cumbersome gear, Mae Wests, parachutes and harness and dinghy, we couldn't get out in ten minutes!)

It was dangerous going out of the top (to be done only if the aircraft ditched or crash-landed) since, in flight, there was the great risk of striking the tail fin and rudder or the tailplane. But, there I was, in a blazing aircraft, spiralling out of control with a 4,000lb bomb still on board. The 'G' pressure was like a heavy weight, pressing me down on to my seat. I did what any man in my position would do: I breathed a quick prayer, 'God, help me.'

Suddenly, despite the heat in the cockpit and my perilous position, a calmness came over me and my mind was clear. A fierce draught fanned the flames so that the whole cockpit was ablaze and full of smoke. There was nothing for it – I had to go: out of the top hatch. I struggled round on my seat to reach behind me to get my parachute from its stowage. As I turned back, my elbow caught the ruined 'Gee' box by my side knocking my 'chute from my hand. It fell down the escape hatch but fortunately it stuck halfway down where I could reach it and clip it onto my harness. In those few seconds, I suddenly remembered reading an account in Tee Em magazine about how a Mosquito navigator had bailed out by climbing out of the top hatch and rolling on to the starboard wing before letting go. I took three deep breaths of oxygen, took off my mask and helmet, threw them down and proceeded to do likewise. I was carried away by the slipstream, clear of the aircraft and, after counting the requisite 'One, two three' I reached up to my parachute pack, which was now above my head, and pulled the release handle. Nothing happened! I reached up with both hands and pulled open the flaps of the pack.

There was a plop as the canopy sprang out and filled with air. There I was floating through the quiet, peaceful sky. Then I looked down and, immediately below me, or so it seemed, there was our Mosquito in a field, blazing away with the 'cookie' still on board. If it had gone up then, I would have gone up with it. I continued drifting a little way away then, suddenly, innumerable fingers were scrabbling at me – I had the fleeting thought of falling into the hands of a lynch mob. But they were twigs – I had come down in a tree! I was dangling there, my night vision completely gone and I couldn't see or feel the ground. I needed to get away as fast as I could. I pressed the release button and I fell ten feet into a bush below the tree. Except for a few scratches, I was unharmed. I was on terra firma, albeit enemy terra firma, but I was down and that was how I qualified for the Caterpillar Club. For my claim to fame – if it can be called such – I am one of a very few men who bailed out from the top hatch of a Mosquito and lived to tell the tale. Also, I am one, probably of many, who climbed down from a tree which he had not climbed up!

I set off walking in a westerly direction, putting as much distance as I possibly could between myself and the blazing Mossie. The 'cookie' did go up after about ten minutes, with a great crump and a terrific orange glow – I felt the blast even at that distance. I was now on my own; my last link with home had gone. I kept going for nearly two days but, on the way through a small village just outside Magdeburg, very late at night, I had the misfortune to walk into a Volksturm patrol who were out looking for the crew of a Flying Fortress that had been shot down earlier in the day. I spent the next three days in the civvie jail in Magdeburg before I was transported to the Interrogation Centre at Oberurssel, just outside Frankfurt-am-Main. A few days later, I was entrained with about 200 others – 180 Americans and twenty British – to Barth in Pomerania on the Baltic coast. I marched into Stalag Luft I with this contingent on Tuesday, 1 August 1944 – my twenty-third birthday – just two weeks after I had taken off from Oakington for the last time. I was to spend nearly ten months in Germany before returning home at the end of the war.

There is a short corollary to this part of my story: an episode that occurred in the PoW camp. The weather in February 1945 was atrocious – freezing cold with ice and snow underfoot. To keep us occupied, the senior officers in the barrack block organised a bridge tournament. In one round, my partner and I were drawn to play against a couple in an adjacent room. As was normal, we exchanged pleasantries before commencing our game – we asked each other about the aircraft which we had flown in and with which squadron, etc.

One of our opponents was a Flight Lieutenant D. L. S. Thompson who informed us that he had been on 571 Squadron when he had been shot down. When I told him that I had been on 571 as well and that I didn't remember him, he said that he had been on the squadron for only a couple of days and had been shot down on his first trip. He went on to say that he and his navigator [Flight Lieutenant John Philip Sargent 'Jack' Calder RCAF] had been due to go to Berlin two nights before but had been taken off the Battle Order and put down as reserve crew. When I asked him when this was, he said that it had been on the 18 July and that they had been shot down over Hamburg on the 20 July. His navigator had been killed. I put two and two together – they had been the crew that Doddy and I had replaced. When I put this to him, he confirmed that the crew who had taken their place on the Berlin trip had not returned and we both realised that 'Doddy' and I had been that crew. I wondered then and I often wondered since, what would have happened if we hadn't taken their flight that night. Perhaps we may have returned from our respective missions and my pilot and his navigator would not have been killed. But this is only conjecture – we can only assume that their number was up and fate stepped in to do the rest. At that time, I had no idea what had happened to Doddy and it was a considerable time after the war that I was to find out what did happen.

This brings me to the second corollary to my story. When a fellow named Barry Blunt was researching the history of 571 Squadron I learned from him what had happened on that disastrous trip. Apparently, we had been tracked and shot down by a German night fighter ace – Oberleutnant Heinz Strüning of 3/NJG flying a Heinkel 219A-5 ('Uhu' – Owl) which was armed with 'Schräge Musik' (the code word for upward firing guns fitting to the aircraft). To enable them to keep up with faster aircraft, as we were, their engines were fitted with nitrous-oxide boosters which could be used for about ten minutes or so to enhance their speed. Heinz Strüning was awarded the Oak Leaves to his Knight's Cross with Swords and Diamonds on 20 July 1944 for shooting us down![1] From an account in the German archives, the body of Squadron Leader T. E. Dodwell had been discovered, with his parachute unopened, in a clump of trees near Laudin, thirty-five miles west of Berlin, close to the site where the aircraft had crashed. From the appearance of the body, it had been deduced that he was dead before reaching the ground having been fatally injured by striking part of the aircraft (the tail?) on bailing out; hence the unopened parachute. Having the fanciful idea of going to Germany to meet Heinz Strüning, I requested further information about him. Apparently, he had been promoted to Hauptmann a few weeks after our incident and posted to 9/NJG as a Flight Commander. He enjoyed considerable acclaim as a night fighter ace with a squadron of Me 110s flying from Holland. On Christmas Eve 1944 a force of our heavies was out and Strüning's squadron took off to try to infiltrate them. Unknown to him the heavies were accompanied by a couple of squadrons of Mosquito night fighters.

Dr Theo Boiten, a member of the Dutch Aircraft Recovery team, reported the following information obtained from German Military Archives. Investigating the wartime crash site of an Me 110, he was told that on the night of 24–25 December 1944 the aircraft in question, Messerschmitt Bf 110G-4, Nr 740162 of 9 NJG, had been flown by Hauptmann Heinz Strüning who had fifty-six night victories including two Mosquitoes with 3/NJG1. Strüning's aircraft had been shot down by a Mosquito night fighter and crashed near Bergisch-Gladbach–Rheinland. The radar operator and air gunner bailed out safely but Strüning hit the tail of the Me 110 when he bailed out and was killed. His body was found two months later and interred.

These incidents make up a remarkable and ironic coincidence. In the first case, a Mosquito pilot, shot down by a German night fighter was killed on bailing out by striking the tail of his aircraft. The German night fighter pilot was shot down by a Mosquito and was killed on bailing out by striking the tail of his aircraft! Truth can be stranger than fiction!

17

AUSSIES OVER EUROPE – THE SECOND WORLD WAR'S BLOODIEST AIR CAMPAIGN

ROLLO KINGSFORD-SMITH DSO AM DFC

Australia brought flying traditions to the air war in Europe, for young as flying was when the war began, Australia already had an air saga. A famous pioneer partnership of the air, for instance, was represented in the RAAF overseas by two nephews of the late Air Commodore Sir Charles Kingsford-Smith MC, the great Australian flying pioneer, and by Pilot Officer John Anthony Ulm, 23, of Sydney, only son of the late C.P.T. Ulm, Kingsford Smith's navigator in many an air exploit. The most famous of these was the first trans-Pacific flight from 31 May to 9 June 1928 in Fokker F.VIIB/3m Southern Cross.

One of 'Smith's' nephews was Wing Commander Rollo Kingsford-Smith DSO DFC. Born 14 July 1919 in Northwood, Rollo Kingsford-Smith was taken as a boy on his first flight by his uncle. He received his Leaving Certificate from Sydney Boys High in 1936 and then attended night classes at Sydney Technical College. In July 1938 he undertook pilot training at the RAAF's Point Cook, in October 1939 he was posted to No. 6 Squadron, Richmond, conducting coastal reconnaissance patrols, and later he was involved in training pilots at

Point Cook, Victoria. In 1942 Rollo was promoted to Squadron Leader and joined Bomber Command in England, initially in the operational training units. In September 1943 he became a Flight Commander on 467 Squadron RAAF, flying Lancaster bombers on night bombing operations over Germany, France and Italy. In November 1943 he was promoted to Wing Commander and CO of 463 Squadron RAAF, a new Australian Lancaster bomber unit based at Waddington, Lincolnshire. Australian prime minister John Curtin visited Waddington in May 1944 and awarded Rollo the DFC, which was followed in August 1944 by an award of the DSO for conspicuous gallantry.

Rollo Kingsford-Smith flew thirty-four bombing operations, including the Normandy coast on D-Day. In April 1945 he took command of 627 Squadron, a Pathfinder unit flying Mosquitoes that dropped flares to mark the path for the following heavy bombers. He returned to Australia in July 1945, but led the Australian RAAF contingent in the 1946 Victory celebrations in London. Rollo left the RAAF in April 1949, with the rank of Wing Commander. Rollo wrote about his wartime experiences in a privately published memoir, *I Wouldn't have Missed it for Quids*. Flying Officer Peter Kingsford-Smith DFC of Sydney reached Britain in May 1941 and carried out many bombing operations, before he was taken prisoner on 20 February 1943. A third brother, Squadron Leader J.W. Kingsford-Smith, had been in the RAAF since 1939. John Ulm became a prisoner-of-war on 6 March 1945. He and Peter Kingsford-Smith, then a flight lieutenant, were liberated in the last days of the war. Rollo died at Bowral on 14 June 2009, one month before his 90th birthday; he was survived by Grace and three daughters, five grandchildren and four great-grandchildren.[1]

As the invading Japanese forces advanced ever closer to Australia in WWII, the gallant fighting by our servicemen in the jungles, the air and the sea was foremost in all minds. The honour given these men by our prime minister and government is well deserved. On the other side of the world there was another more deadly war of repeated battles deep into Germany and across the territories conquered and occupied by the massive military power of Nazi Germany. It was an air war that was inevitable after Hitler's army and air force with their Blitzkrieg tactics quickly conquered the European nations and drove the British into the sea. Only a heavy bomber force from England could take the war to Germany. As Britain built up bomber strength, requests went to Australia, Canada and New Zealand for trained personnel to share on the crewing and Australian aircrew began to arrive in England in 1941. By war's end, although only about 2 per cent of all Australian servicemen of

WWII served in Bomber Command, they lost 3,486 killed in action, 20 per cent of all Australians killed in combat. Another 724 were killed in the bomber operational training units when war training continued in the worst weather and in worn-out aircraft due to the urgent demands for reinforcements from the squadrons. This brought the total killed to 4,210.

The total losses in the AIF divisions in the Middle East against Germany and Italy came to 3,552 killed. Closer to Australia the fighting against Japan cost 1,789 dead in Singapore and over 2,000 in all parts of Papua New Guinea. In later conflicts, 339 were killed from all services in Korea and 519 in Vietnam. Despite these revealing comparisons the Australian government has shown little interest in the young Australians sacrificed over Europe. They were an elite, highly trained force fighting in a separate campaign, yet there is no Bomber Command memorial in Canberra. One has been promised provided remaining veterans find most of the money. The heavy bomber operations saw a very different type of warfare, usually at night, deep into well defended enemy territory. The extra hours of darkness of the northern winters permitted longer missions, when the temperatures at the high altitudes could go down to minus 45 degrees C. It was high technology warfare requiring meticulously trained men to operate and fight with the complex equipment in the four-engined bomber. The seven-man crew, comprising bomb aimer, pilot/captain, flight engineer, navigator, radio operator and two gunners, were isolated in their stations, hooked on to the essential oxygen supply and intercommunication telephony system. The gunners were also plugged into power for their electrically heated clothing. The success of the mission and their safety depended on each man never relaxing his vigilance and determination to attack. It was not glamorous. The bombers, not pressurised or insulated, had one thin sheet of aluminium alloy between the crew and the outside air. The cabin heater was ineffective against the icy draught coming from the front turret apertures and frostbite was not uncommon. Very little help could be given to a wounded crew member until back over England. On the long slow climb after take-off, fully loaded with fuel and bombs, the cabin stank even through the oxygen masks. Most operations meant ten to fifteen hours of concentrated effort from the time the crews reported to the briefing room, longer when the crew member survived being shot down. A sustaining meal before take-off was essential and as the aircraft climbed and the air pressure dropped, the gas in the digesting food was given off and swelled. Repeated farting was inevitable. The Australians arrived in Bomber Command mainly in small groups from their specialist training schools in Australia, Canada or Rhodesia. As in North Africa with the AIF, British government policy was to spread out the Australians under the command of British officers. This delayed the formation of Australian units for some time and the first batches of Australians to arrive were absorbed into RAF squadrons. Even after five RAAF heavy bombers squadrons were formed, many Australian reinforcements continued to be diverted to British units.

This left the RAAF squadrons short of Australians and many crew positions were filled with RAF. They were excellent on operations and in no way detracted from the effectiveness of the units, although adding some administrative work. The writer served in two of the RAAF units, 467 and 463 Lancaster Squadrons, and the remainder of this article will be about these two. Both commenced operations against Germany 60 [sic] years ago in 1943, 467 Squadron in January and 463 Squadron in November. On the formation of 463 Squadron both units were based at Waddington near the city of Lincoln. The two squadrons formed with RAAF and RAF personnel from other units began operations against Germany almost immediately. As reinforcements arrived the Australian content increased but with the high loss rates it was a long process and it never reached 100 per cent. With the output from factories in the conquered countries and masses of slave labour added to the already efficient German defence industries, increased deliveries of tanks, guns, ammunition, aircraft and electronics built the strength of Germany's military forces to an all-time high. By 1943 the new Australian squadrons encountered the world's most effective anti-aircraft defences and losses grew quickly. 467 Squadron lost the equivalent of 100 per cent of its complement of operational aircrew in its first seven months. 463 Squadron lost more than 50 per cent in the first four months. Only a more or less constant supply of new aircraft from factories and reinforcements from the training pipeline enabled them to continue. Yet these men were called 'Jap Dodgers' and some received white feathers from Australia.

From an average strength of 140 aircrew, 467, in 28 months of endless attacks on the enemy, lost an obscene 590 killed in action, including five commanding officers, 117 taken prisoners after being shot down and 84 shot down mainly over the conquered countries but not captured, thanks to assistance from gallant civilians. In its seventeen months attacking the enemy, 463, with similar strength, lost 350 killed in action, 92 taken prisoner and 77 evading capture. Three commanding officers were shot down, two were killed and one escaped capture due to slow-witted German troops and the bravery of a Belgian woman. In 1943 and 1944 most aircrew knew there was a high probability they would be shot down by enemy flak or fighters. Had they survived and come down with only slight injuries it was their duty and very good sense to avoid capture and possible execution in the PoW camp. In Germany capture was almost inevitable but if they landed in one of the countries under German military occupation there was a chance of avoiding capture and even returning to their unit. The success of those who evaded capture was a joint effort of the men involved who had learned the procedures, the air force which issued all aircrew with 'escape kits' and the underground resistance forces, particularly strong in France, Belgium and Holland. The 'escape kit', small and tightly packed, contained concentrated food, energy tablets, water purifying tablets, passport photos in civilian clothing for false identity papers and used bank notes of the appropriate currency.

Improved Lancasters flown by 467 and 463 became the most effective type used by the Allies. Highly manoeuvrable, they could carry the largest bomb load over the greatest distance and as deliveries increased they were chosen for the more difficult targets. The Australians fought their way deeper into Germany and over Norway, Denmark, Holland, Belgium, France, Czechoslovakia and Italy. Losses increased. The bombing objective was to destroy armament factories, oil refineries, transport systems, mainly railways, power generating systems, research establishments and the centres of government. Berlin was a priority target and the fifteen attacks of 'The Battle of Berlin' in the winter of 1943–1944 were a nightmare for the crews. The strengthened defences beginning with radar-guided heavy gun batteries along the coastline followed by constant attacks from the radar-controlled enemy fighter force meant a long gruelling battle before the Lancasters flew into the defence inferno surrounding and over the target. Hitler promised his people that Berlin would never be attacked and he did his best. Over the city the massive anti-aircraft gun barrage, flares, fighters, searchlights, exploding Lancasters and bomb bursts on the ground made an experience the crews did not wish to repeat. But they did, time and time again. Then there was the long return flights. The flak and fighters, which would have landed, refuelled and rearmed, would be waiting. Back over England the tired pilots and navigators had to find their airfield in a winter that was one of the worst on record. Low cloud or fog at times closed Waddington and the returning Lancasters would be diverted to a distant airfield, where they would arrive desperately short of fuel.

On 463 Squadron's worst night four Lancasters out of fourteen attacking Berlin were shot down and 28 crewmen killed. Bad weather held up flying for two weeks, then the survivors attacked again. Taking off well overladen with full bomb load in snowstorms and finding freak winds at altitude and icing, the weather and mechanical failure with the sluggish aircraft killed many more. Was this costly bombing campaign successful? After an earlier attack on industries in Hamburg the Nazi War Minister informed Hitler: 'If these attacks continue a rapid end of the war might be the consequence'.

By mid–1944 the bombing had significantly reduced Germany's ability to wage war. Tank production had been cut by 35 per cent and aircraft by 31 per cent, and the European railway system on which the German Army relied so heavily was severed constantly. The destruction of oil refineries, oil storage centres and synthetic oil plants was increasing. To protect the homeland, one million fit German troops, 74 per cent of all heavy artillery and 55 per cent of lighter weapons were engaged at the expense of their forces fighting the Russians on one front and the Allies on another. The 6 June 1944 D-Day invasion on the Normandy coast by the American, British and Canadian armies was, in the broad scene, the most significant happening in the war. The Lancaster squadrons' involvement started well before June with attacks to destroy railway lines leading to the invasion area, German gun batteries, coastal radar and army tanks. Being over France, the operations were not without loss. Bombing accuracy was essential. Harm to French lives and property was to be avoided regardless of the cost and the bombers attacked at minimum height and not until the target was clearly identified by the Pathfinder Force. This delayed some attacks long enough for the enemy defences to be strengthened. On one such attack on railway yards in Lille the two squadrons lost six aircraft with forty killed, one taken prisoner and one evaded.

Wing Commander Rollo Kingsford-Smith RAAF,[2] CO of 463 Squadron, which operated Lancasters at Waddington, recalls:

In June I heard more and more accounts about the masses of Allied troops, guns and tanks building up in the south of England. It was obvious a very substantial army operation would soon begin but I was too busy with my own war even to think about the Army's activities let alone find out any more details. On the evening of 5 June the Operation Order coming through on our Teleprinter began: 'Main force aircraft from 53 Base will attack'. 'Objective to destroy enemy gun positions at 4.50 am 6 June.' The location given in the operation order was on the Normandy coast and to me it meant that Allied forces could be landing there immediately after we had finished with the enemy gun battery. I say, 'could be landing' because the weather forecast for the English Channel for the 6th was terrible and it seemed quite unsuitable for the small craft that the invasion forces would be using.

We took off at about 2am on 6 June. We had a leisurely flight down England to the south coast and across the Channel to the Normandy coast flying between 6–7,000 feet. There was low cloud most of the way but it started to break up as we approached France. I still did not know whether the Allied Forces would land. But about five miles out from the coast, when I could just discern the dark grey surface of the sea beneath in the early twilight, the fleet of invasion barges right below opened their throttles for the dash to the beach. It was too dark for me to see the boats but their increased speed made white wakes and these showed up clearly. I knew it was 'on'. Some of the wakes were all over the place. There must have been a few collisions at that level. Undoubtedly it was the most thrilling and emotional experience for me in all the years of the war. Until that moment Bomber Command had alone been taking the war to the Germans. For all I knew it would continue on and on until my crew and I finally joined the killed-in-action list. A massive army on the continent meant it was not unreasonable to think that the war might finish and I might get to see Grace and Sue (wife and daughter) again.

The enemy gun battery was at Pointe Du Hoc, a high point surrounded by cliffs overlooking Omaha beach. In my mind this attack would be about the most important my squadron had ever made and we were all determined it would succeed. The battery was well marked by the Path Finders and from a relatively low height, about 6,500 feet; we all took our time, each aircraft dropping 13,000lbs of bombs. The whole Pointe was battered; the battery including its concrete bunkers was destroyed. Even a part of the cliff tumbled into the sea. US soldiers, who about two hours later (had they been on time they would have seen and heard us), scaled the cliff to attack and silence the guns not knowing of our attack, reported the shambles of shattered concrete and steel they saw when they reached the top.

On the first day after the Allied armies had landed, their foothold on French soil was still precarious and they could have been in real trouble had the German armoured divisions been able to get there rapidly. Our squadrons were taken off the long flights into Germany and were kept busy attacking both the German tanks and their rail transport routes in and around the Normandy area. We went back to Normandy to destroy a rail and road junction at Argentan about fifty kilometres from the beachhead. I was Controller for this raid and as it would have been a vital transport junction for the Germans on the following day I was determined it would be pulverized with nil or absolute minimum damage to the adjacent village. At the planning conference I agreed to a bombing height of 6,000 feet but we all bombed lower. The target was accurately marked. I held up the attack for about five minutes to avoid confusion with another target under attack a few miles away. There were a few complaints but not many and it was another successful raid. Milling around the target in the dark and held back by their CO, the operational discipline was always excellent but the radio comments (always with no call sign) were typically Australian pertinent, disrespectful, sometimes rude and usually funny.

The raid report given by Squadron Leader Vowels, my most experienced Flight Commander in briefing session on return: Sortie completed. Cloud base 6,000 feet. Vis good. Cluster of green TIs 0127 hours. 2 ×1,000lb and 14 × 500lb bombs drop height 5,000 feet. Bomb bursts all around and on TIs – straddling and on road junction. Attack went very well, even though it opened about five minutes late through the Controller's order. Control very good and there was no hitch to original plan. TIs were practically bang on. Max error was about thirty yards. Was fired on by British Navy who ceased fire when colours of the period were fired.

Alec Vowel's comment of being fired on by the British Navy was not unusual around D-Day. The English Channel was full of allied Naval ships who continued to fire on us as we went across backwards and forwards – fortunately they were not as accurate as the Germans and I was not aware that they did any harm.

I think I was the last to bomb at Argentan and my approach to the bomb release point was made on a shallow descending dive. Our bombs were always dropped rapidly one after the other and on this occasion they were dropped at about a micro fraction of a second intervals so they fell in a stick right across the target. I was possibly over keen and was too low, so when the first bomb exploded, its blast hit my aircraft with a really severe thump. In a flash I realised that as I was still losing height each successive blast would be harder and heavier. At this late stage being brought down by my own bombs may have showed my determination to press home the attack but it would have been a stupid way of finishing my career.

My own report to the intelligence officer at debriefing states: Sortie completed. Thin layer cloud, base about 6,000 feet. Bombing appeared good and attack successful. Train on fire possibly ammunition train. 4,000 feet. 0140 hours. 2 × 1,000lb ME, 14 × 500lb GP. Attack delayed five minutes to avoid any possibility of the force bombing green TPs of the eastern target which were put down late. Markers quite good. Majority of bombs appeared overshoot slightly and were to the west of the road junction – in the rail siding.

We landed back at base after a very short return flight – one of the best aspects of fighting so close to base. The self-inflicted damage the ground crew found was a fairly small dent under the tail plane.[3]

During the greater part of 1943 and 1944 the average life expectancy of the bomber crews was thirteen operations and they were expected to complete thirty in their first tour of operations. After a period of non-operational flying duties they could be called (and many were) to complete a second of twenty missions. Aircrew ignored these odds. Those detailed for operations were single-minded in their determination to reach and strike the target. Before take-off they meticulously checked their aircraft, its equipment, the weather en route and target details. They absorbed the mass of information at the briefing, took off on time and headed into enemy territory. The successful attacks by the squadrons required leadership, skill and determination of the highest order and this was recognised by the British High Command. The Australians on 467 and 463 were awarded for their gallantry eleven Distinguished Service Orders, three Conspicuous Gallantry Medals, 225 Distinguished Flying Crosses and forty-three Distinguished Flying Medals. Unfortunately the records of the RAF members are not available to be included.

18

A MIDSUMMER NIGHT'S DIP IN THE BALTIC

The RAF bomber airfield at East Kirkby, in east Lincolnshire, received the usual morning notification by teleprinter that both its squadrons would be operating that night. For sixteen crews, it would be the usual pounding of German cities that became synonymous with Sir Arthur Harris, but for another six crews, the orders were different; they were charged with laying sea mines in the Baltic off the port of Swinemünde.

In some ways a 'Gardening' sortie came as relief to the aircrew; it was a break from the still highly effective Luftwaffe night fighters and flak units that resolutely defended the Reich homeland. But gardening was not without its own risks. Low flying over water at night in virtually no moonlight (the New Moon was only two days off) was not a sport to be undertaken lightly, especially where tiredness and any lapse of concentration on the part of the pilot could have fatal consequences. Light coastal flak, ship-mounted weaponry and roaming night fighters could and did both surprise and inflict terrible punishment on the mine-layers.

By the time Sergeant Malcolm Crapper joined 57 Squadron, the practice of specialist briefings was in place. All operating and stand-by flight engineers would be briefed before an 'op' by the engineers' leader. Malcolm's first FE briefing came from Flight Lieutenant Richard Towers Clarke DFM, who was shot down and killed on 31 July on Joigny-la-Roche. The replacement engineers' leader was Flying Officer Blanchard. Bomb aimers, navigators, wireless ops and gunners all had their own specialist briefings by their respective leaders, as did pilots. Final briefings included all crewmembers scheduled to operate or be on standby.

Flying bomb sites were attacked again on 4 August 1944 and the next day. On the 4th oil storage depots, too, were hit and twenty-seven Lancasters, two Mosquitoes and a Mustang of 617 Squadron attacked a railway bridge at Étaples. Some hits were scored but the 1,000lb bombs used failed to destroy the bridge.

At bomber bases the pace was relentless. Sergeant Malcolm Crapper aged 19 from Sheffield, flight engineer on Flight Lieutenant Stanley Leslie 'Stan' Scutt's Lancaster crew on 57 Squadron, recalls:

> The summer of 1944 was a very busy time at East Kirkby. We were doing flying training, attending briefings, flying ops – and sleeping. In the week between 18 July (our first op) and 25 July, when we went on leave, we did five ops and two training flights. In the ten days after our leave, we flew eight ops and two training flights. The weather was pretty good and I don't recall any delays or postponements. I really wanted to join the air force. On my way home from Sunday school (almost 18 years old and still going to Sunday school I ask you!) we saw 617 [Squadron] Lancs low flying over the Derwent Dam. We didn't know what they were up to. No one did; not until after the Dams raid that is. Anyway, those big, dark aeroplanes and their noise really got to me. I knew then what I wanted to do.

The others on the crew were around the same age, although 'Stan' Scutt was 30 years old and had previously served as a flying instructor. Scutt hailed from Chichester. The navigator was Flying Officer Arthur Stienstra from Canada, aged 21. The bomb aimer, Flying Officer R.E. Trindall from Yorkshire, was aged 25. The wireless operator, Pilot Officer Jack Farnhill, from Lancashire, was aged 23. Flight Sergeant J. Shields, the 24-year-old mid-upper gunner, was from Australia. Sergeant Clifford Alfred Harris, the 21-year-old rear gunner, was from Essex.

'On returning from leave on 6 August we discovered that the pace hadn't relented,' continues Malcolm. 'The Lanc we flew our first op in, DX-F PD212, had gone missing and we took Lancaster LM582 DX-B, for a daylight raid on a V-1 storage site at Bois de Cassan, just outside Paris.'

Shortly before noon on 6 August every German fighter unit in the Paris area including 26 Third Gruppe Bf 109s of JG 26 was scrambled to intercept a formation of heavy bombers. Word was that these were American and they were reported to have little or no escort. In fact over 220 aircraft that set out to attack the flying bomb supply sites at Bois de Cassan and Forêt de Nieppe once more were RAF Halifaxes and Lancasters. Bombing was scattered and was no more successful at Hazebrouck where just over sixty aircraft, mostly Halifaxes, attempted to bomb the railway centre. Four Lancasters failed to return from the operation on Bois de Cassan, which proved eventful for 'Stan' Scutt's crew as Malcolm Crapper recalled:

> We were caught by two Bf 109s whilst on our bomb run – the worst possible time – not that any time was a good time to be in a British bomber in daylight, bounced by a couple of Jerries. The Skipper ordered me to the front turret as the bomb aimer was prone working his bombsight. I can't remember if I fired a few rounds in anger or not. It happened so quickly. As soon as it started, the attack seemed to finish and I slid out of the nose turret, avoided trampling our bomb aimer and made my way back to the Skipper's right hand. After a few seconds, he caught my eye and tilted his head at the port wing. I knew that the Lanc's wings flexed in flight – I had seen it so often that I no longer noticed – but this was different. The movement was not only more obvious, but far more pronounced than I had ever seen. I drew breath to speak, at which point the Skipper held up his forefinger to his pursed lips in a semi-theatrical 'Shhh!' mime. I got the message and remained silent. The trip home was largely uneventful and we landed OK. The Commanding Officer of 57 Squadron, Wing Commander Humphries was also attacked by a pair of Bf 109s. He and his crew survived, Humphries being awarded an immediate DFC for his actions.

Next day at dispersal at East Kirkby 'Stan' Scutt's crew were told a cannon shell had hit the spar between No. 1 and No. 2 fuel tanks. Malcolm Crapper recalls:

> Fortunately the spar had not failed. Equally fortunate was the fact that neither tank had received the shell. However, further investigation revealed an even less welcome surprise in the form of an unexploded 20mm cannon shell embedded in the main spar. Had that one exploded ... The only time, as far as I remember, that I visited any of the hangars in my time at EK, was to see the unexploded shell in the main spar. All routine servicing took place on the dispersals, regardless of the weather. And of course, I only saw the summer cycle. How they [ground crew] coped in the ice and snow and screaming winds coming in from the North Sea is beyond me. We were grateful that the Americans had significantly reduced the effectiveness and expertise of the Luftwaffe fighters. I am quite sure more experienced pilots would not have let us off.

On Wednesday 16 August East Kirkby received the usual morning notification by teleprinter that 57 and 630 Squadrons would both be operating that night. By the time Sergeant Malcolm Crapper joined 57 Squadron, the practice of specialist

→ On the night of 12/13 August 1940 Flight Lieutenant Roderick Learoyd was the pilot of a 49 Squadron Hampden, P4403/EA-M, one of eleven dispatched from Scampton to make a low-level attack on the aqueducts carrying the Dortmund–Ems Canal over the River Ems near Münster. Learoyd received the Victoria Cross.

↓ Handley Page Hampdens in formation.

↑ Wellington accident when flying with Sergeant Douglas at Lossiemouth in June 1940. Sergeant Cattle on top of the aircraft retrieving parachutes; Sergeant Cole with back to camera next to Sergeant Cook; Sergeant Douglas walking away from the aircraft; Sergeants Hide and Flanagan inspecting front turret. The picture was taken by Sergeant Butcher with the aircraft's camera.

↑ Part of Geoff Cole's crew at Lossiemouth in 1940. Left to right: Sergeant Hide; unknown; Sergeant Butcher; Sergeant Geoff Cole and Sergeant Cattle.

↑ Squadron Leader John Dering Nettleton, the South African CO of 44 Squadron.

➜ Loading a 4,000lb Cookie bomb into a Wellington at RAF Mildenhall.

➜ Flight Sergeant George Edward Alfred Pendrill DFM, a Manchester pilot on 97 Squadron. On 18 December 1941 he and his crew flew with Wing Commander Denys Finlay Balsdon in L7190 QF-U on the raid on Brest when their aircraft was hit by flak over the target and it stalled and crashed on return to RAF Coningsby. All eight on board were killed.

⬇ Time to go!

→ Cologne, which was devastated by the 'Thousand Plan' raid on 30–31 May 1942.

↓ A Wellington rear gunner lies with his parachute as his shroud in the wreckage of his rear turret.

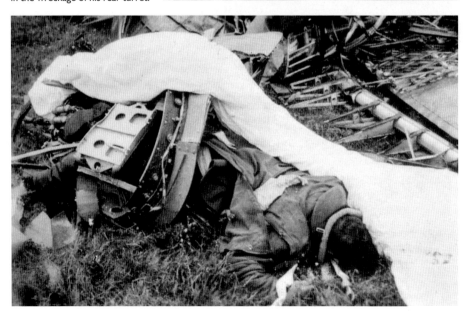

↑ Wellington pilots.

↑ Halifax *Chesty* on 426 Squadron RCAF.

⬆ Halifax II BB194/ZA-E of 10 Squadron at Melbourne, Yorkshire, in December 1942. After surviving operations, this aircraft passed to 1658 HCU, but was destroyed in a crash on 3 February 1943. The pilot, Sergeant J.N. Willoughby, suffered a fractured skull and two of his crew were injured.

⬆ Hauling bombs for Liberator II AL749 in the Middle East.

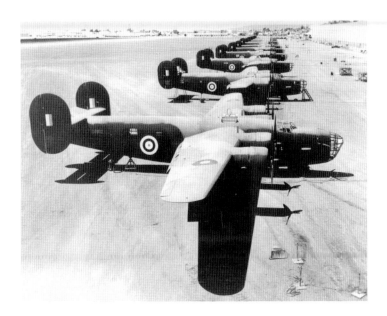

→ Liberators lined up for delivery to the RAF.

→ Albert Pierrepoint, the official British hangman.

← William Joyce, more familiarly known as 'Lord Haw-Haw', who was hanged at the end of the war.

↑ Squadron Leader Joe McCarthy DSO DFC* RCAF, a burly 23-year-old, 6ft 3in Irish-American from New York City, with his crew on 617 Squadron, who flew on the dams raid and the costly operation on the Dortmund–Ems Canal. Far left is Johnny Johnston.

↓ 617 Squadron, the 'Dambusters', pose for the camera at Scampton. Guy Gibson is centre. Joe McCarthy is third from left, back row.

↑ The scene of devastation in the Ruhr Valley after the raid by 617 Squadron.

← Oberleutnant Heinz Strüning of 3/NJG.

↓ George Cash on 20 April 1944, safely back from a 'trip'.

← Portrait of Wing Commander Rollo Kingsford-Smith RAAF.

↑ 460 Squadron RAAF at a briefing at Binbrook.

↑ Wing Commander Rollo Kingsford-Smith's crew on 463 Squadron. Left to right: Flying Officer Norm H. Kobelke, navigator; Flying Officer M.J. McLeod, wireless operator; Flight Sergeant B.W. Webb, bomb aimer; Wing Commander Rollo Kingsford-Smith; Sergeant A. Fairburn, flight engineer; Flying Officer D. Proctor, rear gunner; Flying Officer J.K.R. Rees, mid-upper gunner.

➜ Lancaster *Flak Ship* on 467 Squadron RAAF.

⬇ Two lucky crew members on Lancaster ED986 on 467 Squadron RAAF.

↑ 463 Squadron RAAF crews at briefing for the raid on Juvisy on 18 April 1944.

↑ Bombing up Lancaster *S-Snifter from Sunny Sydney* on 467 Squadron RAAF at Waddington before the raid on Juvisy in April 1944.

→ Flying Officer John McDowall Sullivan and Flight Sergeant Basil Frederick Wilmot of Launceston, Tasmania, on 467 Squadron RAAF at RAF Bottesford, Leicester, on 6 May 1943. Wilmot and his crew were killed on the raid on Düsseldorf on 11 June 1943. Sullivan and his crew were killed in action on the raid on Milan on 15 August 1943 when his Lancaster was shot down by a night fighter over France.

← 'G-George', a 467 Squadron RAAF Lancaster, with beer mugs denoting the number of operations flown.

← Lancaster JO-Q ME580/G on 463 Squadron RAAF about to touch down on 24 April 1944 following the raid on Munich.

← Ted 'the lad' Cachart on 49 Squadron.

↓ 'Tea Up' at a dispersal on an RAF station.

→ The crew of Lancaster 'C-Charlie' on 44 Squadron try to warm themselves in their Nissen hut quarters at Dunholme Lodge, after returning from Stuttgart, 2 March 1944.

↘ Pilot Officer David McQuitty and his father. One of three brothers who all served in RAF Bomber Command in England, 'Mac', who was from Tasmania, was John Joyner's pilot on 1661 HCU Winthorpe. Sergeant William Morrison McQuitty RAAF, the pilot on a 78 Squadron Whitley, was killed on the night of 8–9 July 1941 on the raid on Hamm. Mac's other brother, Flight Sergeant Robert John McQuitty RAAF, was a member of a Stirling crew all killed on a 'gardening' operation on 149 Squadron at Methwold on the night of 23–24 June 1944.

← John Joyner (first left, behind) and fellow crew members on London leave in Trafalgar Square.

↑ VE Day: 'It's All Over!'

↑ 21-year-old Warrant Officer Ron Brunt and his crew on 49 Squadron are debriefed on 23 November 1943 following a raid on Berlin. Fewer than three days later they failed to return from Berlin and all the crew members except the bomb aimer, Sergeant John Burrows, were killed. The navigator, Sergeant Fred Ashman, was just 19 years old; the crew's average age was 21. (John Ward)

briefings was in place. All operating and stand-by flight engineers would be briefed before an op by Flight Lieutenant Eric Blanchard, 57 Squadron Engineer Leader. Bomb aimers, navigators, wireless ops and gunners all had their own specialist briefings by their respective leaders, as did pilots. Final briefings included all crewmembers scheduled to operate or be on stand-by. **Stettin would be the target** for sixteen crews at East Kirkby, but another six crews would sow mines off the port of Swinemünde. In East Prussia, the Red Army had surrounded a large German Army and evacuation by sea from Konigsberg, and thence Stettin, was the only viable means of saving it. Responding to Soviet appeals, Bomber Command were to attack Stettin and lay sea mines in the deep water channel between the port and Swinemünde. Some were timed to explode as the first vessel went over them, some after the second or third and so on.

Blanchard recalls that the abnormally low dropping altitude (300ft) in a shipping channel 157yds wide caused considerable concern among the crews, obliged to operate at that height. Normally 'gardening' was carried out from 12,000 to 14,000ft. All 89 aircrews mining off Swinemünde in the Baltic and Kiel Bay (four more would plant them in the River Gironde) came from 5 Group. Low flying over water at night in virtually no moonlight – the New Moon was only two days off - was a potentially hazardous operation. Light coastal and ship-mounted flak and roaming night fighters could and did both surprise and inflict terrible punishment on the mine-layers. Blanchard wrote: 'Our Station Commander was present at the briefing. I shall always remember him standing there, chipping in with "there will be ships there, big ships – and flak." Not exactly confidence building!' The port of Stettin was to be bombed by 461 Lancasters from high level at approximately the same time as the mining was to take place. Another 348 aircraft (196 Lancasters, 144 Halifaxes and 9 Mosquitoes) were detailed for a heavy raid on Kiel.[1]

LAC Desmond Evans was part of the ground crew which looked after Lancasters on 97 Squadron at Coningsby:

There was a very close relationship between aircrews and the ground crews who serviced their aircraft. During my time on 97 Squadron I lost three aircrews and each time it was devastating. The loneliness of waiting for your particular Lanc to return was awful and when yours didn't return on time there was that awful half an hour to an hour wait until you knew their fuel reserves would have run out and there was no chance they were coming back. Later of course someone would come to your dispersal where the aircraft would be normally parked and tell you, 'Sorry lads - they've had it.' Our dispersal point would be empty for a few days and we would probably help out on another aircraft until our replacement Lancaster would arrive. We would then check the engines and probably later in the day a new aircrew would arrive. In most cases very young and very raw with no operational experience. We would get introduced to the pilot and crew and the whole sequence would start over again. You would look at them, mostly no older than 22 years of age and wonder how long they would be with us.

My particular Skipper was Wing Commander Porter. He was the leader of the first Berlin raids [he had commanded 9 Squadron throughout the Battle of Berlin] and was decorated with the DFC and Bar. His crew were mostly all officers and yet this lovely man and his crew would take my pal and I, just ordinary LACs, out with them for drinks to the local pubs as though we were their buddies. We all went on leave at the beginning of August. The Wing Commander came back two days early from his leave. One pilot due to fly on Ops was taken ill, so Porter said he would fly in his place.

Before they left for the Swinemünde Canal the 97 Squadron crews had long consultations with Wing Commander Guy Gibson, drawing on his experience gained while dam-busting. Gibson had recommended that the three marking aircraft make one low-level run down the canal before turning to drop their flame-float markers. Noel 'Ed' Parker, an Australian pilot who was near the end of his second tour, was master bomber with a scratch crew. He would mark the middle of the canal, Wing Commander Edward Leach Porter DFC★ the south end and Squadron Leader Harry Locke DFC, another Australian, the north.

At East Kirkby after final briefing Flight Lieutenant 'Stan' Scutt's crew wanted to get to their dispersal as quickly as possible to go through the pre-flight checks. Malcolm Crapper recalls:

> Stan Scutt was an extremely conscientious pilot who insisted on strict intercom discipline. We had great faith in him and he was very much the gentleman. We took pride in the fact that we were a daylight formation leader. There was no obvious apprehension amongst the crew because this would be our thirteenth op. Like virtually every wartime crew, we were superstitious, but there was a strong feeling that 'it couldn't happen to us'.

Making their way to the dispersal that was home to Lancaster III, PB384 DX-F, the pre-flight checks proceeded. This was an almost brand new aircraft, the previous DX-F (PD212) having been lost on 28–29 July on Stuttgart whilst the Scutt crew was on leave. It was in this aircraft that they had flown their first operation. Her flying career totalled only 58 hours. With ground checks completed, the aircraft fuelled, the sea mines loaded, guns armed and crew provisions stored, engines could be started to check oil pressures, engine temperatures, compressors, hydraulic systems, generators and magnetos (testing for the dreaded 'mag drop' that could be a justification for an early return).[2]

At 21.17 Lancaster PB384 took off from RAF East Kirkby en route for the Baltic Sea off Swinemünde. In her capacious 33ft-long bomb bay were six Mk.14 sea mines. Her course took her east, out over the famous Clock Tower at Skegness. Malcolm recalls the outward flight as:

> Low level across the North Sea. It was a dank and misty evening. Not at all pleasant. We kept hitting the slipstreams of aircraft in front of us, but never actually saw one. There were short moments when it was possible to relax amid the noise and vibration of a heavily loaded bomber after it had clawed its way upward. Comfortable that engine and oil temperatures were OK and all pressures were right. Check the fuel tanks ... fine. A crackle on the headphones and the all too brief overture of an intake of breath preceded 'Enemy Coast ahead!' Aaah! The eternal bomb aimer's cliché! Very soon, we knew lay The Baltic.

To put the operation into some perspective, it required accurate low-level flying over water and precise air-to-air control. The major risk to survival came from the light and medium flak that would ring the obvious harbour and its approaches. Some commentators have drawn a number of comparisons between the Swinemünde mining operation and the famous Dams Raid of May 1943. One went so far as to state that Swinemünde was a most demanding raid, second only to the Dambusters in terms of the demands made on skill and courage.

The mining force climbed to altitude before crossing the Danish coast with the Main Force at 20,000ft. Malcolm Crapper describes the next phase of the operation:

> We descended to 200 feet over the Baltic and northern Germany. We circled an inland lake that at our briefing was identified as our holding point whilst the mining area was marked by Pathfinder Lancs of 97 Squadron using flame floats. Light flak was encountered, but we were not hit. Our gunners fired back although they almost certainly knew they weren't going to do much harm but maybe make a few heads duck. Wing Commander Edward Leach Porter DFC★ the Master Bomber on 97 Squadron who was coned by searchlights over the canal, called up Squadron Leader Stuart Parkes DSO, one of the deputies, on the VHF that he had been hit by flak and that his aircraft was on fire. I clearly remember Porter saying 'Boys – I'm afraid we have had it. I shall have to leave you now. Bailing out; Good luck everybody.'

And with that, they were gone. You don't easily forget something like that.

After placing their precision marker at the northern entrance to the channel Squadron Leader Harry Locke's Lancaster, with four other Australians in the crew, was to drop mines as far north in the channel as possible. Locke's aircraft lost 'Gee' on the outward run but approached the canal dead on time at 300ft on his preliminary run to find the five flak ships moored by the side of the channel already hosing up fire. The bay was ringed by the horizontal beams of searchlights but Locke put both markers and mines in exactly the allotted area on their second run. Their flame floats had just fallen away when they were engaged by a flak ship mounting cannon, machine guns and searchlights and they plunged towards the water. 'Pull out!' yelled the wireless operator, Tony Boultbee, as he glanced from his window to see the water rushing up at them. Locke climbed away and turned for home. By then both gun turrets and all the hydraulic system of the aircraft were useless and there was a bad petrol leak but through superb calculations by Squadron Leader H. Makepeace the navigator, Locke found a gap in the coast and by crossing Denmark at 6,000ft and dropping down to fly below trees was able to dodge the searchlights and successive defensive positions. Despite leaking hydraulic fluid swamping the H_2S and the lack of almost all navigational aids, dead reckoning by the navigator brought the Lancaster back to England where Locke belly-landed at Coningsby and the crew all walked away.

Blanchard's Lancaster was called in to bomb by one of the deputies. 'The Skipper held the aircraft steady for the drop and all six mines went away. The bomb doors were closed and we increased revs and prepared to climb to miss the high ground at Swinemünde. At that moment another aircraft was on fire and going in – right in front of us.' That aircraft was Stan Scutt's.

Malcolm Crapper recalls:

One of the deputies [Squadron Leader Stuart Parkes[3]] called us in and we started our mining run. The light flak intensified and appeared to be coming from all angles. As we flew straight and level at 300 feet we took hits. It turned out we were hit very badly by light flak from dead ahead. Stan Scutt called for a bail out as he tried to climb from our 300 feet mining altitude. We knew that the aircraft was fatally damaged and we were already on our way out. Our bomb aimer kicked out the hatch under the nose and went through; I followed him. The aircraft was not even at 500 feet altitude. In those short few seconds since the kite was first hit, she was burning quite fiercely. Without hesitation I yanked the ripcord. Despite my fear, I still had the presence of mind to recognise that counting to ten before pulling the handle was not a good idea. It seemed that I fell out of the burning Lanc and into the sea in one movement. One crystal clear memory of those few fleeting seconds was seeing the reflection of our Lanc's flames in the sea below as I jumped. Our aircraft evacuation training must have been pretty good. On hitting the water I hit my parachute release button to avoid being dragged under by the rapidly saturating canopy. Only then did I recall that swimming was not one of my strong points.

Not content with sweeping the water with searchlights, the Germans started machine-gunning what they thought were aircrew struggling in the water. Every time a searchlight swung my way I tried to duck under the water. Whether my four crew mates who lost their lives died when the plane hit the water or were shot struggling in the sea, I don't know.

Somehow I made the shore. It was then that I realised I had lost one of my baggy flying boots. It was the one in which I stowed my revolver. My other boot, in which was secreted the 0.38 ammunition, was still there. What use were bullets without a bloody gun? Bugger! Edging up the shore I came to a sign planted in the sand. It was too dark to read and anyway it would be in German. I guessed, bearing in mind the nature of the English coast since 1939, that it would almost certainly read ACHTUNG! MINEN! On this premise I agreed that discretion was indeed the better part of valour.

Moving back a few yards towards the sea, I found a shallow depression in the sand that would shelter me from the sea breeze and I tried to get some rest, preferably sleep. I must have dropped off. When I woke daylight was breaking and the sign, which had troubled me a few hours earlier, now taunted me. It read 'Baden' (Bathing) and underneath hung a vivid red and white lifebuoy! 'Achtung Idiot! I thought.

Unknown to Malcolm at this time, Flying Officer R.E. Trindall, the bomb aimer who bailed out immediately in front of Malcolm, landed close to Flight Sergeant J. Shields, the mid-upper gunner who somehow had struggled free from his turret and leapt from the fuselage door. He broke his pelvis on hitting a tree on his way down and medical treatment became an absolute priority. Stan Scutt and Cliff Harris, Jack Farnhill and Arthur Stienstra had been killed.

Malcolm Crapper forced himself to think and consider his options. The most promising would be to somehow make contact with one of the Swedish sailors whose vessels delivered iron ore to the port he was helping close off very early this morning. What other options were there? Not many, when he thought seriously. OK - first step is to get close to a Swedish ship. After that work out a strategy for getting on board and sailing off to neutral territory.

He now made his way inland into nearby woodland, struggling through the stamina-sapping undergrowth for an age. Eventually he emerged into a clearing that opened up in front of him. Relief turned to shock and alarm:

Oh Christ! There was a light flak battery at the opposite edge of the clearing. Had they seen me? Do I turn and run? What do I do? What? I didn't want to risk a bullet in my back if I turned and legged it, so I raised my hands. The buggers had not seen me! But by then it was too late. Some young squaddies ran over to me and roughed me up a bit. An older sergeant appeared from nowhere and barked an order. From the tone of his voice, I guessed the NCO was giving the youngsters (they were probably only 17 or 18 years old) a right royal bollocking. I was helped to my feet, taken to the flak battery and basic interrogation took place.

'Your name?'

'Crapper'.

'Initials?'

'M'.

'Rank? '

'Sergeant'.

'Serial number?'

'1591526'.

None of the phoney Red Cross forms and whatnot we had been repeatedly warned about. Coffee and bread were offered. The coffee, or whatever it was, tasted awful but it was hot. The bread, black bread, was inedible but I took it and saved it for later. Later I was put in the sergeant's bed. It had blue and white gingham sheets. Now that detail I have absolutely no doubt about whatsoever. We were supposed to be winning the war and the Germans were supposed to be suffering unbelievable privations. So how come this was the first time in months – no, the first time in years – that I had enjoyed sleep in 'proper' bedclothes?

Even in the drama that had unfolded at Swinemünde, moments of humour emerged. Blanchard's Lancaster mined at the prescribed 300ft but thirty degrees of flap proved necessary to provide extra lift at the relatively low mine-dropping airspeed. On the return journey over Denmark at around 12,000ft, the pilot remarked about the aircraft's sluggishness and poor airspeed. Only then did the penny drop that they had struggled westward across the Baltic still with thirty degrees of flap on!

Of the six Lancasters on 57 Squadron, two turned back, one (Porter's) was shot down. Three completed the task and all three pilots were awarded the DFC. DX-M came home with twenty-six 2in holes in it. No one was hurt.

At Coningsby LAC Desmond Evans was distraught:

It is hard to describe how you feel about the loss of a whole crew. One minute you are chatting and having a smoke before they take off and four or five hours later, they have gone – just a memory. Wing Commander Porter's crew took off at 21.40 and at 01.33 a radio message came in: 'We are hit – burning, burning – abandoning ...' That was all they had time to transmit. One [Sergeant Terence Michael Twomey DFM, the rear gunner] is buried on the Island of Bornholm [in Peders Kirke churchyard]; four including Wing Commander Porter are buried at Poznan Polish War Cemetery – three were never found. Anyone who says they were full of fun before they went on a raid and that they hadn't a care in the world are fools. These young men knew exactly what lay before them; they were tensed up and nervous and that's what made them brave – they still went and did what they had to do.[4]

19

THE BIG RAIDS
PILOT OFFICER JOHN A. MARTIN DFC

We reached Berlin, dropped our bombs at 25,000 feet and as we were leaving the target area, our two port engines were hit by flak and set on fire. My skipper ordered us to abandon the aircraft but at that point a German fighter, attracted by our plane on fire, came in to attack us. A shell from the fighter seared across the top of my head and knocked me out. When I came to, I was in the wreckage of the bomber. It had crashed into the side of a huge pine forest. I was very bruised, the only injury I received was from the shell of the German fighter, my head was split wide open. I then gave myself up at a German railway signal crossing. Next day I found out that all six of my crew were killed when they bailed out of the plane, they said they saw my plane spiral down and hit the side of the ground.

Sergeant William Burnell

Sergeant William Henry Burnell was mid-upper gunner on Lancaster ME635 AS-C on 166 Squadron on the evening of 24 March 1944 on a bombing raid on Berlin that became known to Bomber Command as the Night of the Strong Winds. The skipper, Flight Sergeant Ernest Brown RAAF, and Sergeant John Eric Scruton; Flight Sergeant William Mitchinson; Sergeant Russell Boyde; Sergeant Joseph Flavell and Sergeant William Charles Mason were killed.

All were buried in Berlin war cemetery. Sergeant Burnell, the only survivor after surviving a fall of 25,000ft inside the Lancaster, was interned in Stalag

Luft VI, then Stalag 357 Thorn and finally 357 Fallingbostel. Here he remained until the end of the war when in April 1945 he was injured by American attacks on the camp, causing him to lose a lung. He was flown home on 4 May 1945.

✧ ✧ ✧

Pilot Officer John A. Martin DFC:

We were involved in most of the big raids. We went to Berlin on 24–25 March 1944 when the forecasters gave us the wrong winds by which to navigate. There were ninety aircraft shot down that night out of 700 aircraft. I was in the astrodome and could see, 'there's one going down, there's another one going down, there's another one going down.' They were just going down like flies. Including the ninety that were shot down and those which crashed, there were 120 aircraft lost that night, just because of the wrong winds being given. Even then we were lucky and got back.

On being briefed for Manheim, the briefing officer would tell us that we had had a good spell of dry weather and this town had a large number of wooden structures, it should burn well tonight. We went to Italy also, we flew over the Alps and en route I was admiring Mount Blanc. It was a beautiful night; there was snow on the mountain. 'Mac' McDonald, the skipper, said he could see the TIs (Target Indicators) going down now. Instead of being over Turin, we were over Milan. We went around again and on to Turin. We were the only aircraft there at this time; the others had been and gone. We got an aiming point and dropped our bomb load and returned to base.

The next night we were briefed that we were going to bomb the Fiat works in Turin. We had to climb over the Alps and do a low level bombing and then climb back up to get back over the Alps again. When we were on our way over the Alps, Mount Blanc was above our level of flight. The journey time for the raid was about eight or nine hours, which was very close to the limit for a Stirling. Part of the duties of a flight engineer on a Stirling was the balancing of the seven fuel tanks fitted to each main plane. Your main tanks were two and four. They held 250 and 300 gallons of fuel. On the trailing edge you also had fuel tanks. If you were caught by a fighter you couldn't use the trailing edge tanks as the fuel wouldn't run from them to the engines so you had to change to tanks two and four during combat. During the flight over the target you also went on to tanks two and four so that you could get out of the target area as quickly as possible, which meant that you were juggling all the time with the tanks so that you finished with fuel in tanks two and four. During the flight I kept a watch on the oil pressures and temperatures and advised the pilot what engine settings to use so that we could save as much fuel as possible. If there were any leaks we had materials to carry out a first aid repair.

One night I was in the Sergeant's Mess along with three mates having a small celebration. We had arranged that in case I had any difficulty getting home, two of my mates would ensure that I got there safely. Wireless operator Gamble came into the mess and thought that the two mates were going to assault me outside. Gamble tried to pull them away to save me. One of the two lifted a five gallon drum and hit Gamble a blow on the forehead with it, a scar he carries to this day. Because of the injury Gamble couldn't fly with us the next night when we were briefed for an attack on Mönchengladbach. I was sitting up in the second dickey seat and 'Mac' McDonald, the pilot said, 'The flak seems heavier on the north of the town, I think we'll go in from the south and then we'll dive out of the heavy stuff.'

Gamble wasn't with us that night and as soon as we went in from the south the flak stopped in the north and opened up on us in the south. The flak shot out our 'Gee' box, which was our navigation aid. They also shot out our identification indicator, which signalled 'friend' or 'foe'. There was other electrical equipment damaged, but we couldn't do anything about it. We got away from the flak and were on our way home. We hadn't a notion where we were. We thought we were crossing the English coast when the Dover gunners started shooting at us with 'hose pipe flak' (a type of tracer ammunition). This flak was coming up all round us. 'Mac' told me to fire off the colours of the day (an emergency procedure in case of radio loss). I got the gun out to fire the colour of the day, but the gun slipped and fired the colours down inside the aircraft. We turned away from the coast and tried going round again, but again the Dover gunners opened up with more flak, so we shouted at them, 'Mayday, Mayday. Mayday, Mayday.' The ground forces then put up a cone of searchlights over an airfield at Ford, where we were able to land. At the same time Gamble was waiting in our control tower for us to return and he was most distraught thinking that we had been hit by ground fire and crashed. We had no radios left working as we crossed the English coast. That was the only trip Gamble missed.

I visited the mess at RAF Feltwell one day and saw this wee insignificant warrant officer pilot standing at the bar and he and I had a drink, we continued and may have had one or two more. He said during our conversation, 'I'm looking for an engineer, I'm going back.' (Returning to flying bombing operations.) He had already carried out 39 trips in the Middle East. We had a further libation or two and at one stage I said I would go back with him. He said that was OK and he would go and have a word with the wing commander in the morning. I got up the next morning and didn't quite remember exactly what had happened. The wee warrant officer pilot said he had had a word with the Wingco who had OK'd my return to operations with him. That was the start of my second tour. We started our trips on Stirlings and then went to Feltwell to finish on Lancasters; but Gamble whom I had previously flown with was at Feltwell and expressed some amazement at my return to take on a second tour; especially going back with a 'Sprog' crew, who had never been over Germany in their life, apart from the pilot. Gamble said that yes, he was going back, but at least he was going back with a seasoned crew who had flown over Germany before. They were all intelligent officers who had been to Germany before. The next time I met Gamble was in 1945 and he told me that he went with his new crew on his first operation; they never even got the bomb doors open. They were shot down and he was taken prisoner. So much for his telling me I was stupid for going with a 'sprog' crew. Gamble had to walk the long march when the war was almost finished; he was in one of those long treks where the prisoners of war were moved in retreat as the Allied armies advanced. He was on the road for weeks and weeks, walking.

We were over Hamburg and I saw this plane being coned by searchlights, there were several searchlights and the plane was in the middle of the cones of lights. There was a fighter outside of him, pumping, shooting away at him. The pilot was Johnny Johnston. When we went outside the next morning after landing, we looked at the plane, it was riddled, I don't know how he ever got it back. There were seven of a crew on board and none of them had been injured, but the plane was riddled. The crew escaped injury, but it was riddled. Isn't it amazing?

We went in that night as usual for a briefing and it was Hamburg again. Johnny and his crew went out to the aircraft, but the crew said to Johnny, 'We would like a rest tonight, because of what happened last night.' Johnny said to them, 'If you feel like that there is nothing I can do about it,' and brought the crew back into the briefing room. They were arrested and taken to Stradishall and put into military custody by the MPs. They were kept in jail overnight and the next morning they were taken to a place called East Church to face punishment for their misdemeanour. When they arrived at East Church and their case was heard, they were stripped of their brevies (brevets are the wings worn on the tunic, denoting the job of the wearer) and their Sergeant stripes. When they came back up to Chedburgh, they were sent to the airman's mess and made to peel spuds. That was a demonstration of the others on base not to 'go LMF' (lack of moral fibre) whatever you do! That gave us a good warning, you might not want to go out on a mission, but you were scared not to go. I felt sorry for the crew, the whole lot of them. All the crew were disciplined, except the pilot, Johnny Johnston. He picked up another crew and went on as briefed.

We went out one night on a bomb raid and the tacticians thought they would be very crafty. After the main force went out, at a certain stage, the Lancasters and the Halifaxes went to Hanover and the Stirlings went to Bremen. While we were at Bremen the wireless operator was at the rear throwing out propaganda leaflets. The seat where the wireless operator normally sat in the aircraft, near the pilot, had armour plating right behind it. While the wireless operator was at the rear, a fighter came in and started to fire at us. I was in sitting at the wireless operator's seat with my feet up trying to miss the bullets that were being fired at us. The wireless operator was at the rear trying to avoid the strafe that was being fired around him. We managed to get away from the fighter. Gamble, who was throwing the propaganda leaflets out the rear, came up and said, 'Paddy, Paddy, I've been hit, but don't tell the pilot till we get out of trouble.' I took my torch out of my flying boot and looked at him to see how badly injured he was. What had happened was, the bullets had penetrated the hydraulic system and jets of hydraulic fluid had hit Gamble on the face, his face was covered in hydraulic oil and he thought it was blood, in the dark. He was greatly relieved when I told him it was 'only' oil. Thankfully we got away from the fighter.

We weren't due to fly one day during 1943 and I had a WAAF to see in Cambridge, when Mac McDonald came out and said, 'Paddy, we'll have to go to Stradishall and bring an aircraft back.' We went to Stradishall and collected the aircraft. As we were coming in to land, right in front of us, two Stirlings collided. Right in front of our eyes, in mid-air. The whole lot came down, everyone on board was lost. The worst part was, they had taken up some ground crew for 'a trip'. There were nineteen lives lost in that accident. We were about the only crew to finish our first tour in Stirlings, the majority of the others were shot down. Stirlings were lethal, Air Chief Vice Marshal Harris said he wouldn't send 'the boys' out in Stirlings any more, they were too dangerous. There were so many lost, the top ceiling for them was 13,000 feet. The Lancasters, at that time were able to climb to 20,000 feet. In comparison with other aircraft going up, we were in the middle of them.

During my time at Chedburgh, I was on 620 Squadron and there was another Squadron there; it was 214. I met another chap there – [Sergeant Richard] 'Paddy' Mailey, from Bangor – he was also a flight engineer. It's quite natural for Irishmen abroad to 'stick' together. Paddy told me that he was going on a mining trip tomorrow [3–4 July 1943]. I said that I wasn't flying tomorrow and I would come to the airfield and see him off. I went up the next day and saw 'Paddy' off in the aircraft and wished him 'all the best'. Paddy had just got off the ground and the whole aircraft blew up. The mines had exploded prematurely. The aircraft fell down like confetti. The complete aircrew were all killed, that was the last of Paddy Mailey. There wasn't a piece of the aircraft left. [1]

When we were out carrying out an air test on our aircraft at Chedburgh, flying above the River Cam, our pilot used to fly so low that he was able to tip over the yachts. He would call to a member of the crew who was keeping watch out the rear, 'Have I got it?' The crew member invariably replied, 'Yes it's gone.' You can imagine how low he must have been flying to direct the slipstream from the props to overturn the yachts.

I've asked myself many times since the war ended, 'Was it all worth it, given the lives that were lost during the war?' I was at Waterbeach as a Flight Mechanic and I then went to train as a member of aircrew and afterwards joined the squadron. I had flown about 25 bombing operations. I was an old sweat by that time. Everyone else had gone and Taffy Whitfield, the fellow who slept in the next bed to me, he arrived as a Flight Engineer. He was attached to an Australian crew. They went in to get briefed for their mission that night; it was an attack on Berlin. They came out from briefing and we went in for ours. I asked him whenever we came out, 'What do you think of the operation tonight?' He said to me, 'With this crew, I have got no hope, no hope in this wide world. Getting through with this! They're hopeless.' We got to Berlin and I was in the astrodome. Berlin was like flying down Royal Avenue in Belfast; all the lights were on, everything was as clear as a bell. Once you start into Berlin, you never think you are going to get to the other end of the city. It's so long. While I was in the astrodome, I saw Taff going over ahead of me. The next thing I saw, a fighter came up and shot him down and that was the end of Taff. It all happened right in front of me, he was shot down. I was able to read his aircraft registration on the side of his aircraft. That was Big Taff Whitfield. You realise just how close you were to being shot down yourself and wonder how did you get through the war? You were so close to combat and didn't get any injuries.[2]

20

'SUNNY'

Ernest 'Sunny' Gledhill was born in Halifax on 4 June 1921 and lived in Odsal, Bradford, in West Yorkshire. He was a good-natured young man, 5ft 7½in tall, with brown hair, hazel eyes, a fresh complexion, and was the apple of his mother's eye. His older sister, Margaret, spent a lot of time looking after him after their father died when 'Sunny' was 9 years old, which left their widowed mother to build the family pawnbroker's shop and keep them fed and clothed. He was an assistant in the business before volunteering for the RAF and joining up on 5 October 1941 to train as a wireless operator-air gunner. By the late spring of 1943 he had successfully completed his training, at 2 Radio School and 7 Air Gunners School at Stormy Down, Wales, where he trained in air gunnery on Whitley bombers. 'Sunny' gained his sergeant's stripes shortly after his 22nd birthday, on 9 June, with 78 per cent marks in his training, and he moved to 9 Observer Advanced Flying Unit at RAF Llandwrog, near Caernarfon, Wales, training on Avro Ansons. Llandwrog was a very pleasant base, being positioned on the coast directly next to the beach and in the shadow of the mountains of Snowdonia. From there he joined 12 Operational Training Unit on 13 July, the unit being re-organised as 1657 Conversion Unit at RAF Stradishall, Suffolk, where Sunny remained until 6 December 1943.

'Sunny' became part of Sergeant John Clare Gilbertson-Pritchard's all-NCO crew on the Stirling. Gordon Kenneth Woodward, navigator, was from Ardwick, Manchester. James McGahey, who was from Exeter in Devon, was the flight engineer. Deeply religious, before volunteering for the RAF he was a scoutmaster and carpenter, working on various churches and cathedrals in his area. He was also a talented musician, and would often play the piano and accordion, among other instruments. He surprised his whole family when he volunteered for the RAF, as they were expecting him to be a conscientious objector. His brother, Frederick, remembers the whole family being shocked when Jim came home to Exeter on leave once in a pair of sheepskin flight boots, knowing that in doing so he was breaching regulations. The winter of 1943–44 was the coldest on record and Jim was determined that his feet would not get cold! Frederick believed that Jim was 'led astray' by William Earle Brown, the Canadian bomb aimer from Calgary, Alberta, who apparently was a bit of a rascal! Jim McGahey became 'Sunny's best friend.

Ernest Walter Haigh, mid-upper gunner, born in Walton, Liverpool, on 27 August 1915, was the third of four children. He was a bottle hand prior to enlisting on 1 August 1936 and was initially an aircraft hand on general duties. But Ernie, who was 5ft 4in tall, with fair hair, grey eyes and a fresh complexion, had always wanted to fly so he immediately volunteered for flying duties as an air gunner. On 10 April 1937 he realised his ambition and became acting air gunner (unpaid) and was promoted to AC1. War was rapidly approaching when, on 13 August 1939, Ernie had married Josephine Agnes Putterill. On 30 September 1940 Ernie and Josephine had a baby girl they called Josephine Doreen. Ernie Haigh was serving on 611 Squadron when war was declared in September 1939, by which time 611 had swapped bombers for fighter aircraft, so obviously there was no need for air gunners, but he made steady progress as a trainee armourer. Throughout 1941–43, 611 Squadron was heavily involved in the defence of Britain. Knowing the dangers, in July 1943 Ernie volunteered for flying duties in order to become an air gunner again and was immediately posted to 10 Air Gunners School. He crewed up on Gilbertson-Pritchard's crew at 12 OTU on 31 August. At 28 years of age, Ernie was the 'grandpa' on the crew. He had much in common with Jack Birch, the rear gunner, who was from Chesham, in Buckinghamshire. Jack was also married, to Nan, and they too had a baby daughter, Ann. In November 1943 Ernie's wife Josephine was pregnant with their second child, Ernest Benjamin, who was born on 9 November. Tragically, the baby died a few months later.

Just before Jack Birch and Ernie Haigh went missing over Duisburg on the night of 21–22 May 1944, Jack visited his nephew and niece one Sunday morning. Jean Leithall remembered the visit well. Jack had almost completed thirty operations and was looking forward to ending his tour. Sadly, they never saw him again. He and Ernie Haigh were killed when Lancaster II DS781 JI-R, skippered by Pilot Officer Bernard William Windsor DFM RNZAF, was lost without trace in the North Sea. The aircraft was one of three lost on 514 Squadron that night. Birch and five other members of the crew, which included William Earle Brown and Gordon Kenneth Woodward, are commemorated on the walls at Runnymede. Ernie Haigh's body was recovered and is buried at Kiel War Cemetery.

Gilbertson-Pritchard's crew had been posted to join 218 Squadron at RAF Downham Market, Norfolk, on 6 December. The new crew flew just four operations on the Stirling, beginning on 16 December with a short duration mining trip off Frisian Islands when thirty-five aircraft dropped mines off the Friesians and off Biscay ports. Gilbertson-Pritchard lifted Stirling III HA-S LJ452 off at 17.05 hours and two B204 and two B218 mines were released over the allotted area before returning at 20.05 hours with 'nothing of interest to report'. On 22–23 December, on Stirling III HA-R EF124, they took part in raids by fifty-one aircraft on flying bomb sites between Abbeville and Amiens, taking off at 21.05 hours and landing back at 00.05 hours. One site was bombed accurately but the other could not be located. Bombs were dropped on TI markers and light flak was experienced but all aircraft returned safely.

The crew flew no further operations until the night of 14–15 January 1944, when Stirling III HA-M EH942 was one of 82 aircraft – fifty-nine Stirlings, thirteen Halifaxes and ten Mosquitoes – that attacked flying bomb sites at Ailly, Bonneton and Bristillerie without loss. Gilbertson-Pritchard's crew went to south Cherbourg and the Hazebrouck construction works, where they bombed from 14,000ft on Red TI markers but no built-up area was seen. It was flying bomb sites once again on the night of 21–22 January; their last on 218 Squadron, when 111 aircraft – eighty-nine Stirlings, twelve Lancasters and ten Mosquitoes, bombed six V-1 sites in France without loss. Stirling III BF504 HA-P 'Peter' took off at 18.10 hours to bomb a 'special target (Blackcap)' in the Pas-de-Calais from 9,000ft. Bombs were seen to burst near the TI Markers but 'P-Peter' landed back at 21.10 hours with all eighteen 500lb bombs intact due to 'hang-up'.

On 23 January 1944 Gilbertson-Pritchard's crew was transferred to 1678 Conversion Flight at RAF Waterbeach, Cambridgeshire, and joined 514 Squadron as a complete crew, on 4 February.[1] The crew flew their first operation on 1–2 March, to Stuttgart, on Lancaster II, 'P' LL683. The only change was the mid-upper gunner position; Sergeant George A. Henry replacing Ernie Haigh, who was on compassionate leave following the death of his daughter. 'Hawkeye Henry', as he was known, was from Fulham in London and before joining the RAF at 18 years old, worked in a chiropodists' equipment factory. George had flown seventeen operations on 15 Squadron before being posted to 514 Squadron in December 1943 and was a 'spare' mid-upper gunner, filling in on different crews until eventually hooking up with Gilbertson-Pritchard's crew. George completed his tour of thirty operations on 514 Squadron and then trained air gunners for six months, before being posted to India to crew Liberators until the end of the war. Gilbertson-Pritchard took 'P-Peter' off at 23.41 hours with a bomb load of one 2,000 pounder, one 500 pounder and incendiaries. They had only reached Cambridge when the W/T receiver went U/S and they were forced to return early. Gilbertson-Pritchard jettisoned the bombs to reduce the load before landing at 02.05 hours.

On 15–16 March Gilbertson-Pritchard's crew were one of 863 crews on 617 Lancasters, 230 Halifaxes and sixteen Mosquitoes that were detailed to bomb Stuttgart once more. Gilbertson-Pritchard took Lancaster II LI734 'S-Sugar' off at 19.14 hours and dropped the load of 1,000lb bomb, seventy-two x 30lb, 1,050 x 4 and ninety 4lb incendiaries at 23.20 hours from 21,000ft. There was very thin cloud and the attack was not concentrated. 'S-Sugar' received holes in the fuselage due to flak on the homeward leg near the French coast but landed safely at 02.39 hours. Three nights later, on 18–19 March, Gilbertson-Pritchard's crew took Lancaster II DS882 'T-Tommy' to Frankfurt, taking off at 19.30 hours with a load of one 4,000lb bomb, 1,350 x 4lb bombs, ninety x 4lb incendiaries and thirty-two x 30lb incendiaries. The weather was hazy but they bombed at 22.04 hours from 21,000ft. 'Incendiaries scattered round TIs. Fires to South and East. Monica and Gee U/S homeward. Holes in port wing by heavy flak.' S-Sugar, landed safely at 01.04 hours.

Gilbertson-Pritchard's crew were stood down on the night of the disastrous 30–31 March trip to Nuremberg but 'Sunny's best friend, Sergeant James McGahey, stood in as flight engineer on Pilot Officer Donald Charles Cameron Crombie RAAF's crew. Crombie, of Ascot, Queensland, and his crew were on their fourteenth operation. Pilot Officer Harry G. Darby, the bomb aimer on the crew, recalled:

The war found me racked by conflicting emotions – on the one hand an intense patriotism coupled with a desire to match my father's bravery and fortitude in the First World War and on the other a haunting fear of having my life squandered in some action on the lines of the disasters of 1914–18. In my young, immature mind I rationalized these thoughts by deciding that I would serve but that I would join an arm of the forces where individual courage, skill and verve were at a premium (or so I thought). It now seems ironic that I should have finished up by flying with Bomber Command in the winter of 1943–44, the arm that had to take the war to the enemy, that had to display the 'Press on' spirit that had characterized the offensives of the first war and that suffered a higher proportion of casualties than any other branch of the forces. That winter was a tough time to be operating and the losses were appalling. It didn't require an actuarial mind to see that the chances of surviving a tour were slender in the extreme. I find it difficult to recall just what it was that sustained us – fear of showing the white feather I suppose. By the time of the Nuremberg Raid the morale of our crew was undoubtedly getting rather worn and even our phlegmatic Australian pilot was showing signs of strain.[2]

When the crew carried out the final checks on their aircraft, Harry Darby exploded with rage:

The perspex through which I used to peer for most of the trip was very dirty with oil and dust. It may be a measure of my tension that I flew into a rage and ordered one of the ground-crew sergeants to send the rigger responsible to me. I severely reprimanded the man but also explained that our lives could depend on having good vision. I often wondered how that airman must have reacted when we failed to return.[3]

Crombie's crew were intercepted over the target by 23-year-old Leutnant Wilhelm Seuss, pilot of a Bf 110 in 11./NJG5 at Erfurt, near Weimar in Saxony. Seuss had been due for leave and had thought that he would not be flying at all this night. The moonlit night had seemed to confirm it but he and his comrades had been ordered off at 23.17 hours with orders to fly west. With him in his Bf 110 were *bordfunker* (radio operator) Bruno Zakrzewski and Fritz Sagner, his *bordschütze* (gunner). They shot down a Lancaster and then, keeping a sharp look-out, Seuss flew quite near to the searchlights and his crew was able to see another bomber catch fire and dive to the ground. It had been caught in the beams.[4] Seuss then called Sagner and told him to change the ammunition drums on the oblique guns. Meanwhile, Zakrzewski was able to lead his pilot on to another *viermot* (four-engined bomber) at 22,000ft and drawing close to the final turning point. It was Lancaster DS836 flown by Donald Crombie. In his excitement Sagner took longer than usual to change the drums and Seuss had to shadow the Lancaster, keeping 120 metres beneath it while he followed all its movements. Without warning, Crombie corkscrewed, although Seuss was certain the crew had not seen them, at the moment he decided to attack from behind using the horizontal guns. Sagner reported that the oblique guns were now working. Seuss tried again to land his shots between the two port engines but the Lancaster suddenly swerved to port so that his fire landed in the port and starboard wings. Both wings burst into flames and the Lancaster dived sharply. This shooting-down was probably south-east of Schweinfurt.

Crombie and four of the crew were killed. Sergeant James McGahey died going to the aid of the rear gunner, Sergeant Harold Roy Hill, who was trapped in his turret and died when the aircraft crashed. Flight Sergeant Claude Charles Payne, a Londoner from Stratford, and fellow Londoner, Sergeant Morris Joseph Tyler, of Wembley, were the other two men who died when the Lancaster crashed with a full bomb load just outside the Bavarian village of Eichenhausen, a district of Bad Neustadt.[5] Only Flight Sergeant A. McPhee, navigator, and Harry Darby, the bomb aimer, survived. Darby wrote: 'I was immediately overcome by a feeling of profound relief that never again would I have to run that gauntlet. I experienced a distinctly warm glow, almost of elation. I had done my bit and now, given a shade of luck, I would survive and live to a ripe old age. I swore a solemn oath that I would never go in the air again.'[6]

Flight Sergeant John Clare Gilbertson-Pritchard was to be posted on 19 April[7] and his crew became 'spare bods', so for the first time 'Sunny' Gledhill would be without his regular crew. On 18 April he found himself on that night's Battle Order for the trip to bomb the railway yards at Rouen on Lancaster II DS882 'T-Tommy', piloted by 20-year-old Flying Officer Maurice Linden Morgan-Owen, whose regular wireless operator, Sergeant F. Barrett, was in Ely Hospital recovering from an accident. Altogether, 273 Lancasters and sixteen Mosquitoes of 1, 3 and 8 Groups were detailed for the raid. Morgan-Owen was from Wandsworth in London. He volunteered for the RAF on his 18th birthday and had trained to be a pilot in Canada, sending very spirited letters home to his family. Fun loving and liking a pint or two, he was a round-faced and rather cheerful person, having endured a long and snowy Canadian winter to obtain his pilots' wings on 16 April 1943. At one time he and his fellow pilots had to pitch in and shovel snow to rescue a snowbound locomotive from a nearby railway line.

The crew's navigator was 23-year-old Flight Sergeant Alan William Green. Flying Officer George Alexander Jacobson, the 27-year-old bomb aimer, was from Gunalda, Queensland, and was born on 25 March 1917, in Gympie. He enlisted on 5 April 1940 in Brisbane and embarked for England on 7 September 1942. Sergeant Alfred Douglas Tetley, the 23-year-old rear gunner, was one of three brothers. His family owned and ran a greengrocer's shop in Starbeck, an area of Harrogate, North Yorkshire. The mid-upper gunner, 27-year old Sergeant Herbert Stanley 'Bub' Hayward from Bishop's Stortford, was one of five brothers and four sisters. Stanley's fiancée, Mary, lived at Hunstanton, Norfolk. George Alexander Jacobson was Sunny's bomb aimer in his final crew. Sergeant Henry Leo Sadler, known as Leo, the kindly, good-humoured 25-year-old flight engineer, was born in Brighton on 21 October 1918. He had a younger brother and three sisters, two of whom were WAAFs. Leo's family had moved to Birmingham in 1922 and he joined the RAF in 1936. His mother was very proud that he was trained by Rolls-Royce. Somehow Leo got himself into the Fleet Air Arm and served on the carrier *Eagle* in Crete and Ceylon. His family were not sure how or why he got into Bomber Command. In 1941 Leo married Joan from West Hartlepool at the Rosary Church, Saltley, in Birmingham. They had a daughter whom they named Maureen after one of Leo's sisters.

Lancaster II DS882 'T-Tommy' took off at 22.41 hours for Rouen with ten 10 1,000 Medium Capacity bombs and five × 500lb MC bombs. Weather was clear en route and visibility good. 'T-Tommy' bombed at 00.52 hours from 13,500ft after the target was identified visually. The TI markers were scattered but bombing was well concentrated and much destruction was caused to the target. 'T-Tommy' made it back safely despite one of the 1,000 pounders getting hung up in the bomb bay. Their luck seemed to hold.

On Saturday, 22 April 'Sunny' discovered that he was 'on' again that night and would be on Flying Officer Maurice Morgan-Owen's crew once more. Altogether, 596 aircraft – 323 Lancasters, 254 Halifaxes and nineteen Mosquitoes – were on the Battle Order for Düsseldorf. That same night 238 Lancasters of 5 Group and seventeen Mosquitoes and ten Lancaster 'active observers' of 1 Group were to attack Brunswick and another 181 aircraft were to bomb the locomotive sheds and marshalling yards at Laon in France. Morgan-Owen took Lancaster II DS682 'N-Nuts' off from Waterbeach at 22.58 hours with an 8,000lb bomb, forty-eight x 30lb bombs, 486 x 4lb bombs and fifty-four x 4lb incendiaries and 1,360 gallons of petrol, which allowed about 6½ hours' flying time. The anticipated duration of the flight was approximately four hours and seven minutes and 'N-Nuts' was due to return at 03.00 on Sunday morning.

At Düsseldorf 2,150 tons of bombs were dropped, mostly in the northern districts of the city, which caused widespread damage. This 'old style' heavy attack allowed the *Nachtjagd* to penetrate the bomber stream and twenty-nine aircraft – sixteen Halifaxes and thirteen Lancasters – were lost. Three of the missing Lancasters were on 514 Squadron. Two of them had collided and crashed at Ecke Rethel. All fourteen men died. At 02.56 an SOS message was received giving 'N-Nuts' position as approximately 70 miles west of the Dutch coast. Nothing more was heard from the aircraft. All seven of Maurice Morgan-Owen's crew were posted missing. According to acting Squadron Leader Barney Reid, at first light an ASR aircraft was dispatched to look for the crew. Reid personally took part in this. However, despite good visibility, nothing was found. Two of the crew were eventually washed ashore in the East Frisian Islands, off the northern coast of Germany. They were Leo Sadler, originally buried on the island of Nordeney, and Alfred Tetley, originally buried on the island of Baltrum. They are now both buried in the Sage War Graves Cemetery in Germany. The other crew names were added to the Runnymede memorial.

One of Bub's nieces tells a very strange tale indeed. This is what she wrote:

I remember as a child hearing the family talk about Uncle Bub and how my grandmother was not told of his disappearance because she had been extremely ill, near death in fact. One night she dreamed she saw Bub in the water, with his dark hair floating all around him. The next morning, she said she knew that Bub had been trying to tell her that something had happened and insisted on being told the truth. According to one of his two surviving sisters, at the time this happened, Bub's mother did not know that anything had happened to him; least of all that he had come down in the Sea.

21

THE SKIES OVER MAILLY-LE-CAMP

SIDNEY LIPMAN

Just before the war broke out, in September 1939, I was contacted by the District Surveyor's office in Stepney where I lived. They were in the process of setting up a Heavy Rescue Party, as war was imminent and I was asked if I was willing to join them. This would mean that if we had any bombing I would be in a group of men whose job would be to shore up dangerous structures, cut off main water and gas supplies in buildings and, of course, rescue people who were trapped. I was suited to this work as I was working for my father in the building trade. I willingly accepted the task and also took a course and passed out as a PT instructor, to keep the men fit and active for their arduous tasks.

It wasn't a pleasant experience in the Heavy Rescue Party and we were on duty twenty-four hours on, twenty-four hours off. Many of my colleagues were lost on those long and dangerous nights when we had to pull people out of the wreckage. We thanked God if they were alive and unhurt, but all too often it was too late to save them. On one occasion my own house was bombed to the ground and another night I was called upon to rescue relatives of mine out of a bombed building.

After two and a half years there was a lull in the bombing and four of us from the Heavy Rescue Party volunteered for the Royal Air Force as aircrew. In the interview I was told that I would be accepted. Unfortunately the other three men did not pass the selection procedure. I had another hurdle to pass, which involved three days of rigorous mental and physical examinations. I got through these to their satisfaction and was given an RAF volunteer reserve badge and told that they would call for me. I didn't have long to wait! The training was an exciting and mind-broadening time for me. I had the opportunity to test my physical strength and abilities to the limit and was very proud of studying at Clare College, Cambridge, for a few months for Initial Training Wing. At this period Lancasters had just come out and flight engineers were being trained for them. It sounded an exciting challenge and I volunteered to go for training, which was at St Athan, South Wales.

After passing out as a Sergeant flight engineer I went to Wratting Common and it was there that I met my crew. I was walking towards a Stirling aircraft when a voice from behind said 'hello, my name's Ron. Have you got a crew yet?' He explained that he was looking for a flight engineer to make up the rest of a seven-man bomber crew in which he was a wireless operator. I went with him to meet the other chaps, all looking very young and keen. We were a cosmopolitan group; included in our numbers were a New Zealander pilot and an Australian bomb aimer. We started on our training on the Stirling four-engine bomber and after passing out we were transferred on to Lancasters. After a 9-day conversion course with them we were sent to 166 Squadron at Kirmington in Lincolnshire. It was from there that we started our tour of operations.

There were 21 Lancasters on our squadron. On the first operation that I was involved in, to Essen, Germany, we lost two Lancasters and were down to nineteen. On the second raid, over Nuremburg, Germany we lost another four. This Nuremburg raid was known as the massacre because 94 air force planes were lost that night. The loss of six Lancasters out of 21 in my first two flights brought home to me the full extent of the terrible odds that were stacked against the bombing crews.

The first two raids that I flew in were with strange crews which were short of a flight engineer while waiting for my own crew to be ready. Subsequent to those first two flights I flew a further twenty-nine operations with my own crew, piloted by Alan Gibson (Gibby), the New Zealander. Many of those flights were very eventful and hazardous; the most dangerous of all being, perversely the very last one, but that is another story. However, the flight which will be forever etched in my mind is the trip to Mailly-le-Camp.

The raid against Mailly-le-Camp on the night of 3–4 May began well. The briefing was optimistic – a 'piece of cake', we told each other afterwards. We collected our parachutes from the stores, took our log books and made sure we each had our lucky mascots. The uncertainty and danger bred an atmosphere of superstition and I never flew without a little toy monkey to bring me luck. We were looking forward to getting going as we fastened our flying helmets, donned silk gloves and pulled on leather fur-lined boots to protect us from the severe cold of the altitude. The code name for our Lancaster was 'K for King' and we waved regally to the loyal WAAFs who stood outside the runway to wave us off.

As usual we flew in formation like a flock of birds each protecting the other. We were birds of prey tonight, carrying in our bellies the weapons of destruction. The flight across the channel was uneventful and the raid went according to plan, although the searchlights were out over the target and there was a great deal of flak in the area.

Approaching the target, the bomb aimer gave instructions to our pilot to enable him to line up directly above the target in readiness for dropping the bombs. Gibby managed this time to avoid being caught in the searchlight, although others that night were not so fortunate and we watched them helplessly as they weaved and turned like moths around a flame. Bombs were dropped and the 'K for King' lurched up sharply, relieved of all that extra weight. Our mission had been accomplished; now for the return flight home.

We congratulated ourselves on a job well done and were looking forward to a well-earned tipple when we arrived back at base. However, as we came away from the target we saw really heavy flak; tiny sparks of light shooting up into the sky like beautiful fireworks. We had no time to admire the display. They were German anti-aircraft guns, aiming at us with German thoroughness and German precision. We watched in horror as two of our companion planes burst into flames. We managed to pick out a tiny figure escaping from his inferno, looking like a little toy parachutist suspended in mid-air. We weaved in and out to escape the same fate, when a German fighter flew across from starboard to port and then came into port quarter down. He hit us and we opened fire at him. The enemy aircraft continued to strafe us. We experienced damage to the control surfaces, petrol supply system, edging starboard mainplane, coolant, flank, magneto system and engine structure, and the pipelines to the mid-upper turret were severed. Apart from these minor irritations we were unharmed!

The German fighter followed us for about eight minutes, taking pot shots from approximately 600 yards, and our pilot weaved and lost height. He attacked us again from port quarter down, determined to finish us off this time. At 500 yards our rear gunner, Alf, opened fire with a three-minute burst and tracer was seen to enter the fighter's front cabin. A huge explosion followed when the enemy aircraft burst into flames. 'I've got the basket,' shouted Alf and we cheered with relief as we watched the enemy aircraft plunge to the ground. We were out of immediate danger but were conscious of the terrible damage that had been inflicted on 'K for King' and aware that the bomb aimer's parachute had opened during the fighting and was strewn about the cockpit. This meant that he would be unable to parachute out in an emergency as we didn't carry spare parachutes. The conflict had lasted about twelve minutes over a distance of 35 miles, but we still had a long way to go home.

We were down to 2,000 feet and climbed up to 14,000 feet on track. Taking stock of the damage, I feathered the starboard outer engine as it was giving trouble and noticed that the fuel gauge was very low, obviously due to the leaking pipeline. I tried to balance the fuel to no effect. We crossed the French coast and set off for Selsey Bill, losing height. Fuel was now very low and we sent out a distress call. We were desperate to cross the Channel before the fuel gave out, but all we could do was hope. For a long time we received no signal but at last, to our relief, we received confirmation that our distress call had been accepted.

Finally, our hearts in our mouths, we crossed coast at Selsey Bill. As Gibby knew that our engines were about to cut, he lowered the wheels as all the red lights had come on. He gave the order for the crew to assume the crash position. Although it would have been perhaps safer for us to have bailed out, no order was given to parachute because the bomb aimer would not have been able to parachute with us as his 'chute was damaged. So we stayed in the Lancaster and took our chances with him.

Shortly after crash positions were taken, all engines cut as fuel ran out and Gibby decided to make a glide landing. As we came in to land, an aerodrome with 3 ambulances was seen, prepared for the inevitable casualties. Incredibly, the landing, with 30° flap and no engine assistance, was faultless (one of the best we ever made) and none of us needed medical assistance.

'Miraculous' was the word the newspapers used to describe the landing, which was carried out in darkness and without any engine assistance. I felt very keenly that nothing short of a miracle could have brought us through our ordeal unscathed. Although I am not an emotional person, instinctively I kissed the ground with relief after jumping down at last from the aircraft. I shall never forget the moment of truth when each of us knew that our innermost prayers had been answered.

22

FRIDAY THE 13TH

Somewhere on a distant airfield stood a neglected 1934 Standard 10 motor car, much used, even ill-used, in the past, but nobody cared. The three men from the aircrew that drove it had gone missing, together with four additional crew members of Lancaster PB842/Y, on an operation to an oil plant at Pölitz, near Stettin, on 13–14 January 1945.

A few weeks before, in December 1944, Flight Sergeant Frederick Woodger Roots, air gunner; Brian Curran, his Australian pilot; and Bob Wilson, the Scottish navigator, had visited the Roots in Cockfosters, London, and had acquired the car. Mr Roots, a newspaperman on the *Daily Mail*, spent a lot of time helping them patch it. They froze as they grovelled beneath it, tracing broken circuits and tightening loose controls, for garage staff were in short supply. In RAF parlance there was no 'joy' in the battery, no 'joy' in the self-starter. Eventually they drove it off on the way back to more bombing operations with 619 Squadron from Strubby, Lincolnshire, a 5 Group Lancaster station near Alford, not far from Skegness and Mablethorpe.

Twenty-one-year-old Fred Roots was formerly on the staff of the Press Association, Fleet Street, and had joined the RAF in 1942. He spent his period of training in Canada and the Bahamas, passing his Elementary Flying Training School final air and ground examinations for pilot on 29 September 1942. He was then posted to 38 EFTS at Estevan, where he soloed on an Anson II and continued flying Ansons until 3 January 1943, when he was taken off the course; it was thought that he would not make a service pilot in the required time! Roots then underwent gunnery training in Canada, eventually receiving his air-gunner brevet. Coastal Command training in Nassau in the Bahamas followed and he was allotted to a crew that flew Mitchells and Liberators. However, the crew was disbanded and they returned to the United Kingdom to be retrained on Wellingtons, Stirlings and Lancasters for 5 Group Bomber Command.

Roots' crew started bombing operations early in October 1944. All went well until 13–14 January 1945. One morning soon after, the Roots received a telegram. It did not 'stun' – it was less merciful. It admitted them to a vast community that mourned in every country or grimly and bleakly fought for hope. Their air gunner son was reported missing on a bombing trip over Germany. Friends and neighbours are very kind at such times. Some came bravely in to help, others as kindly stayed away. Two pressed whisky into their hands. 'Give her a drop tonight,' they said. 'It'll help a bit.' The RAF was kind, too. The wing commander wrote in practical, encouraging terms, stressing the sound experience of the crew, the qualities of the pilot.

Their grey sojourn was mercifully brief. On the third day came another wire: 'Safe but interned'. The speed of it shook them. How the neighbourhood leapt with them! Even the telephone girls, whom they never saw, rejoiced as the calls sped in and out. The butcher and the baker, the parson and the milk girl heard the news. Everyone called. Someone brought more whisky. 'For a toast to your boy and his pals – and all the others, too.' (The giver's son-in-law was home with her, with his legs shot off.)

Friday the 13th had begun like most other nights on operations for Fred and the rest of his crew, as he recalls:

We set off in the usual way from Strubby, having gone through the usual preliminaries, including briefing, inspection of our aircraft, guns and turrets, etc, and of course our special egg, chips and bacon meal as always. We climbed into PB842 'Y-Yoke' and settled down into our respective positions in the aircraft. As always I was in the rear turret, with its four Browning .303 machine-guns. Our usual bomb aimer, Sergeant Charlie Lockton, was sick and his place was taken by Flight Sergeant M. R. Quigley. He and Sergeant Johnny Haigh, the wireless operator and Sergeant David Drew, the flight engineer, all came from Huddersfield. The mid-upper gunner, Flight Sergeant F. A. M. 'Abdullah' Blakeley, completed the crew.

As usual, the commanding officer, padre and many of the station personnel were facing the runway to wave us off with the 'thumbs up' sign as we took off. We were routed over Sweden and the flight was comparatively quiet with only the occasional anti-aircraft activity. Over Sweden the Swedish anti-aircraft gunners opened up, to comply with international requirements from a neutral country. However, the aiming was intentionally 'friendly' and we had no need to take evasive action. Closer to the target was a quite well-defended area because of the oil refineries at Pölitz and the number of warships with anti-aircraft guns and the flak became more intense. However, we flew safely on until we reached our bombing run to the target.

I was obviously keeping an alert look out for enemy night fighters. It was during the last few minutes of our run-in that I saw the Me 410 night fighter. Because he was sufficiently distant and flying a parallel course to us, I knew at that time that there could be no immediate danger and it was better that the bombing run continued so that we could get rid of our bombs.

However, immediately I saw the Me 410 turn towards us – the pilot had to turn his aircraft towards us in order to sight his guns – I opened fire with my four guns at the same time, giving the order to Brian to corkscrew to port – the evasive action devised by Bomber Command. The Me 410 continued to close in until he was within point blank range and I continued to shoot. Just before the German night fighter came in, our bomb aimer had released the bombs on to the target. I imagine the enemy pilot had been waiting to see the bombs released, knowing of the danger to himself if they were to explode!

By this time I imagine that the Me 410 must have been extensively damaged, for he fell away from us and the fight came to an end. I claimed the enemy aircraft to be damaged, as I did not actually see it fall to the ground. David, our flight engineer, later my brother-in-law, claimed that he definitely saw the Me 410 fall away to earth. Just before this we felt a judder in the aircraft and a few minutes later our engineer noted that the fuel indicator for the port inner tank registered empty. A shell from the enemy fighter's cannon had entered the tank, causing a hole and the fuel to leak out. The miracle was that it did not burst into fire. By this time we had left the target area and were starting our return journey home again across Sweden.

Discussion then took place on the intercom and estimates were made as to how much fuel we had left and how far we could reach. The progress of the Allies in France was by now well advanced and we wondered whether we could fly back, away from the main stream of bombers and alone across enemy territory, in the hope of reaching Allied lines and bailing out. It was doubtful whether we would even reach our own lines; it was also more likely that our lone aircraft would be attacked and shot out of the sky. The only reasonable alternative was to make for Sweden and either bail out or land the aircraft. The machine was flying well so it was decided to make for Rinkaby satellite airfield of the Swedish Air Force.

As we approached the airfield we shot off emergency cartridges from our Very pistol. The airfield, apparently, was not equipped with night flying equipment, so all available cars and lorries were driven on to the runway and we landed by their lights, finishing very close to the boundary fence. We destroyed all our secret radar equipment and one of the lorries with armed guards led us to the administrative buildings. We were interrogated very briefly and, of course, revealed only our names, ranks and numbers. We were then fed and entertained with beer in the officers' mess. We had a very friendly evening with the officers and were supplied with sleeping accommodation.

Next day we were taken for a walk, under armed guard, along one of the snow-covered country roads and were put on the train at the local station. We travelled to Stockholm and on to the office of the Air Attaché at the British Embassy. We were told not to make any attempt to escape as the Air Attaché would do his very best to get us home. There was nowhere to escape to and the attaché's office would be much speedier. We were then put on a train and transported to Falun for another brief interrogation and a medical examination. I believe arrangements were made for us to cable home so that we could reassure our families that all was well. We were taken by army coach to our 'internment camp' (Internezingsager IV Korsnas) where we were to spend our internment. Here we were given a warm welcome by the proprietress and her staff. The cook, a plump motherly lady, described herself, in what little English she knew, as our 'Swedish mother'. They all became our good friends. Our internment camp was a small hotel and we were waited on with good food and comfortable surroundings.

During my stay at Korsnas there were thirteen British internees. We were the only crew who had been able to land our aircraft; the others had parachuted out, one member being badly burned, while another was the only survivor of his crew. We had nothing to do but enjoy ourselves. It was an enforced holiday. We were allowed into the village and into the town of Falun and were advanced some of our pay by the Swedish Army and the Air Attaché's office in Stockholm. We were taught to ski by an instructor from the Swedish Army and we met local people, who were very friendly. Our stay was all too short, however. The Air Attaché, true to his word, made arrangements for our pilot, navigator, mid-upper gunner and myself to be flown home on 27 February 1945, as special envoys aboard a Dakota of BEA. We were debriefed at the Air Ministry by senior officials on our return to London.

In Cockfosters, north London, Mr and Mrs Roots awaited the return of their son. The post office had looked up the Roots' telephone number to get the telegram from Stockholm to them more swiftly. The girl who dictated the telegram said, 'Is it the good news we thought?' and they heard her call to other girls – 'It is, it is!'

At the Air Ministry, a pleasant WAAF corporal said, 'I wish we had thousands more cases as happy as this.'

They made them feel comfortable and easy in little rooms with deep chairs. They sent an officer with a file of signals. Yes, there were ways to write, wire and send parcels. So who cared about an old, battered treasure of a car standing idle on an airfield? The Roots could only wish that other parents might have the same comforting news. But how did it happen that, days after all this, the airfield chaplain sent a long, handwritten letter of consolation, encouragement and hope in their grief and anxiety? Did no one tell the padre anything but the bad news?

23

'TED' THE LAD

'Ted' Cachart was born on 15 June 1925 in Gorleston-on-Sea in Norfolk, one of five children to Benjamin and Dorothy Cachart. Benjamin, a former regimental sergeant major (RSM) and First World War veteran, studied to be a chartered accountant and, when he was newly qualified, the Cachart family moved to Wealdstone and eventually Pinner. After leaving school, 'Ted' attended The City of Westminster Catering College in Vincent Square. But there was a war on and his older brothers were already in the army and his sister was joining the WAAF. He was dissuaded from joining the army by his brothers.

At around 2.30am on Sunday, 2 January 1944, 'Ted' Cachart was alone in a forest in northern Germany – cold, soaked to the skin and with severe cramp in his left leg from a knee injury. A member of Bomber Command, he had parachuted from the remains of his Lancaster during a bombing operation to Berlin. In all, twenty-nine Lancasters were lost on Berlin.

I wanted to join the RAF, rather than be conscripted into the Army or Navy, as it seemed the best option to me. It also appealed as the RAF were known as the Brylcreem boys in those days and believed to be more attractive to the young ladies. There was a poster that showed a young woman kissing an airman and a queue of young women waiting to kiss him. The slogan read: 'The girls will queue for the boys in blue.' And I wanted to be a boy in blue! In 1941, although only fifteen years of age, I went to the local Recruiting Office where

I was told I could not volunteer until I was 17¼, with my parents' consent. I took the forms home and asked my father and a priest to sign them, telling them: 'It's just to make sure I get into the RAF.' No lies passed my young lips! I sent the signed forms off having entered my birth year as 1923 rather than 1925. In April I attended a medical examination board at Edgware Hospital and was passed as A1. In May I was told to report to Oxford University, where, with others, I took a written exam, followed by an interview with the Air Crew Selection Board. Only too aware of my young age I declined to train as a pilot and trained as a wireless operator/air gunner. I was then sworn in and on 13 May 1941, a month before my 16th birthday, I became a member of the RAF.

I turned sixteen in June and received my call-up papers in October. My father was quite annoyed, but when I told him I knew he had joined the Army underage in the First World War, he accepted and said, 'OK but I'll bet you will want me to get you out before Christmas comes.'

After completion of training in wireless and gunnery I was promoted to Sergeant and proudly sewed on an air gunners' brevet and three stripes. I am sure I swaggered home for ten days leave. Further training followed when I joined with four others to be a crew. They were Flying Officer Johnny Young, pilot; Pilot Officer Jack Scott, navigator; both Canadians in the RCAF. Pilot Officer Les Orchard was the bomb aimer; Sergeant Len Crossman, rear gunner. Like myself, both were in the RAF. Two months later we added Flight Sergeant Allen Vidow, flight engineer, RAF, and Australian Sergeant 'Spud' Mahony, mid-upper gunner. As a group we would sleep, eat and play together. We were no longer individuals, we were a unit. It was quite natural to go to the cinema together where we would sit all seven in a row. It made us confident that each person would do their job to the best of their ability.

On 13 October 1943 we were posted to 49 Squadron at RAF Fiskerton near Lincoln, as part of Base 52 in 5 Group, Bomber Command. I can only speak for myself when I say what it was like to go on an operation with Bomber Command and I can honestly say that it was something very special. It was never, 'Oh we're on ops' said in a gloomy tone, it was always, 'Hey we're on ops tonight!' It started with our regular WAAF driver, Dot Everett, who drove us to our Lancaster, EA-N (NAN), or 'Nancy Pants' as Dot renamed her. The adrenaline kicked in as you thought about the target, the number of night fighters and if there would be heavy flak and searchlights. It was incredibly exciting.

During an operation I would stand with my head in the astrodome as I listened to the radio on a long lead, while also acting as an extra pair of eyes. I can only say it was like watching an exciting film, as everything was going on outside, not in our Lancaster. At least not until our final op! The most critical time in any bombing operation is the last few minutes as the pilot flies the aircraft straight and level at a fixed speed to allow the bomb aimer to adjust his bombsight and give instructions for alignment. I am sure we all held our breath until the magic words 'bombs gone'. Targets were bombed on a number of occasions when approaches were made from different directions to ensure that the entire target was attacked. Our approach to the target was via a turning point sixty miles north of Berlin. As we dropped our starboard wing to turn on to the new course, another aircraft, which had already turned, flew straight into our starboard wing, which snapped off close to the inboard engine. As I looked from the astrodome I saw part of our aircraft disappear.

In the collision I lost my helmet and oxygen mask and at that height, if you're lucky, you have about two minutes before you pass out through lack of oxygen. I worked my way along the darkened fuselage and saw both gunners standing at the open door. I couldn't talk to them and don't remember if they gave me the thumbs up to bail out. I do know I sat on the steps and rolled out. I don't remember pulling the rip cord; I just remember descending in the chute. I could have been court-martialled for having abandoned the aircraft without permission. At that moment I was more concerned to see the aircraft fly away into the clouds, perhaps back home, than what lay ahead of me in Germany below.

Then my thought was 'how do I keep warm?' as I was frozen. The temperature was probably around 30 below that night. It was a snowy, windy night with 75mph winds. I wished desperately that I'd chosen another role as the other crew members had thick jackets, sweaters and gloves. I just wore battledress and boots as mine was the hottest seat in the aircraft. As I looked down I saw a black area among the clouds and thought I was coming into clear air. But my feet crashed through the branches of a tree and I hung there from the parachute straps in the darkness and pouring rain as I tried to work out how far I was from the ground. Eventually I managed to swing over and grab the tree trunk with my legs; I then released the parachute harness and slid about three feet to the ground.

The impact of the landing injured my knee and made it difficult to walk. I have no memory of how long I struggled through the forest, but eventually I found a remote farmhouse. I sat on the doorstep and banged on the door. Someone shouted at me to go away. I kept on banging using the handle of my sheath knife. Eventually a woman opened the door. I held the knife up to her, holding it by the blade to show I meant her no harm. She took it from me, helped me up and inside and into a downstairs bedroom where her husband was in bed. He didn't want to know I was there. She sat me in a chair and gave me a towel to dry myself with; she put a blanket round my shoulders and took a piece of wood from the tree out of my hand and bathed and bandaged it. The bandage on my knee was now too tight and as I struggled to loosen it she took over, removed it and re-bandaged my knee. She gave me a cup of cold coffee and although we didn't speak each other's language we made ourselves understood. I learnt that her son had been killed onboard a U-boat. There was a photograph of him on the mantelshelf with a piece of black ribbon round it. I believe she treated me the way she would have wanted her son to be treated had he been captured.

A car arrived and I was taken to the local Burgermeister's house where I was briefly interviewed, before I was taken to a nearby Luftwaffe base. The German sergeant in the guard room let me sit by a fire and shared his rations with me in the early hours of the morning before he locked me in a cell when he went off duty. Later five officers entered and one tapped me on the shoulder and said 'Liverpool fünf times' and another said, 'London acht times'. Another, who spoke good English, put his hand on my shoulder and said, 'You're a very lucky young man as your war is over. We have to fight on.' There was no animosity. They were no different to us; they were just doing the job they were told to do. There was great respect between the RAF and the Luftwaffe.

I was eventually taken to Trollenhagen Airbase where I was interrogated by the Commanding Officer who asked why I carried a sheath knife. When I told him it was to puncture the tins of orange juice that we drank on operations he said, 'You took drink on operations?' He was even more incredulous when I told him it was to wash down the sandwiches and cakes we ate on ops. Needless to say they confiscated the knife. All our crew were brought in one at a time until we were all seven together.

The commissioned officers – the pilot, navigator and bomb aimer – were sent to Stalag Luft III at Sagan in Silesia, which was the camp of the great escape, where fifty PoWs were executed.[1] I and the other NCOs went to Stalag IVB near Mühlburg, to the south of Berlin. After two months I was sent to Dulag Luft for further interrogation when some new radio equipment was discovered in the wreckage of the Lancaster. I was then sent to Stalag Luft VI, Heydekrug, on the borders of Lithuania, and later moved to Toruń in Poland and then to Bad Fallingbostel in Western Germany. I was repatriated in 1945 and continued to serve in the Royal Air Force until 1949 and for a further six years as a reserve.

After post-war service in the RAF, 'Ted' moved into light industry, first with Hoover Ltd and then his own domestic appliance business. It was during this period that he married Betty and raised two children, Tony and Jackie. A career change from selling to training happened when he was appointed by Derbyshire County Council to manage its Youth Training Scheme workshop. It was here that 'Ted' developed his passion for computers, a subject that became a very important aspect of his life. Hugely proud of his military career, 'Ted' joined the 49 Squadron Association and soon became a very proactive member, eventually becoming the chairman. He was persuaded to write a book about his miraculous escape from a doomed bomber and subsequent life as a PoW. The title for the book was *Ted the Lad*, a name that was to stick with him for the rest of his life. It epitomises 'Ted' so well. He was a man who lived a full and active life, despite his deteriorating health in recent years. In fact, as he had throughout his life, he relished challenge and refused to be beaten by adversity.

Asked about the Bomber Command Memorial, 'Ted' said:

It's finally politically acceptable to recognise Bomber Command. Winston Churchill turned his back on Bomber Command at the end of the war when he made no mention of us in his post-war speech. From then onwards Bomber Command was a political hot potato. No one wanted to be seen to do anything to recognise it. It took more than sixty years to get the Memorial. The Bomber Command Association, along with Robin Gibb of the Bee Gees and others started a campaign, which was supported very strongly by the *Daily Telegraph* and *Daily Express* and with their help £5 million was raised in two years. The memorial was unveiled by Her Majesty The Queen in 2012 and I had the honour to be there.

I have feelings of both sadness and pleasure when I visit the Bomber Command Memorial as I remember the comrades who failed to return and those I Served with who did. I think of the 55,573 who made the ultimate sacrifice, 25,000 of whom flew from Lincolnshire. I hope the Memorial will make people appreciate the sacrifices they made. At long last we have been given the Bomber Command Clasp and I wear mine with a great deal of pride, but I just wish it had been given many years ago.

During the early hours of Monday, 9 September 2013, 'Ted' sadly passed away, aged 88, holding the hand of his devoted daughter, Jackie.[2]

24

DESPITE THE ELEMENTS

ROY SIMMONDS

Around the beginning of 1943 there was a feeling amongst several of us aircraft engineering apprentices that life could be far more interesting in the services and because of the close proximity of Hornchurch aerodrome and the flying activity to be seen on a daily basis, the thinking was towards the Royal Air Force, in a flying capacity. About the beginning of March I went and signed on in Romford and after a satisfactory medical exam, was sent off to Cardington near Bedford for another more thorough medical examination, a written exam and an interview by several elderly senior officers; They were quite satisfied for me to join their club, But, I had opted to become a pilot and they pointed out that the training time for a pilot was about two years and they offered me the alternative of Flight Engineer with a training time of about 9–10 months; now the signs were that the end of the war was in sight, some contracts at work were already being cancelled, so to get into the war it was sensible to go for the flight engineer option, which I did. As an engineer, I had a trade test, which when I had completed the Flight engineers course credited me with an extra half a crown [2/6p – 25p] a day pay. There was still a problem, because I was in a 'reserved' occupation, as an engineer and the Company would not release me; but by the end of October to start the system working, I was made redundant and sent to work at Briggs Bodies, a company which in peacetime made the bodies for Ford cars; I worked in the tool room there until I was called up at the beginning of December 1943.

I reported to Lord's Cricket Ground at St John's Wood near Regent's Park in London on 6 December 1943. It was known as a reception unit where we were issued with uniforms, including a white flash for our caps which denoted air crew under training. We had another medical, which included a chest X-ray which was till then unknown to me, a dental check which caused me to be sent for urgent treatment, which proved to be on the wrong victim and also showed that the system was fallible; so beware!

The next three weeks we spent marching around and generally being taught how to operate in a service environment; the system again played up when I failed to get a pass out to go to Southend for Christmas. On Christmas Day, I went to a performance of the Messiah in the Albert Hall, so persuaded a colleague to join with me and walk to the Albert Hall to see what was going on; when we got there, the doors were open and we wandered in, to find not what I had expected, but a concert put on by and for the London Fire Brigade and Auxiliaries.

A few days after Christmas we went by train overnight to Bridlington, up on the north-east coast, to an ITW (Initial Training Wing), which should have been a six weeks course. We were billeted in a large house in a district which had suffered from bombing with bombed and derelict houses around us, with us frozen stiff and forbidden to use all the damaged timber wanting to be tidied up.

Much of our tuition took place in a large hotel suffering from bomb damage and considering the time of year it was a most uninspiring area. After about three weeks I finished up in sick quarters with influenza. I was sent home for two weeks sick leave, a few days of which I spent at Telscombe, with Auntie Cis. When I returned, I reported to the orderly room and on the notice board was a memo stating 'The flight engineers course is closing at Bridlington and reopening at Newquay'. I had to be interviewed by the education officer and I suggested that it would be better for me to start the course again.

Getting out of the train at Newquay station was like dreamland with golden sand and blue sea and despite the fact that it was only January, I felt that this was going to be a very pleasant six weeks. In my favour, was the fact that I had already done half of the course at Bridlington and the most difficult subject was learning the Morse code, which I had already broken the back of before joining up, at the ATC, which I had been recommended to join. This left me with a fair degree of freedom. On Sundays, which was our day off, apart from the occasional Church parade, we used to go for walks, one of which was to Perranporth about six miles away and our route apparently went across a rifle range because we seemed to be experiencing shots flying over our heads!

The cliffs northwards were very good, as well as the River Gannel to the southland when the sun was shining. There were plenty of spots to sit out of any wind to just enjoy the sunshine. This was a happy six week course and to crown it we were all sent off to various Advanced Flying Units (AFUs) to get some flying experience.

I went to Babdown Farm near Tetbury, flying in Airspeed Oxfords. The real task of the unit was to train pilots to fly twin engine aircraft, after having been taught on single engine machines; we 'sprogs' were to fly with the trainee pilot and instructor. Sitting on the wing spar behind the other two pilots who were sitting side by side, our task was to take an interest in what was going on.

My first trip was with the flight commander, who as far as I can remember was taking a senior [to him] pilot as student. We set off from Babdown and then crossed the river Severn at low altitude. In fact, I felt I could have dipped my fingers in the water if the window was open. It was a good job the tide was out! We then proceeded across the Forest of Dean, still hugging the tree tops up hill and down dale, until I saw the Sugar Loaf Mountain, at which point we turned back on a different route. This time we seemed to be flying at river level along the River Wye, with steep hillsides on either side. This may have been Symonds Yat Rock.

The next day the pilot who had me under his wing took me on a night flying 'air test' and I was able to sit in the second pilot's seat, which was good fun, especially when he said 'have a go'. We also had some ATC cadets in the back and I bet they were very envious of me. I enjoyed this so when another pilot was off on a night flying test, I invited myself aboard, but what I had not noticed was that it was slightly foggy, for which at a much later date, I found the remark in my records, 'keen on bad weather flying'. My last flight of note was an obligatory night flight, with one Pilot Officer Liquorish as instructor on a 'cross country' flight of just over an hour. What I found interesting was firstly the instructor seemed very 'twitchy', which meant that either he had been warned that there could be enemy aircraft around; or that he had had a rough time on operations before becoming an instructor. Secondly, I was surprised at the poor standard of blackout, yet I could recognise Oxford by the road layout. I left Babdown at the end of March for a week's leave.

My next assignment was to a School of Technical Training at Locking, just east of Weston-super-Mare in Somerset. Here we were given instruction on airframes and engines, mostly in fairly general terms. This culminated after each session, on working on engines, with practical experience of running the engine at full throttle, exercising the propeller and checking the magnetos. The first engine was a Gipsy Major, mounted on a stand. The second was a Hercules on a Beaufighter. This was quite exciting – sitting in the pilot's seat.

The third was a Merlin mounted on a Spitfire. When the throttle was wide open at 1,000hp plus, the aircraft really felt that it wanted to fly, which was difficult because there was a hangar in the way and flying was lesson two which I had not yet reached! This was possibly the highlight of the course.

One of the evening entertainments was a twice-weekly music appreciation group held in a large carpeted room furnished with armchairs, with tea or coffee and biscuits half-time. One night in the week was a set programme, the other night was members' choice from a rather limited selection. The gramophone was clockwork, needing winding up on each disc, the discs were 78s, they ran at 78 rpm and the needles were fibre, which needed sharpening for best results for each side played. The real killer was Bach's toccata and fugue in D minor which sounded a bit rough, often before one side had completed. I was asked to give a programme one evening, which turned out to be D-Day. One of my choices was Beethoven's 5th Symphony, which fitted in very well with the occasion.

One evening, I was wandering towards the NAAFI, when coming towards me was my friend Sergeant Len Cooke. He had been on a pilots/navigators course and as had been anticipated, the course had been cut back and he had been transferred to the flight engineers course, hence his presence at Locking. Once he had got his bike on the camp, we were able to do quite a bit of exploring around the Mendips and Bristol, including an exploration of one of the caves in Burrington Combe.

The course lasted eight weeks and after another week's leave I was sent to St Athan in Glamorgan, just west of Cardiff. This was a sixteen-week course, concentrating on specific aircraft. The first part of the course was generally about one particular aircraft, in my case it was the Lancaster. At the end of this phase, we were given a choice as to which aircraft we wished to concentrate on. This was a Lancaster or Halifax, though there were other options like Sunderland, Liberator and Catalina all used in Coastal Command; but I had already concluded that the Lancaster was the best of the bunch and opted for it without hesitation. It looked right and the systems all appeared to be straight forward and the simple systems usually have the fewest problems. The standard engine was the Merlin; but I was impressed by the workmanship on the Hercules. These were only fitted to about 300 Lancasters. As it transpired the Supercharger on the Hercules was poorly designed and ran out of power at about 18,000 feet, whilst the Merlin was doing well at 22,000 feet; a crucial difference where anti-aircraft fire was concerned.

The second part of the course concentrated on the Lancaster in every detail, including the Merlin engine, as well as performance. We climbed over the aircraft, ran the engines and carried out operating procedures in a fuselage, with all the instruments behaving as for real, although controlled by an electronic system out of sight at the back somewhere. This was very much like the present day 'flight trainer'. We were taught to 'fly' the Link Trainer, which enabled one to learn to fly using the 'blind flying' instruments on a panel, which was common to all British-made aircraft. This meant that I could fly the Lancaster night or day without looking out of the window; in fact looking out only confused me!

Len Cooke, who was possibly four weeks behind me, eventually turned up and with our bikes we were able to get around the Vale of Glamorgan, to see the sights and visit the odd pub away from the camp environment. In St Athan there was a large theatre where we watched films; and saw concerts by the BBC Symphony Orchestra who were based in Cardiff. We also went to one or two operas. Then around the middle of October in 1944, after successfully passing all my exams, I gathered my brevet and sergeant's stripes and was given a ticket to Chedburgh, in Suffolk, to meet a crew and start flying with them.

After a week's leave, during which I was rather disturbed by flying bombs tearing across hell-bent on London, I set off through rural Suffolk on a single track railway to Bury St Edmunds. An American officer shared the compartment with me and he took out a box of Dairy Milk chocolates and offered me one or two. This was a rare treat during war-time rationing, that the Americans shared their luxuries with us. He came from Lavenham airfield and probably purchased them in the mess, which is more than I would expect in our mess.

From Bury St Edmunds I caught a bus to Chedburgh. After registering with all the different sections on the site, a ritual to be performed on any new station, I met up with my crew, who were of a similar age. The pilot Eric Kitson was the same age as me and we hit it off straight away. The rest of the crew I also found very friendly and as time would tell, very competent. The unit was known as a heavy conversion unit, i.e. from twin engines to four engines. The crew I met had already spent several weeks working as a team on twin-engined Wellington aircraft. I had now joined them to help manage the greater complications of a four-engined machine. To my chagrin, the aircraft they were flying were Stirlings, which I was not familiar with and not particularly enamoured with, but we had to get on with it, though luckily for not very long.

Kit and I spent two days being briefed on the characteristics, engines, fuel systems and all other flying systems necessary to get the thing off and back on to the ground. I was then taken out to an aircraft and never having been in one before, was blindfolded and asked to locate the fire extinguishers; luckily I had noticed such things on our way up to the flight deck from the entrance, so all was well.

We got airborne without much delay with a pilot instructor, with Kit and our earlier instructor showing me the ropes. One important task was to check the undercarriage, which was electrically operated, and to establish that it was down and fit to land on. The number of revolutions turned by the electric motor had to be the same as that required to retract it, which meant memorising the number on a counter before you took off! Then check that it is the same before landing; the problem was trying to remember it whilst worrying about many other things like engine temperatures and pressures.

We completed our take-off and landing exercises, a total of twelve hours, and on the penultimate landing, whilst taxiing, we heard a terrific explosion and the aircraft keeled over and stopped. We had had a tyre burst and as they were about 6 feet in diameter, they contained a lot of high pressure air. On our last attempt to take off, two engines on the starboard side stopped and could not be started. It appeared that the cables from the flight deck to the engines had stretched enough for them to be turned on in the 'cab' but remain off at the engines. It was obviously time for the aircraft to be retired! The unit was transferring to North Luffenham, near Stamford, and we were given a week or so leave whilst the transfer was actioned and then we were to continue the course on Lancasters.

Our first introduction was on a taxi trip to Ossington to ferry someone for an unknown reason and we [our crew] were travelling as passengers. The familiarisation of the aircraft was to take place on the return journey. Unfortunately the undercarriage would not lock down and all tricks were played, including the last resort which was to use the emergency air, supplied for the purpose, all to no avail. This meant an 'emergency' landing and everybody had to sit in the crash position behind the rear spar, for the landing. We landed with no problem, but having used the emergency air, the aircraft was no longer flyable, so we had to ride back to North Luffenham in the back of a lorry. Before we left the aircraft, I had a quick look around the undercarriage and the lock was just about one inch from safe.

The following day, after a practice run with instructors, we were on our own. We practised circuits and landings for the next few days. After that we were sent on several exercises of longer duration, the first of which I suggested we timed the minimum time up to 20,000 feet. It took us twenty minutes and I had hiccups just to prove it. The flying went quite smoothly, including night flying, until on 5 February, when we went on a cross country exercise of about five hours in freezing weather. The airspeed pitot iced up, giving us no registered aircraft speed, and the carburettor on one engine iced up causing the engine to over-speed and making the propeller control inoperative. We realised that if we stopped the engine in the freezing environment we would never start it again and the air pump for the braking system was on that same engine. I throttled it back until the visible exhaust flame went out and then opened the throttle until the flame just appeared and left it like that. By the time we arrived at base, the pitot head had thawed out at the lower altitude. We were instructed to 'feather' the propeller, everybody [except me] had to go once more to the crash position and Kit landed us very smoothly, considering the circumstances. We were now beginning to understand how one should never take the moods of airframe, engine and weather for granted. You should always keep your wits about you.

We completed the course on 7 February and we were posted to 115 Squadron at Witchford near Ely. The Squadron motto was 'Despite the Elements'; was there any connection with our exploits?

Our first flight, by way of introduction to the squadron and the local landmarks, was with our flight commander. He was a Squadron Leader who, unusually, was also an air gunner and had the brevet to show it.

The Squadron was in 3 Group, which specialised in radar-controlled precision bombing. This was usually done in daylight in any reasonable weather, from above cloudland in formation, known as a 'gaggle'. We flew in groups of three. The leader did the aiming and the other two dropped their bombs when the leader dropped his.

Our first trip [on 1 March 1945] was to Kamen in the Ruhr, on an oil refinery.[1] As we approached the target we could see an enormous cloud. This was anti-aircraft fire, above the target. My immediate thought was 'oh dear' or thoughts to that effect; but when we actually got there, we could see the explosions just beyond our wing tips but no closer. The return flight was uneventful, until we crossed the English coast. Then the whole squadron spread out in line abreast and returned to Witchford in that formation at about 500 feet. This was a sight I had never experienced before, or seen since. Of course we were entitled to egg and bacon for breakfast before we left and the same again when we returned; we also had a mug of coffee laced with rum as soon as we landed. It was not a bad life, as long as you survived.

Our second and third (operations as they were called) were [on 5 and 19 March] to Gelsenkirchen, also an oil refinery in the Ruhr, and both in daylight and with rather less gunfire. As we approached the target it looked ominous, but died away when they saw us coming. On several of these daylight ops we had an escort of Spitfires or Mustangs, the pilots of which would invariably wave as they flew past.[2]

We then spent a week at Feltwell, in Norfolk, for the navigator to learn about the radar bombing system and then for us to fly off to gain some practice, by photographing a turret on one of the transepts of Ely Cathedral. The airfield was of pre-war origin, with no concrete runway and had a country lane running across it, where the traffic had to wait whilst we were flying in or out.

We had the feeling that the war was soon to end, because a barrel of grapefruit appeared in the mess. All the more remarkable because for several years this had been no more than a dream. Eating them was rather messy because after removing the outer skin one had to skin each segment because, of course, we had no sugar.

The next trip to Bruchstrassa, in the Ruhr, was eventful in an unexpected way; we were on our way home at about 3,000 feet with the automatic pilot doing the work. We had just put our cigarettes out, when the nose of the aircraft dropped like a brick, pointing us straight at the sea. This sort of situation calls for some very rapid thinking and fortunately Kit [the pilot] and I reached the same conclusion and grabbed the control column and pulled it back as hard as we could, to bring the aircraft back on an even keel. The cause was fairly obvious; it was the automatic pilot; so the need was to switch the autopilot off! It was possible to overcome the autopilot, by a bit of manhandling, so our reaction was quite correct; but the impact on the loose bits and pieces in the aircraft was, including the crew, quite devastating. The bomb aimer in the nose did a backward somersault from his unofficial seat right in the nose. Kit and myself hit our heads on the cabin roof, the pilot should have been strapped in but was not. I noticed the camera magazine, which was on the deck at my feet, rise up to head height and slowly sink as we pulled the nose of the aircraft up. The navigator had his bag of maps rise up and settle on his table. The navigator and wireless operator, situated near the centre of gravity of the aircraft, did not feel too much influence from our sudden change of direction. The mid-upper gunner probably had the worst deal. To get into his turret, he had to climb in, then pull his seat behind and hook it on a rail at the side of the turret. Unfortunately, when the aircraft nosed over, he went up and the seat went up, but the seat did not hook up on the way back down, so the gunner had no support. He fell out of his turret, into the fuselage and was not too pleased about events. The rear gunner told us that he was out of his turret sorting out his parachute as soon as he realised that things were not as they should be. The aircraft was quite alright, but the fuel tank must have had a good shake up because the fuselage reeked of petrol fumes. It was a good thing that we had already put our cigarettes out, otherwise things could have been quite unpleasant.

When we returned to base, it transpired that the autopilot was not clutched in; the lever in the cab was in its correct position, but had not been checked for engagement by the pilot by moving the controls full travel in each direction; thus the gyroscope was slowly processing until it hit the stops. When it toppled, we toppled with it! We were issued with an instruction card to tell us what we should have done, but the damage had been done. I no longer had any confidence in autopilots.

The next operation was to Bruchstrassa. It does not bring back any memories, except the perennial thought that, with about 12,000lb of high explosive on board, what if an engine gets a bit moody on take-off; there is no simple answer to that, except that with four engines, once you have gathered enough speed to make it difficult to stop, the remaining three engines should be adequate to get you airborne except for a little cold sweat to deal with.

A similar situation occurred on the next operation. Münster was the next target and on the approach to the target, the starboard inner engine started to run a bit hot. I should point out that flying in formation, in a cloud of protective 'Window' to confuse the radar, to leave the formation was exposing you to predicted gunfire, so it was not a good idea to go on alone at a reduced altitude because in isolation the guns could get 'a bead' on you. So, I throttled the engine back, to see if it would cool off, but after several minutes when I opened the throttle again, it went all 'lumpy', so it was decided to opt out and 'feather' the engine and turn for home.

This was quite an exciting event. First we had to jettison the bombs over the sea, which made quite a splash because the 'cookie' was a bit touchy and all 4,000lb exploded, which rocked the boat a little. As we approached the coast, a Spitfire arrived and flew alongside and required us to identify ourselves by firing off the identifying 'colours of the day', which we did and he went home. When we landed, going through the normal routine, Kit unfortunately levelled out a bit high and we bounced rather higher than was sensible, so he caught it on the throttles. That is he opened up the engines to full power, to fly round again, remembering that we only had three engines. This was not the recommended procedure, but by now we were committed. So we immediately raised the undercarriage and lifted the flaps from full down to the normal take-off position and sat tight hoping the aircraft would increase speed, which it thankfully did and we landed satisfactorily next time round.

As soon as we had landed, the trestles were up and the cowling off the engine to see what was wrong. I did not find out at the time, but subsequently heard that the cylinder head was prone to crack if the temperature changed too rapidly, such as when formation flying. As with the autopilot problem, we were issued with a foolscap sheet with all the flying limitations, one of which said that once you had committed to a landing with flaps fully down, then land you must. We were gradually getting the hang of the business!

We did one more daylight operation, to Hamm [on 27 March]. This was more uneventful.[3] Then we were switched to a few night operations. The first was [on 9–10 April] to Kiel,[4] when the first person to see the target was the rear gunner. This suggested that we had gone too far, so we made a big circle round to join the stream to have another go. When we saw the target, we dropped our bombs. It was about this time [on the night of 4–5 April] that my friend Len Cooke, lost his life when the Halifax bomber he was flying in crashed in the North Sea off the east coast of Scotland near Wick.[5]

We went back to Kiel again on 13 March when, halfway across the North Sea, another aircraft flew straight across in front of us, missing us by a matter of feet. Of course in the dark it is very difficult to see anything at any distance, so there is little warning when another aircraft does get close. Collisions were not unknown and people rarely survived.[6]

Someone was lucky enough to sink the battleship *Admiral Scheer*; it could have been us but I very much doubt it. It happened to be Friday the 13th. It was nearly bad luck for us but certainly bad luck for the sailors.

Our 9th operation [on 18 April] was to Heligoland. This was an island in the corner of the North Sea, near Germany. It was a beautifully clear day and we flew out in our usual gaggle. From what I could see, bombs were dropping all over the island. There was no obvious opposition, so I suspect that bombs were dropped on any obvious target of opportunity.[7]

Our penultimate operation [on 14–15 April] was at night to Potsdam, near Berlin. It was also in clear sky conditions. This was the only time we had an opportunity to observe a raid on a good sized city and it was all that photographs have shown. There was a sea of fire at ground level, a blanket of light 'cloud' of anti-aircraft fire at about 10,000 feet. It appeared to be aimed at aircraft flying a lot lower than we were and the hope was that the gunfire stayed at that altitude. Nothing untoward happened to us, but it was an experience to see what a city looked like under bombardment.[8]

The European war finished on 4 May, but before then we were doing some practice drops of sandbags, a repeat of an exercise carried out a few weeks earlier for reasons neither known, nor understood at the time. But the purpose was now revealed and it was to drop bags of food to the starving population of The Netherlands. They were surrounded by German troops as a last pocket of resistance. This we did at about 1,000 feet on to the racetrack at Den Haag past German gun sites, where the gunners just stood and watched. It was what you might call a pleasant day out with the object of doing some good, rather than destruction for no sensible purpose. We went out again on 5 May to drop more food, in sacks and packages, on the same target. This food dropping operation was called 'Operation Manna', as from Heaven. A few years after the war, an association was created in conjunction with the recipients of the food to liaise, via the Manna association, which was a mysterious club of elite members who appeared to be reluctant to divulge their activities!

The next task we had, after spending a bit of time practising 'circuits and landings' was to ferry ex prisoners of war back home from France where they had been carried by lorry, usually from Eastern Germany. The original specification for the Lancaster bomber was that it should be capable of conversion to troop carrying; this was accomplished by providing all passengers with a leather cushion, on which they could sit on the top of the bomb bay. In total we did seven of these trips, which were very satisfying when they set foot on mother England; our pick-up airfield was Juvincourt near Reims, in France, and Brussels in Belgium. The journey was at a relatively low level and passed over many of the First World War cemeteries, which were a sight never to be forgotten.

25

ON HIS MAJESTY'S SERVICE

PETER ANDREWS

11:37 On His Majesty's Service PRIORITY:
For Mr Andrews, 48 Priory Road, Tonbridge, Kent
Deeply regret to inform you that your son, Flight Sergeant Peter Frederick
Andrews failed to return last night from night operations – letter follows
– Please accept my profound sympathy – further information will be
wired you immediately – pending receipt of written confirmation from
Air Ministry. No information should be given to the press – from the
Adjutant 10 Squadron, Melbourne.

15th February, 1945.

I was on 10 Squadron at Melbourne, near York, and we were one of the veteran
crews. We'd done over twenty operations over German targets and we were
briefed to drop mines off the coast of Denmark. We took off and we were
attacked by the night fighter over the Danish mainland and it set the port

175

wing on fire which was a mass of flames and the aircraft blew up at 18,000ft. By which time the rear gunner and the mid-upper gunner and the flight engineer had managed to bail out through the main escape hatch at the back of the aircraft and we were all in the front of the aircraft. That's the pilot, the navigator, the bomb aimer and myself, the wireless operator air gunner. We were all clustered together in our positions in the front of the aircraft and it blew up. The pilot was killed, the navigator was killed, I was blown out of a gap in the front when the aircraft separated and the bomb aimer had the same fate.

I came to in a world of silence because my ears had blacked out because you're dropping at 120 mph. I looked up and saw my chute was unopened and I reached up and pulled the ripcord and my chute opened; because my harness was slack, it did quite a bit of damage to me. I landed in a field and went to a group of houses and I approached a group of people who were out chatting at their front doors. It was around about nine o'clock and we were hit at about twenty past eight. They didn't want to know because obviously they were frightened that if they helped in any way they would be shot by the Germans but they directed me to a house. I knocked at the window of that house and they took me in and bandaged me up and tended to cuts and bruises. I got my escape kit out and they indicated where we were, which was Holbaek, near Copenhagen, and they sent for an ambulance for the civil hospital, which arrived and I was stretchered into the back. A short distance down the road we stopped again and they wheeled the bomb aimer in. He looked a shocking site, covered in blood. It wasn't as bad as it looked but there were superficial penetrations to the face from Perspex and it was bleeding and it looked terrible. We were taken to the hospital and we went into a sort of examination room. There were two beds and they worked on us to dress whatever was wrong with us; mainly surface wounds and in my case it was extreme bruising to the lower part of my body through the delayed drop.

While we were in there we were approached by a Dane in a cloth cap and he spoke to us through one of the doctors who could speak good English. He said that he was a member of the underground or the resistance and if we were able to walk in the morning they'd get us away. Unfortunately during the night somebody had blown the whistle on us in the hospital and the Gestapo walked in and collared us, took us away by stretcher and interrogated us and shoved us in some dungeon. After about twenty-four hours of quite bad treatment the Germans handed us over to the Luftwaffe, who took us to an airfield with a hospital unit [at Vaerlose] and they looked after us really well. I had sunray treatment for my bruising and we were both treated quite well. The bomb aimer had a couple of broken ribs and a lot of superficial damage, the same as I did. His name was Stan Chaderton, who at this moment in time is very ill in a hospital in Liverpool.

Stan was with me throughout the rest of the war. We were transported by ship across the Baltic to Lübeck and then we had two guards for the two of us and we travelled through Germany down through Hamburg. We rolled into Hamburg late one evening and we'd got a reserved compartment but it hadn't stayed reserved for very long. The people who were moving around Germany could not see why a couple of RAF blokes with a couple of guards should have a private compartment, so they crowded in. They were trying to push me out the door, indicating 'your colleagues' [i.e. active RAF bombers] because that part of Hamburg we were going through then had been completely flattened, but the guards with their guns eventually forced them back. We had one or two incidents like that in our trip down to Dulag Luft, which was near Frankfurt, it was the interrogation centre for all allied air crew. They shoved you into solitary confinement and practised the art of sleep deprivation by turning radiators on and off through the course of the night ... whipping you out for interrogation with somebody who could speak perfect Oxford English and offered you a cigarette and 'would you like a jam sandwich?' and something like that. I suppose it was the old 'good guy, bad guy' treatment. We spent a few days in that solitary confinement and they eventually came to the conclusion that we knew even less than what they did. They knew that we'd recently had a new CO on the squadron, they knew as much as we did, if not more and so they knew there was very little they could get out of us. We were released into the larger compound where they kitted us out with some kind of boots that would withstand heavier treatment and then we were set off on the march.

We marched from there on the tail end of the 'death march'. We weren't on it from Northern Germany, we were on it from Frankfurt right through to Munich, Moosburg. It was the biggest collection of allied prisoners of war in the whole of Germany, there were 110,000 there at the end because they were funnelling in from all over Germany. So we were all piled in an unsavoury area there. We had a lot of incidents on the march where we were attacked by friendly fire: the squadron attacked and killed a number of people on the march thinking we were a German column I suppose. After a lot of weeks on the march we got to Moosburg and we sat it out there till the end of the war, that's just the bomb aimer and myself, with very little food. I was suffering from dysentery and I don't think I would have survived if it hadn't been for my friend the bomb aimer, who was two or three years older, and he managed to drag me through it. We eventually were liberated by Patton, the head of the American probe through that part of Germany.

We eventually got to a German airfield. We were flown by Dakota to Reims in France and Lancasters were coming in there. They were piling prisoners of war into Lancasters and flying them back to England where we were promptly stood in a line and they fired delousing guns. We needed it badly, then we were bathed, had checks and were fed and then sent on indefinite leave. It was quite a few years before I saw the bomb aimer again, I think in actual fact you got on with your life. The rest of the crew, they've got individual stories to tell.[71]

The flight engineer, Maddock-Lyon, is not there. As I say, he was killed, the navigator, Red Berry, and the pilot, Johnny Grayshan, was killed. That's the rear gunner, who's alive today, and that's the mid-upper gunner and the wireless op. The flight engineer, he doesn't wish to be included, he wants to wipe it all out, he doesn't want to know about it. Stan Chaderton, the bomb aimer, a great fellow, saved my life. These two plus myself, went out to Denmark on 4th May 2005, which is Danish Liberation day, and they invited us over, all expenses paid. They had a big ceremony where they unveiled a stone, where part of the aircraft had come down, with all our names on: The stone is like a monolith with an image of the Halifax on the top of it and an inscription in Danish: 14th February 1945, Styrtede, nr Holbeck. Halifax NZ793ZA/X RAF 10th Squadron John Graysham; Albert James Berry (both of whom died); Stanley Chaderton; Peter Frederick Andrews; Roy Maddock-Lyon; James Petre; Horace Lesley Mills.

26

THE GOOD COMPANIONS

John Joyner was one of thousands of Bomber Command airmen who completed the lengthy training process before joining an operational squadron. His training began in October 1943 and his first operation was not flown until 18 March 1945. When, in 2012, the Ministry of Defence began awarding the Clasp to veterans of Bomber Command, the qualifying rules were nonsensical. It was stipulated that a veteran had to have served on a Bomber Command 'unit' for a minimum of sixty days. In fact, the Ministry of Defence (MoD) requires 120 days, so any aircrew who joined a squadron after 8 January 1945 will not qualify for the clasp, no matter how many operations he has completed. On the other hand, anyone who joined a squadron before 8 January 1945 and completed one operation and remained with the unit until 8 May 1945 would be eligible for the award! What has been overlooked is that aircrew such as John Joyner (who under MoD rules was just eight days short of the 'qualifying period') also served lengthy spells on units such as ITW, EFTS, Air Gunnery School, OTU and HCU – all of them 'units' in Bomber Command![1] OTU airmen flew on pointless leaflet raids, on the 1,000 Bomber Raids in 1942 and on 'Freshman' operations, and many never returned to serve on a squadron. It must never be forgotten that airmen put their life on the line every time they flew on a training flight and on operations, and that 8,195 airmen were killed in flying training or ground accidents.[2]

It was 1940. It was a significant year for Britain and young men and women, clerks and shop assistants were given the promise of another life and another world full of unknown opportunities. I was sixteen years old, living in Ilford, Essex, where I was born on 4 June 1924. My father worked in a rubber factory in Hackney where they made dinghies. He would cycle there and back every day. An accomplished artist, he would paint pictures every moment he could. My mother was a furrier in Luton. My 19½-year-old sister Jean joined the ATS. I joined the local Air Training Corps. We paraded and drilled under the stern eye of Warrant Officer Ash one evening in the week and on another learned the Morse Code. This, together with Algebra and Geometry, which I had never encountered before, broadened my horizons and prepared me for my application to join the Royal Air Force Volunteer Reserve at 17¼ years. In the interim we learned the rudiments of navigation and I studied Teach Yourself To Fly; one of an optimistically titled series. One could use an imaginative joystick and rudder bar on the front seat of the bus. My year or so included an opportunity to fly, which I did in a Miles Magister, which prompted me to write 'My First Flight', now lost to posterity. Waiting for my call-up I sported an RAFVR badge, while marking off the days on the locker room door of the warehouse where I worked.

In October 1943 my parents saw me off on the train to London, as I had already been summoned to the Air Crew Receiving Centre (ACRC or 'Arcy-Darcy' as it was nicknamed) at St Johns Wood, where those of us who had not been inoculated and vaccinated received this painful procedure and we were kitted out. We were told that a sixpence tip to the barber would ensure a tasteful haircut but this proved to be a fallacy, as was a collection for our discip corporal's marriage. (I recall that my father kissed me, possibly believing that he might not see me again. This loving gesture was fortunately misplaced, however, for I was home on leave in a week). We were taken to Seymour Hall Baths where the prospect of young men swimming in what were euphemistically called 'dips' up and down decided their destiny for Initial Training Wing (ITW). In November those who demonstrated their ability to swim a length were sent to 12 ITW at St Andrews in Fife in Scotland and those who could not, to Scarborough, which, unlike Scotland, provided swimming facilities! Foolishly, the swimmers could not get leave home from Scotland as easily as the non-swimmers at Scarborough. It was one lesson among many which one learns in life. At ITW we came to grips with navigation, astronomy, signals and the inevitable drill. Our drill instructor managed to demonstrate movements from one of the concrete blocks defending the sea shore without disappointingly falling in and for our part he leapt from one block to another miserably clad in singlet and shorts.

Eventually, in April 1944 we were posted to what promised to be and was, actual flying. Perhaps some were deemed more suitable for training as navigators or bomb aimers but for my part I went to Elementary Flying Training School (EFTS) at Theale in Reading and Belle Vue, Manchester. We actually flew in Tiger Moths from a grass field. A three-point landing was rarely accomplished in practice, for the instructor had to bear much leaping from terra firma into the air before the blessed moment when the plane came to a halt. I do recall the 'spin' however. It showed that you need this manoeuvre to lose height. Pull back the stick as far as it will go while closing the throttle. The plane will go into a stall. At the moment, apply full rudder to either port or starboard and the plane will commence a dive. This is not recommended after a greasy breakfast. To get out of the spin you put the stick forward – full throttle and opposite rudder and do none of it unless you have reasonable height.

I never did solo but in any case before we had finished our training we were all summoned to Heaton Park in Manchester for a series of psychological and aptitude tests. At the end of the week we were all considered suitable for training as air gunners, including one of our number named memorably Snooks, who had soloed. I think that it was because the PNB (Pilot-Navigator-Bomb Aimer category) had choked up the training programmes in Rhodesia, Canada and even America as I recall, or equally Bomber Command needed more air gunners. We were posted to No. 7 Air Gunnery School, Stormy Down, Glamorganshire, on 18 August where I met a fellow trainee named Bill Jones. Bill came from a village named Garnant where his father was a miner and we hitch-hiked there whenever we could get a weekend pass.

We learned now to take a Browning .303 to pieces and put it together again. We also practised with shot guns too and learned hydraulics, which was to understand the working of a gun turret. We went to St Athan where three of us went up in an Avro Anson and rendezvoused with a Harvard towing a drogue. Each of us took our turn in the gun turret, from which we fired at the drogue, using belts of ammunition covered with wet paint in distinctive colours. The idea was that when (and if) one's bullets hit the drogue, then as the bullet entered it there remained a hole ringed with the colour of the gunner's bullet. The drogue was then dropped over the airfield and WAAFs had the unenviable task of counting the hits of each gunner. Also we sat in a darkened room identifying flashed on silhouettes of aircraft.

The time came for our final exams and oral tests. Much of what I had learned about hydraulics eluded me but the examiners said, 'Do you want to be an air gunner?' and when I said 'yes please' (I was brought up to be polite) they said, 'Right – you've passed!' I think that this had to be because Stormy Down was being turned into a PoW camp for German officers. So we were given our sergeant's stripes and air gunner's half wing. Bill Jones and me and three other air gunners met up in London on 22 August, having our photo taken with the pigeons in Trafalgar Square and going to see Phyllis Dixey – 'England's Popular Pin-Up Girl' – in *Peek-A-Boo!* at the Whitehall Theatre on the corner of Trafalgar Square.

On 31 August we went to 16 OTU (Operational Training Unit) at Upper Heyford, where crew members of all trades were assembled in a hall and told to sort ourselves out into crews. Bill Jones and I stayed together. As Bill was shorter than me they put him in the rear turret and me in the mid-upper. I cannot explain the chemistry which formed crews but ours became six. Sergeant David McQuitty, our pilot, was a Tasmanian we called 'Mac'. Our bomb aimer was a Scot called John Bennett Orr, but he had to settle for 'Jock' because we couldn't do with three Johns. Our wireless operator was an Irishman; a volunteer from neutral Eire called, appropriately, Danny. Our navigator was Stanley Annetts. As a policeman he was only permitted to join the forces as a volunteer for aircrew, which he did. He was 29 and a source of guidance in more ways than one. Just as we were about to go on the squadron Danny took off for Eire and never came back. His place was taken by another Scot, John Cameron, who was given the title 'Cam'. Later, at 1661 Heavy Conversion Unit (HCU) Winthorpe, Peter Gillespie joined us as flight engineer when we went from Wellingtons to Lancasters.

We practised on Wellingtons at Barford. The Wellington did not have a mid-upper turret, which meant that I had to stand with my head in the astrodome. I didn't have guns until we flew on Lancasters. We did circuits and bumps by day and night and bombing exercises. I was useful in my astrodome keeping an eye out for other aircraft in the circuit. It is a sobering thought that over 8,000 aircrew were killed on training exercises. Later it was Bill's and my opportunity to demonstrate our skills against an 'attacking' Harvard. We took turns in the rear turret with a gunsight linked to a camera. The film was developed later and showed to the crew. During this gunnery exercise the pilot responded to directions from the gunner to 'dive starboard' or 'climb port'; a manoeuvre called the 'corkscrew'. The principle of this is to climb away at right angles from a diving fighter or dive at the same angle from a fighter climbing in pursuit with its fixed cannon or guns bearing on a key area of the bomber; often the rear gunner with his four Brownings, or engines and fuel tanks. Searching was a key exercise to avoid a surprise attack; turrets turning through 180°, bomb aimer vigilant for head-on attacks with two guns, prone in his bomb aimer's position and pilot contributing to a general awareness of threats from attacking fighters. Once the fighter had committed to its attack the bomber would perform the 'corkscrew', presenting a difficult target. Chat over the intercom was kept to a minimum and to the necessary essentials.

The crew commenced training at 1661 HCU Winthorpe, just north of Newark in Nottinghamshire, on 24 February 1945 and for two months became familiar with H_2S and three engine flying, stalls and circuits and landings on Lancasters. During February and up until 16 March, each training flight was flown with an instructor pilot with 'Mac' (now Pilot Officer McQuitty) as second pilot. Two days later we stood by for our first operation. The allies were advancing across France and 'Monty' was about to cross the Rhine into Germany. On 18 March with Flying Officer Paul as skipper and 'Mac' as second pilot once more, we carried out an operation code-named 'Sweepstake' on Strasbourg in France in 'Q-Queenie'. This involved [66 Lancasters and 29 Halifaxes from training units on a sweep over northern France to draw up German fighters] entering the area partially occupied by the Allies, in particular to divert fighter aircraft away from the Main Force, which was bombing Wesel just beyond the Rhine in preparation for Montgomery's crossing. 'Sweepstake' employed 'Window', which was dropped by the bomb aimer in handfuls according to a pre-arranged plan. I reported a single-engined fighter on our port quarter which I took to be a Focke-Wulf 190, but I could have been wrong. I reported it but almost immediately it fell back and disappeared. It was said that fighter aircraft were less likely to attack if their quarry appeared vigilant. Nothing else happened to us before we returned to base. With 'Mac' as skipper, on 23 March we flew our second 'Sweepstake' operation [involving 78 training aircraft on a sweep across France and as far as Mannheim] when we dropped 'Window' at Saarbrücken in support of the main force bombing Wesel just over the Rhine ahead of the alliance.[3]

What happened next proved tragic and kept us on the ground while we were transferred to a holding unit. It had been decided that 'Mac', who had lost two brothers on Bomber Command operations, as the surviving third brother on active service, should be taken off ops and he ended the war in Transport Command. Statistically this was common, for the chance of surviving a tour of aircrew operations unscathed in the war was less than one in two. As many as ninety aircrew failed to return from a raid and one squadron lost seventy aircraft in a month. The operational life of a Lancaster was forty hours' flying time and aircrew, whose 'tour' consisted of thirty ops before an interval and future operations.

We were now a 'headless' crew. So we companions, no longer in arms, were due to be sent back to a holding unit to pick up a new skipper. The evening before this happened I was having my hair cut in the Mess when Bill Jones came in to tell me that I was on the Battle Order for that night to replace a mid-upper gunner who was either absent, sick, or dead – I never enquired. I attended the briefing, which was, as I recall, to an oil refinery and as the hour grew near, kitted up and was given a Wakey-Wakey pill. Out on the dispersal, we ran up the engines and ready to taxi to the runway when a Very light went up from the control tower and the op was scrubbed.

Flight Lieutenant Harrison, who pre-war had been a civil pilot, took over as skipper of the 'headless' crew and they were posted to 189 Squadron at Bardney, and then to Acaster Malbis. On 101 Squadron at Ludford Magna in July 1945 Harrison's crew were among those who flew Operation Dodge flights to Pomigliano, near Naples in Italy, to bring British PoWs home for demob or going on leave. A *Daily Mirror* reporter wrote of the flights to Italy:

> Long before you awoke this morning Lancaster and Halifax bombers were winging their way over the British coast and across France on the same routes they'd taken months ago to bomb the Reich. But in their bomb-bays were no bombs, the twin Brownings had gone from the gun-turrets and inside the fuselage were rows of cushions. For the bombers were off to Italy to bring home nearly 20,000 men a month. Transport Command too, will fly a big number back. After six or seven hours in the air all bombers will circle airfields near Naples and Bari before landing to pick up twenty men each for the homeward trip. All the flying is done by day and at low altitude, so that the men, unused to air travel, will be as little fatigued as possible. Air crews rest in Italy for a day and a half before making the long trip home. Only fully trained crews, many with one or two tours of thirty operations to their credit, are picked for the job.

Harrison's crew were transferred to 9 Squadron at Waddington. In January 1946, with the independence of India looming, Lancaster crews on 9 Squadron and 617 Dambusters Squadron were sent to Salbani in Bengal, where, recalls John Joyner:

> We were later bombed up with 500lb bombs at Nagpur en route to Karachi and each of us was provided with .38 calibre revolvers. I have no idea why.
> Four months later, in April, at home in Britain I was designated 'embarkation assistant', collecting boarding cards from WAAFs and sick airmen sailing on the *Ulster Monarch* and the *Western Prince* to Heyshaw in Lancashire. Fit aircrew

were obliged to go north to Larne for the crossing to Stranraer. Finally, I was transferred to a maintenance unit at Attlebridge in Norfolk, where I came face to face with the enemy. German PoWs were employed to pick up freight from the railway stations and I sat beside the German driver with others behind. Then, kitted out in suit, raincoat and trilby, I returned home for three weeks' leave before coming to grips with commerce. As the old lady said as she breathed her last: 'It's all been most interesting.'

27

'SUNSHINE TO SADNESS'
TERENCE C. CARTWRIGHT

Flight Lieutenant Owen Scott DFC served on 170 Squadron in 1 Group Bomber Command and was stationed at Hemswell, Lincolnshire:

I joined up at the age of 19 and trained as a pilot. Later in the war I flew Lancaster bombers and I served the full term of thirty operations over enemy territory in the period 1944–45. The first time I went out with a bombing crew, I was being trained by a more experienced pilot. It was a daytime operation and, as we made for the Kentish coast, I looked down and saw Ramsgate, where I grew up and pointed out my old school, Chatham House.

I and my crew were often airborne for ten and a half hours. Our take-off time could be at any time of day, depending on the weather and was a secret to us until we were briefed to report for duty. We might be wakened by our batman and told, 'Briefing in 50 minutes, sir!', or receive a radio message while on a training flight. Our aircraft had to be fully operational. Sometimes, with the crew ready in position, the green light which told you to take off was replaced by a red one, telling you that your operation had been cancelled because of the weather or a change in tactics. Then, feeling somewhat relieved, you went back to bed.

Ninety per cent of our operations were at night, flying over enemy territory in the dark, dependent on maps and instruments, aware that enemy fighters would be on our tail. We flew manually and 'rolled' the 37-ton loaded plane to see whether any enemy fighters were underneath us. To avoid fighter attack, we performed a 'corkscrew' operation. Being caught in a searchlight was a terrifying experience as it made our plane an easy target for enemy shells.

Accuracy was of vital importance. The crew had to synchronise watches to the second to ensure that every operation went according to plan, that bombs hit the right target on schedule. The pilot would give the order, 'Synchronise watches, 12.05. Hit target 12.10!' In front of every bombing flight flew the Path Finders, usually Mosquito aircraft, to drop coloured flares indicating the position of the different targets. This was doubly important when the air was filled with black smoke from exploding shells, spread by the wind into a dark haze, making it impossible to see for any distance. It was terrifying to be flying 'blind' and put us at grave risk of collision with other aircraft. We were never warned of the danger of collision and were not fully informed about the number that took place at the time, though we experienced the enormous explosion that took place when two bomb-loaded planes collided. We were not aware of casualty numbers. All we knew the following day was that a friend or colleague was not to be seen and later heard that he had 'bought it'.

I remember vividly the bombing raids on V-1 flying bomb launching pads in France. We had to fly in at a height of 7,000 feet, but the Path Finders had to fly much lower than that. As we straightened up ready to drop our bombs, we were at grave risk from enemy fighters, who knew the exact position of our targets and were waiting to attack. Coming up to the target it was 'Left a bit, right a bit, steady, hold it, Skipper!' As soon as our bombs, seven tons in weight, were gone, the aircraft 'leapt' into the air. We closed the bomb doors, opened up the throttles and went into a shallow dive to increase our air speed to leave the area. It was not until the war was over that we learned of the massive losses incurred by Lancaster and Halifax bombers and their crews; 7,000 bombers, 7,000 pilots, 55,000 men over all. The chances of survival were one in three.

I have vivid memories of the night we bombed Dresden. We had no idea then of the damage our bombs had done but I shall never forget the sight of the city in flames. It seemed an easier mission than usual owing to the lack of ground fire and enemy fighters.

I felt a twinge of guilt as I smeared the lard on my rusting bike chain. Lard was on ration, but oil and grease being hard to come by left me with little option. I pumped away at my treadles, well-patched tyres (acquired from our local rubbish tip) trying hard not to notice the numerous cracks and bulges which grew alarmingly with each stroke of the pump. I tightened the strand of wire (substitute for a missing brake rod) and as my back brake blocks had disintegrated some time ago, hoped that the single remaining front blocks would at least help slow me down in an emergency! I then tightened the string holding on my front mudguard and, with a sigh of satisfaction, declared to my friend ... 'I'm ready.'

It was Sunday, 8 April 1945. A beautiful sunny spring morning. Birds were singing, buds were bursting and temperatures were rising. We had decided to take a 'bike-ride'. So, with tyres resembling python snakes that had swallowed a colony of rabbits, we set off along 'Cut-throat Lane', (Coleman Road) towards Evington Village. We rattled and clanked our way past 'Blacky Fields', scene of many 'raids', on to farmer's potato clamps to supply requirements for our campfire feasts and then eventually Shady Lane PoW camp. It was here, only a year before, at the age of twelve, I had the unforgettable experience of tasting my first Wrigley's spearmint chewing gum. Tents had appeared over night, like Magic Mushrooms ... and within these miniature Aladdin's caves, trestle tables groaned under the weight of 'Camel' Cigarettes, chewing gum, tins of exotic meats and foods we had never seen or tasted before. These 'Treasures' were dispensed by 'Gods' (who spoke like the 'Dead End Kids' and 'Roy Rogers' combined) to the hordes of grubby, green-candled nosed, ragged trouser-bottomed 'Dennis the Menace' and 'Just William' look-a-likes who descended on the camp like locusts ... Yes ... The Yanks had arrived!

On to Stoughton airfield. Scene of many a fascinating hour, watching the Dakotas and gliders taking off and landing in almost round the clock training for D-Day and the Rhine crossing. With the absence of traffic and petrol fumes we were able, above the rattle of our bikes, to take in the fleeting sounds of *Family Favourites*, hand-pushed mowers, cows mooing and lambs bleating, which mingled and blended with the tantalising smell of roasting beef (evidence that the locals and farmers were not restricted to the meat ration.) Newly cut grass, blossoms and farmyard manure all produced a cocktail of sensations, which could only portray a typical peaceful English summer Sunday. The war was coming to an end; rations were easing and it felt good to be alive.

We arrived at the junction of Station Road and Uppingham Road. Our bicycle inner tubes were porous, as well as being the wrong size, so we decided that we needed to stop for a rest and feed our tyres with a few more 'rabbits'. Looking over the countryside toward Scraptoft, there was a simmering haze covering the rolling green fields and in the distance we heard and then saw, a Lancaster bomber with an accompanying Spitfire tagging behind, droning majestically towards us. We had seen many bombers over the years, but as always, the sight never failed to arouse our interest. We turned our attention back to our bikes. A minute or so later the drone of the engines changed abruptly to a high-pitched scream. We looked up in alarm and to our horror as we saw the Lancaster in a vertical dive, descending at terrifying speed toward the ground, only a few yards from where we stood. We tried to run, but our legs could not move. We were rooted to the spot. Just when we thought that our end had come, a miracle happened, with engines howling, the plane suddenly began to pull out of its dive, as if trapped inside a giant invisible U-bend of a waste-pipe. The wings bent to breaking point as it swooped over Station Road at treetop height and began a vertical climb over Coles Nurseries. Our fear changed to relief and then to anger and indignation where we found ourselves shouting abuse at the pilot for 'acting the fool'. Our anger, however, was short-lived and quickly turned to horror when we witnessed the plane, high over Thurnby railway station, turn on its back and plunge earthwards once more in another vertical dive. We saw its black silhouette disappear below the horizon of the railway embankment and a split second later a tremendous orange/red/black mushroom of fire clawed its way into the blue sky, followed by a delayed hollow booming thud. Our legs came back to life and with childish visions of heroic rescue of airmen from burning wreckage we sped down Station Road, over the embankment and ran along the back of gardens where people were standing like statues. I passed a woman with a baby in her arms. Tears were falling from her cheeks.

The site of the crash was covered in a layer of smoke, but as we got nearer we were confronted with an incredible sight. There, in the meadow, stamped as if by a giant's hand, was a scarred outline of the Lancaster. A large crater was created by the fuselage, with four others made by the engines. Unbelievably, the leading edge of the wings, tip to tip, could be clearly seen, marked purely by scorched but otherwise undamaged grass. The field was strewn with small pieces of debris no larger than the page of a newspaper. Our hopes of rescue vanished as we jumped over the small brook and ran to the edge of the main smoking crater.

As we looked into this pit, ammunition was exploding, sending puffs of ash into the air like a volcano ready to erupt. We were not sure if any bombs were in there, so we retired to a safer distance. It was then that I saw that the local 'Bobby' had arrived. He was looking at what I thought was a meaty bone a dog had brought into the field. He had a strange shocked look in his eyes and when he said, 'Don't touch it' the tone of his voice prompted me to look again. With a numbing sense of shock I realised I was looking at what appeared to be a human shoulder blade! I then saw a sock. Inside was half a foot. Up to this point it had been as if it was all a dream, but now reality and shock began to filter through my brain and I felt sickened, sad and helpless.

The accompanying Spitfire returned to check the scene. I could clearly see the pilot as he banked his plane to view the smoking craters below. The sound of bells announced the arrival of the fire engine and at this point the 'Bobby' asked us to leave. The day had changed. Sounds of music, animals and mowers were abruptly replaced by the thud and crackle of exploding ammunition, fire bells and tears. The smells of the countryside had dissolved into an unforgettable stench of burnt fuel and flesh. The summer haze now acrid smoke. We made our way slowly to Station Road. The woman with the baby was still rooted in the same spot. I found myself thinking of the unfortunate families of the airmen, who were soon to receive those awful, heartless, Buff Telegrams. We regret to inform you …

I don't remember the journey home.

NOTES

Chapter 1

1   Acting Flight Lieutenant Roderick Alastair Brook Learoyd, 49 Squadron,
    Hampden P4403. Awarded for action 12 August 1940, *London Gazette*,
    20 August 1940.

2   James Anderson 'Jamie' Pitcairn-Hill was awarded the DSO for the attack
    on the Dortmund–Ems. The son of a Scottish minister; he excelled in
    sport and played rugby for the RAF. On 29 August he was forced to ditch
    in X2897 after running out of fuel on the return from Berlin, having been
    in the air for more than nine hours. On 18 September Squadron Leader
    Pitcairn-Hill DSO DFC was killed when his Hampden was literally shot
    to pieces over the target area during an attack on Le Havre.

Chapter 2

1   Quoted in *Wings on the Whirlwind*, compiled and edited by Anne
    Grimshaw (North West Essex & East Hertfordshire Branch Aircrew
    Association, 1998).

2   Warrant Officer Trevor Horace Bagnall was killed in action (KIA) on
    17 December 1942. Sixteen Stirlings and six Wellingtons of 3 Group
    were detailed to attack the Opel Works at Fallersleben. Five Stirlings on
    75 New Zealand Squadron, led by Wing Commander Victor Mitchell
    DFC, a 27-year old Scot, with Bagnall as his second pilot, took off from

Newmarket for the Opel Works. The New Zealand squadron, which had only recently re-equipped with Stirlings after having flown Wellingtons since April 1940, suffered disastrously. Mitchell and his crew were lost without trace and all fourteen men on the two other crews were killed. A fourth Stirling flown by Flight Sergeant K.J. Dunmall was shot down by a combination of flak and fighters and crashed in the Westeinder Plas in Holland. All seven crew were soon taken prisoner.

3   On the night of 7 March a 1662 HCU Halifax with an all-Polish crew and a 1667 HCU Halifax were involved in a mid-air collision. There were no survivors from either aircraft. *RAF Bomber Command Losses, Vol. 8 Heavy Conversion Units and Miscellaneous Units, 1939–1947* by W.R. Chorley (Midland Publishing, 2003).

Chapter 4

1   *RAF Bomber Command Losses of the Second World War, Vol. 1 1939–41/ RAF Bomber Command Losses of the Second World War, Vol. 9 Roll of Honour 1939–1947* by W.R. Chorley.

2   Four aircraft did not hear the recall signal and, with the 3 Group aircraft, proceeded to the target where fifty-three aircraft bombed the estimated positions of German warships through a smoke-screen. No aircraft were lost but two Wellingtons crashed in England.

3   Contributed by C. Findlay, the nephew of Pilot Officer Law.

Chapter 6

1   In all, 898 crews claimed to have hit Cologne and almost all of them bombed their aiming point as briefed. Fifteen aircraft bombed other targets. The total tonnage of bombs was 1,455, two-thirds of this tonnage being incendiaries. Post-bombing reconnaissance certainly showed that more than 600 acres of Cologne had been razed to the ground. The Air Ministry reported after reconnaissance had been made that 'In an area of seventeen acres between the Cathedral and the Hange Brücke forty or fifty buildings are gutted or severely damaged. Buildings immediately adjacent to the south-eastern wall of the Cathedral are gutted. There is no photographic evidence of damage to the Cathedral, although the damage to the adjoining buildings suggests that some minor damage may have occurred. The Police Headquarters and between 200 and 300 houses

have been destroyed in another area of 35 acres extending from the Law Courts and the Neumarkt westwards almost to the Hohenzollernring. An area of three and a half acres between St Gereon's Church and the Hohenzollernring has been completely burned out.' The fires burned for days. In his report to Chief of Police Himmler, Gauleiter Grohé recorded that 486 people were killed, 5,027 had been injured and 59,100 rendered homeless. A total of 18,432 houses, flats, workshops, public buildings and the like were completely destroyed, 9,516 heavily damaged and 31,070 damaged less severely. 'The immense number of incendiary bombs dropped' had caused 12,000 fires, of which 2,500 had been major outbreaks. Albert Speer, Minister for Armaments and War Production, was with Goering at the Veldenstein castle in Franconia when the Reichmarschall was told of the reported weight of the attack. Speer said that Goering shouted: 'Impossible! That many bombs cannot be dropped in a single night!' It was estimated that from 135,000 to 150,000 of Cologne's population of nearly 700,000 people fled the city after the raid. Thirty of the fifty-three bombers that were lost were believed to have been shot down by night fighters between the coast and Cologne. It was estimated by Bomber Command that sixteen of the twenty-two aircraft that were lost over or near Cologne were shot down by flak.

2   A total of 1,067 aircraft were detailed to attack Bremen on the night of 25/26 June. Although only 960 aircraft, including 272 from the OTUs, became available for Bomber Command use, every type of aircraft in Bomber Command was included, even the Bostons and Mosquitoes of 2 Group which, so far, had only been used for day operations. There were a total of 472 Wellingtons, 124 Halifaxes, 96 Lancasters, 69 Stirlings, 51 Blenheims, 50 Hampdens, 50 Whitleys, 24 Bostons, 20 Manchesters and 4 Mosquitoes. Five further aircraft provided by Army Co-Operation Command were also added to the force. The final numbers dispatched, 1,067 aircraft, made this a larger raid than that on Cologne at the end of May. The entire 5 Group effort – 142 aircraft – were to bomb the Focke-Wulf factory. Twenty Blenheims were allocated the A.G. Weser shipyard; the Coastal Command aircraft were to bomb the Deschimag shipyard; all other aircraft except for 5 Group were to carry out an area attack on the town and docks. This raid was the last flown operationally by Manchesters, after which the type was withdrawn. Bomber Command never before, or after, dispatched such a mixed force. After Churchill had intervened and insisted that the Admiralty allow Coastal Command to participate in this raid, a further 102 Hudsons and Wellingtons of Coastal Command were

sent to Bremen but official records class this effort as a separate raid, not
under Bomber Command control.

3   Flight Sergeant Spratt and the rest of the six-man crew also landed safely
and were taken into captivity. Their aircraft crashed at Luttenberg
in Holland.

Chapter 8

1   AL574/0 crashed on a night take-off at Fayid on 16 March 1942.
AL566/P bombed Tripoli harbour, Libya, on 10–11 January 1942; the first
bombing mission for a Liberator anywhere. AL566 also bombed Taranto
naval base, Italy, on 6 June 1942, a thirteen-hour flight; another Liberator
first. AL566 later became 'Y' of S.D. (Special Duties) flight. AL530/Q had
a Wellington rear turret fitted. Its letter was changed to 'Z' for S.D. flight.
AL530 had been retired from operational flying but was brought out for
one more S.D. operation because it was rated the fastest of the Liberators.
Later it suffered battle damage and was struck off charge on 31 May 1944.

2   Amos returned to flying duties. He was killed in 1943. Gerry Molloy of
Carlingford and friends, Co. Louth, Ireland, has erected a plaque at the
crash site commemorating those who lost their lives.

3   After completing operations over Europe, Flying Officer J.R. Anderson
was posted to the Middle East, 37 then 108 Squadron. He stayed in the
RAF post-war, spending some time in the Air Ministry Intelligence
Unit. Leaving the RAF, he set up a sail-making business on the south
coast, enjoying some success with his innovative designs. His burn injury
of one leg needed a dressing at all times for years until, in 1970, cancer
developed necessitating amputation of the lower leg. Flight Lieutenant
J.R. Anderson DFC★ died in 1983.

Chapter 9

1   Leonard Reginald Gribble (1908–1985) was a prolific English writer.
His family came from Barnstaple, Devon. He married Nancy Mason in
1932 and served in the Press and Censorship Division of the Ministry
of Information, London, 1940–1945. He was a founding member of
the Crime Writers' Association in 1953 and also wrote Westerns and
books on criminology and other subjects. Gribble also wrote as Sterry
Browning, James Gannett, Leo Grex, Louis Grey, Piers Marlowe, Dexter

Muir and Bruce Sanders. As Leonard Gribble his series character was
Superintendent Anthony Slade. As Leo Grex he wrote about Paul Irving
and Phil Sanderson. Despite his voluminous output he probably remains
best known for his football-based mysteries, namely *The Arsenal Stadium
Mystery* (1929) and *They Kidnapped Stanley Matthews* (September 1950).

2   *Handley Page Halifax; From Hell to Victory and Beyond* by K.A. Merrick
(Chevron Publishing, 2009).

3   Robbie Robinson was killed when his Halifax was shot down during the
raid on Berlin on the night of 23–24 August 1943. Of the 719 bombers
dispatched to Berlin – 117 of these PFF aircraft – fifty-six failed to
return, including two 'Station Masters': Group Captain A.H. Willetts at
Oakington and Group Captain Basil Vernon Robinson DSO DFC* AFC.

Chapter 10

1   A few years after his birth, the family returned to Galway, Ireland. Joyce
attended the Jesuit St Ignatius College in Galway from 1915 to 1921.
Unusual for Irish Roman Catholics, both Joyce and his father were
strongly Unionist. Joyce later said that he had aided the Black and Tans
during the Irish War for Independence and had become a target of the
Irish Republican Army. In 1921 he left for England, where he briefly
attended King's College School, Wimbledon, on a foreign exchange. He
joined the Worcestershire Regiment but was discharged when it was
discovered that he had lied about his age. He then applied to Birkbeck
College of the University of London (obtaining a First Class degree)
and to enter the Officer Training Corps. He also developed an interest in
fascism. In 1924, while stewarding a Conservative Party meeting, Joyce
was attacked and received a deep razor slash that ran across his right cheek.
It left a permanent scar that ran from the earlobe to the corner of the
mouth. He claimed his attackers were Jewish communists. In 1932 Joyce
joined the British Union of Fascists under Sir Oswald Mosley and swiftly
became a leading speaker, praised for his power of oratory. In 1937 Mosley
sacked him and Joyce promptly formed the National Socialist League.
In late August 1939, shortly before war was declared, Joyce and his wife
Margaret fled to Germany after he had been tipped off that the British
authorities intended to detain him. Joyce became a naturalised German
citizen in 1940.

2   Joyce also broadcast on and wrote scripts for the German Büro Concordia
organisation, which ran several black propaganda stations, many of which

pretended to broadcast illegally from within Britain. Joyce's other duties included writing propaganda for distribution among British PoWs, whom he tried to recruit into the British Free Corps. His book, *Twilight Over England*, unfavourably compared the evils of allegedly Jewish-dominated capitalist Britain with the alleged wonders of National Socialist Germany. Adolf Hitler awarded Joyce the War Merit Cross (First and Second Class) for his broadcasts, although they never met.

3   Thanks are due to Margaret Fielden for this story from the memoires of Nick Carter, written for his children, grandchildren and great grandchildren: Maggy, Lissie and Nick Jnr. Thanks also to Bill Jeavons of Virginia, USA, Nick's friend of many years, who died in August 2003. Nick Carter died on 4 February 2002.

4   War Report, BBC dispatches, AEF 1944–45. (1946).

Chapter 11

1   Halifax II JB871 MP-V.

2   See *Hell On Earth: Dramatic First Hand Experiences of Bomber Command At War* by Mel Rolfe Grub Street, 1999).

3   D/R being dead reckoning navigation on a time and distance flown basis with an allowance made for possible drift.

4   Feldwebel Karl Gross and his *bordfunker* (radio operator) Unteroffizier Geck of 8./NJG4 flying a Bf 110G-4 from Juvincourt were guided on to the tail of the bomber by the ground radar of 15./Ln. Regiment 203 and in a single long burst of cannon fire Gross shot DT775 down; his sole victory of the war. While serving in 11./NJG6, Gross was KIA in a crash at Urzenici, Romania, on 11 July 1944, cause unknown.

5   Halifax DT775 crashed in a field at Anoux near Briey (Meurthe-et-Moselle) in east France, where it burned out. Sergeant Jack Adams and five of his crew bailed out safely and all were PoW. Sergeant Joe Enwright, a married man with a small daughter, was KIA by cannon fire and his body was found near the remains of his rear turret the next day. (Of the ten 78 Squadron crews who returned to Linton-on-Ouse from Frankurt, six were shot down on ops, 16 April–15 July 1943.) Twenty-two aircraft failed to return (FTR) from Frankfurt.

Chapter 12

1   *The Everlasting Arms: The War Memoirs of Air Commodore John Searby DSO DFC* edited by Martin Middlebrook (William Kimber, 1988).
2   Lancaster I W4886 crashed near Furth with the loss of all seven crew.
3   *The Dambuster Who Cracked the Dam: The Story of Melvin 'Dinghy' Young* by Arthur G. Thorning (Pen & Sword, 2008).
4   Priscilla Lawson, a graduate of Brearley School, New York and Bryn Mawr College. *The Dambuster Who Cracked the Dam: The Story of Melvin 'Dinghy' Young* by Arthur G. Thorning (Pen & Sword, 2008).
5   Eight Lancasters had set out with the new 12,000lb light-case bomb (not the 12,000lb Tallboy earthquake bomb developed later). While over the North Sea a weather reconnaissance Mosquito reported that there was fog in the target area and the Lancasters were recalled. *The Bomber Command War Diaries: An Operational Reference Book 1939–1945* by Martin Middlebrook and Chris Everitt (Midland, 1985, 1990, 1995).
6   The body of David Maltby, who was 21 years old, was picked up by the Cromer lifeboat and taken to the morgue at RAF Coltishall. He was buried later at Wickhambreux near Canterbury in Kent, where he had been married.
7   *The Dam Busters* by Paul Brickhill (Evans Bros London, 1951).

Chapter 13

1   Eric Blanchard would fly as flight engineer on seven operational trips and Ray Francis, thirteen trips.
2   The abnormally low dropping altitude (300ft) in a shipping channel 157 yards wide caused considerable concern among the crews, obliged to operate at that height. Normally 'gardening' was carried out from 12,000–14,000ft. All eighty-nine aircrews mining off Swinemünde in the Baltic and Kiel Bay (four more would plant them in the River Gironde) came from 5 Group. Low flying over water at night in virtually no moonlight – the New Moon was only two days off – was a potentially hazardous operation. Light coastal and ship-mounted flak and roaming night fighters could and did both surprise and inflict terrible punishment on the mine-layers. The port of Stettin was to be bombed by 461 Lancasters from high level at approximately the same time as the mining was to take place. Another 348 aircraft (196 Lancasters, 144 Halifaxes and nine Mosquitoes) were detailed for a heavy raid on Kiel. At Stettin much damage was meted

out to the port and industrial areas with twenty-nine factories destroyed and more than 1,500 houses destroyed and another 1,000 homes damaged. Around 1,500 bodies were recovered from the ruins and more than 1,600 people were injured. Five ships were sunk at their moorings and eight other vessels were seriously damaged. Two of the four Lancasters lost went down in the Baltic and a fifth Lanc crashed in Sweden, killing the pilot. The rest of the crew were interned. The raid on Kiel was only partially successful. Four Halifax aircraft and two Lancasters were lost on Kiel docks, another Halifax crew ditched off Scarborough and a sixth crashed in England. Three Halifaxes mine-laying in Kiel Bay also failed to return. Five aircraft were lost on Swinemünde. A total of six other aircraft were lost; three Halifaxes in Kiel Bay, two Lancasters off Swinemünde and a single OTU Wellington. Just under 1,200 sorties were dispatched in a wide-ranging and geographically dispersed series of operations. *The Bomber Command War Diaries* by Martin Middlebrook and Chris Everitt (Midland, 1985, 1990, 1995).

3   Wing Commander Edward Leach Porter DFC★ on 97 Squadron was the master bomber. He was coned by searchlights over the canal and called up Squadron Leader Stuart Parkes DSO, one of the deputies, on the VHF that he had been hit by flak and that his aircraft was on fire. All the crew perished. Sergeant Terence Michael Twomey DFM, the rear gunner, is buried on the Island of Bornholm in Peders Kirke churchyard; four including Wing Commander Porter are buried at Poznan Polish War Cemetery and three were never found. Squadron Leader Stuart Martin Parkeshouse Parkes DSO was killed on 26 August 1944.

4   Königsberg, an important supply port for the German Eastern Front and the capital of East Prussia, was first attacked on Saturday night, 26 August, by 174 Lancasters of 5 Group. The eastern part of Königsberg was bombed and four Lancasters failed to return. On Tuesday night, 29 August, 189 Lancasters of 5 Group carried out one of their most successful attacks of the war when the target was Königsberg again. There was heavy fighter opposition in the target area and fifteen Lancasters failed to return. Königsberg was renamed Kaliningrad in 1946 after the death of chairman of the Presidium of the Supreme Soviet of the USSR Mikhail Kalinin, one of the original Bolsheviks. The survivors of the German population were forcibly expelled and the city was repopulated with Soviet citizens. The German language was replaced by the Russian language. The city was rebuilt, and, as the westernmost territory of the USSR, the Kaliningrad Oblast became a strategically important area during the Cold War. The Soviet Baltic Fleet was headquartered in the city in the 1950s.

5   Some 217 Lancasters and ten Mosquitoes of 1 and 5 Groups took part in what was the only major raid carried out by Bomber Command during the war on this medium-sized target. Some 909 tons of bombs were dropped in an accurate raid and widespread destruction was caused; the post-war British Bombing Survey Unit estimated that 36 per cent of the town's built-up area was destroyed. One Lancaster and one Mosquito were lost. *The Bomber Command War Diaries* (Martin Middlebrook and Chris Everitt).

6   Fred worked in personnel at Rolls-Royce in Derby until taking the position of personnel manager at Rolls-Royce, Anstey, near Coventry in 1967. He remained personnel manager at Rolls-Royce until he retired at the age of 59. Fred and Dot celebrated their sixtieth diamond wedding anniversary on 10 April 2004.

Chapter 14

1   Small forces of Ju 88 G-6s and Bf 110 G-4s of I., II. and IV./NJG6 were directed to the Dessau force, but the majority of the *Nachtjagd* crews did not get at the bomber stream due to conflicting ground control instructions and due to heavy jamming by 100 Group, rendering the SN-2 radar all but useless in the target area. Still, at least two experienced crews of II./NJG6 managed to infiltrate the bomber stream, Oberleutnant Spoden and Hauptmann Schulte claiming three Lancasters shot down over or in the vicinity of Dessau between 22.00 and 22.29. After claiming two Lancasters, one of the engines of Oberleutnant Peter Spoden's Ju 88G-6 2Z+DP was put out of action by return fire from a vigilant Lancaster gunner and the crew was forced to bail out. Oberleutnant Spoden came down safely and survived the war as Gruppen Kommandeur of I./NJG6, credited with twenty-four confirmed night victories, plus one probable B-17 kill in daylight on 6 January 1944.

2   In the course of almost six years of war, Bomber Command lost 8,655 aircraft on ops, plus 1,600 through accidents and write-offs. Of a total of approximately 125,000 aircrew serving in front-line units, casualties amounted to 73,741, of whom 55,500 were killed.

Chapter 15

1   On 6–7 June 1,065 bombers (589 Lancasters, 418 Halifaxes and 58
    Mosquitoes bombed rail and road centres on the lines of communication
    behind the Normandy battle area. A total of 3,488 tons of bombs were
    dropped on nine choke points, including bridges and road and rail centres
    behind the Normandy battle area, at Achères near Paris, Argentan, Caen,
    Châteaudun, Condé-sur-Noireau, Coutances, Saint-Lô, Lisieux and Vire.
    The important road and rail bridge at Coutances was badly damaged by five
    squadrons of Halifaxes of 6 Group RCAF, who bombed visually on to red
    and green TIs dropped by two Lancasters and three Mosquitoes of 8 Group.
    One aircraft on 420 'Snowy Owl' Squadron RCAF scored a direct hit while
    the remainder bombed Condé-sur-Noireau. Much of the town was hit
    and set on fire, and 312 civilians were killed. (About 100 aircraft each of 3
    Group and 6 Group RCAF attacked Lisieux and Condé.) The Canadian
    Group suffered no losses but a 426 'Thunderbird' Squadron RCAF Halifax,
    which was hit by a bomb while over the aiming point, was damaged but the
    pilot managed to get the aircraft back across the Channel and abandon it
    over Slapton Sands on the south coast of Devon. At Lisieux, a Lancaster was
    lost. In all, 11,500 tons of bombs were dropped on the targets. *The Bomber
    Command War Diaries: An Operational Reference Book 1939–1945* by Martin
    Middlebrook and Chris Everitt (Midland, 1985, 1990, 1995).

2   A total of 105 Halifaxes and seventy-six Lancasters of 6 and 8 Groups
    carried out the first large raid on this target since June 1942. It was also
    the last Bomber Command raid of the war. The force was escorted, first
    by Spitfires and then by 8th Air Force P-51 Mustangs. Only one Lancaster,
    that of the deputy master bomber, 23-year-old Flight Lieutenant Granville
    Wilson DFC DFM, on 7 Squadron, was lost. Wilson's aircraft took a direct
    hit from a flak shell and he was killed instantly, together with his navigator
    and bomb aimer, Sergeants Dennis Jones and Edward Ronald Brunsdon.
    The five other members of the crew bailed out safely. The bombing
    was accurate and Emden was seen to be a mass of flames. *The Bomber
    Command War Diaries: An Operational Reference Book 1939–1945* by Martin
    Middlebrook and Chris Everitt (Midland, 1985, 1990, 1995).

Chapter 16

1   Heinz Strüning BXVI was also credited with shooting down Mosquito
    BXVI ML984, crewed by Flight Lieutenant Thompson and Calder.

Chapter 17

1   In retirement, Rollo became active in the debate about Australia becoming a republic and adopting a new national flag. He formed the group Veterans for a Republic, having become a republican in April 1944. This followed the British Government's attempt to prevent RAAF bomber crews returning to Australia after their tour of duty in England in order to fight in the Pacific War and the resultant diversion of RAAF reinforcements to RAF squadrons. In his view, Australian interests should not be subservient to British interests and Australia should leave the British Empire when the war ended. Rollo also joined Ausflag as a director. He explained his position on the flag in an article in *Australian Geographic*, stating: 'As a serviceman in World War II, I saw my share of fighting and witnessed the deaths of far too many Australians in combat. However, I certainly didn't fight for the flag and I didn't know anyone who said they did. Success and survival in war depends on luck, skill, determination and discipline – when you're in the thick of it, there isn't time to worry about something as irrelevant as a flag.'

2   A nephew of Sir Charles Kingsford-Smith MC who, with fellow pilot C.T.P. Ulm and crew, made the first trans-Pacific flight 31 May–9 June 1928 in Fokker F.VIIB/3m *Southern Cross*.

3   'The final raid on my tour of operations was a few days later on 14 and 15 June when we attacked a German Panzer (tank) force concentrated at night, hiding under cover of trees in a wood. With information from the French Resistance we knew exactly where they were. On 17 June my replacement, Wing Commander Donaldson RAAF, arrived and the next day I started my end of tour leave.'

Chapter 18

1   Other supporting operations consisted of a diversionary sweep over the North Sea (145 aircraft); Berlin (23 Mosquitoes); Deelen airfield (5 Mosquitoes); Dortmund (3 Mosquitoes); Kamen (3 Mosquitoes); Sterkrade (3 Mosquitoes); radio counter-measures sorties (33); intruder/anti-night fighter patrols (47 Mosquitoes); mine laying in the River Gironde (4); and OTU sorties (24).

2   Early returns citing 'Mag drop' were in some instances seen as, if not grounds for accusation of LMF, possibly a precursor to it, particularly if the trouble seemed to repeatedly afflict a specific pilot. 'Mag drop' was a

phenomenon inherent in the basic design of these early magnetos, which both produced the electrical energy to fire the engines' spark plugs and distributed the electrical impulses to the correct plugs in the engines' firing cycle. If the magneto produced a reduced sparking voltage to any of the spark plugs, it would produce a smaller spark to ignite the fuel/air mixture in the cylinder, which resulted in incomplete ignition. Over a relatively small period, carbon and/or oil could accumulate on the plug, rendering it virtually useless and thereby reducing the efficiency of the engine, ultimately resulting in total failure.

3   Locke, Wing Commander Porter and Squadron Leader Parkes were awarded immediate DSOs and messages of congratulations from the AOC followed. Squadron Leader Stuart Martin Parkeshouse Parkes DSO was killed on 26 August 1944.

4   At Stettin much damage was meted out to the port and industrial areas, with twenty-nine factories destroyed and more than 1,500 houses destroyed and another 1,000 homes damaged. Around 1,500 bodies were recovered from the ruins and more than 1,600 people were injured. Five ships were sunk at their moorings and eight other vessels were seriously damaged. Two of the four Lancasters lost went down in the Baltic and a fifth Lanc crashed in Sweden, killing the pilot. The rest of the crew were interned. The raid on Kiel was only partially successful. Four Halifax aircraft and two Lancasters were lost on Kiel docks, another Halifax crew ditched off Scarborough and a sixth crashed in England. Three Halifaxes mine-laying in Kiel Bay also failed to return. Five aircraft were lost on Swinemünde. A total of six other aircraft were lost, three Halifaxes in Kiel Bay, two Lancasters off Swinemünde and a single OTU Wellington. Just under 1,200 sorties were dispatched in a wide-ranging and geographically dispersed series of operations. *The Bomber Command War Diaries: An Operational Reference Book 1939–1945* by Martin Middlebrook and Chris Everitt (Midland, 1985, 1990, 1995).

Chapter 19

1   Stirling III EE882 BU-J took off from Chedburgh at 23.10 on 3 July. All of Sergeant R.G. Armsworth's crew were killed.

2   These stories were submitted to the *People's War* site by a volunteer on behalf of Pilot Officer John A. Martin DFC (retired) Larne, N. Ireland.

Chapter 20

1   Steve Smith, the 218 Squadron historian, gave this explanation as the reason Sunny and his crew were posted so soon into their operational tour. 'It could have been the disbandment of 623 Squadron on 6 December 1943. 623 Squadron was formed from 218 Squadron in August 1943 and, like 218, it operated from RAF Downham Market. On the squadron's disbandment, a number of former squadron crews were posted back to 218. Another factor was that at the time 218 Squadron's losses were exceptionally low: between 1 December 1943 and 1 February 1944 only one crew were lost. This meant that the squadron had its full complement of crews, plus spares. Thankfully the Stirling-equipped squadrons of 3 Group were not participating in the bloodbath over Berlin. This was left to the Avro Lancaster-equipped squadrons, one of which was 514 Squadron. During the period December 1943 to February 1944, 514 Squadron lost, I believe, twelve crews. On the 21–22nd January attack on Berlin 514 Squadron lost four crews in one night. I feel it is a combination of 218 having too many crews and losses suffered by 514, which saw the crew posted.'

2   Quoted in *The Nuremburg Raid* by Martin Middlebrook (Allen Lane, 1973).

3   Quoted in *The Nuremburg Raid* by Martin Middlebrook (Allen Lane, 1973).

4   Later, they learned that it was one of two Lancasters that had been shot down by their Kommandeur, Hauptmann Gustav Tham.

5   In 1984, the local German parishioners erected a stone memorial with a bronze cross and plaque bearing the names of the five men who died.

6   Quoted in *The Nuremburg Raid* by Martin Middlebrook (Allen Lane, 1973).

7   Warrant Officer John Clare Gilbertson-Pritchard was killed on 31 March 1945. He had joined 154 Squadron in Fighter Command at RAF Hunsdon, Hertfordshire. At the time of his death Gilbertson-Pritchard was a fighter pilot flying Mustang Mark IVs.

Chapter 23

1   It was every officer's duty to escape and at Stalag Luft III three tunnels – 'Tom', 'Dick' and 'Harry' – were started from under barracks in the north compound, although when one was discovered it was decided to put all energies into 'Harry'. On the night of 24 March 1944, in what has since gone down in history as 'The Great Escape', no fewer than seventy-six Allied air force officers used 'Harry' to flee the supposedly 'escape proof'

camp before their flight was discovered. Only three of the escapers made 'home runs'. The rest were captured and Hitler ordered that fifty were to be shot in cold blood.

2   Adapted from an interview with Catherine Goodier, editor of *Blind Veterans UK*, and biographical material provided by John Ward of *The 4T9er*, the 49 Squadron Association Magazine.

Chapter 24

1   A total of 151 Lancasters of 3 Group attacked the oil plant through cloud. No aircraft were lost. *The Bomber Command War Diaries: An Operational Reference Book 1939–1945* by Martin Middlebrook and Chris Everitt (Midland, 1985, 1990, 1995).

2   On 5 March Gelsenkirchen was attacked by 170 Lancasters of 3 Group, who carried out a G-H attack on the Consolidation benzol plant. No results were seen. One Lancaster was lost. On 19 March the plant was attacked again, by seventy-nine Lancasters of 3 Group. Smoke and dust from the bombing prevented observation of the results. No aircraft were lost.

3   Some 150 Lancasters of 3 Group carried out G-H attacks on two benzol plants in the Hamm area. No results were seen because of cloud but dense smoke rose through the cloud from both targets. No aircraft were lost. *The Bomber Command War Diaries: An Operational Reference Book 1939–1945* by Martin Middlebrook and Chris Everitt (Midland, 1985, 1990, 1995).

4   A total of 591 Lancasters and eight Mosquitoes of 1, 3 and 8 Groups bombed the Deutsche Werke U-boat yards. The pocket battleship *Admiral Scheer* was hit and capsized and the *Admiral Hipper* and the *Emden* were badly damaged. Three Lancasters were lost. *The Bomber Command War Diaries: An Operational Reference Book 1939–1945* by Martin Middlebrook and Chris Everitt (Midland, 1985, 1990, 1995).

5   Pilot Officer N.W.N. Tanner RCAF had taken the Halifax off from 1652 HCU Marston Moor at 22.35 for a briefed Bullseye target on the fleet at anchor at Scapa Flow. The bomber crashed after midnight in the Moray Firth. All eight crew – four of whom were Australian – and including Sergeant Leonard Alexander Cooke, were killed. *Bomber Command Losses, Vol. 7 OTUs 1940–1947* by W.R. Chorley (Midland, 2002).

6   Some 377 Lancasters and 105 Halifaxes of 3, 6 and 8 Groups were dispatched. Two Lancasters were lost. *The Bomber Command War Diaries: An Operational Reference Book 1939–1945* by Martin Middlebrook and Chris

Everitt (Midland, 1985, 1990, 1995).

7   A combined total of 969 aircraft – 617 Lancasters, 332 Halifaxes and
      twenty Mosquitoes of all groups – attacked the naval base, the airfield and
      the town on this small island. The bombing was accurate and the target
      areas were turned almost into crater-pitted moonscapes. *The Bomber
      Command War Diaries: An Operational Reference Book 1939–1945* by Martin
      Middlebrook and Chris Everitt (Midland, 1985, 1990, 1995).

8   All told, 500 Lancasters of 1 and 3 Groups and twelve Mosquitoes of
      8 Group took part in the operation on Potsdam. Although Mosquito
      bombers of the Late Night Striking Force (LNSF) had attacked the 'Big
      City' almost continually, this was the first time the Reich capital had
      been attacked by heavies since March 1944. One Lancaster was lost to
      an unidentified night fighter over the target. *The Bomber Command War
      Diaries: An Operational Reference Book 1939–1945* by Martin Middlebrook
      and Chris Everitt (Midland, 1985, 1990, 1995).

Chapter 26

1   'Bomber Command contained a considerable number of its own
      training units, in which airmen who had received a basic training in their
      respective speciality – pilots, navigators (earlier known as observers),
      wireless operators, air gunners, bomb aimers (officially "air bombers")
      and flight engineers – were gathered together for crew training at OTUs
      (Operational Training Units) and, for those crews intended for four-
      engined aircraft, at HCUs (Heavy Conversion Units). Many of these
      training units dispatched aircraft on active-service operations. Most of
      the OTU flights were by pupil crews which carried out a short sortie to
      a target in Northern France just before finishing their training courses at
      the OTU; most of these flights only carried leaflets. The HCU operations
      were mainly flown by mixed crews of pupils and instructors in 1942,
      when training aircraft were added to Bomber Command's Main Force
      for the Thousand-Bomber Raids and for other major raids. The OTUs
      also contributed to the 1942 Main Force raids, but more instructors than
      pupils provided the crews on these occasions. In total, 24 OTUs and eight
      HCUs sent crews on operations. (OTU aircraft flew 4,068 sorties and
      120 aircraft were lost. HCU aircraft flew 167 sorties with 13 aircraft lost).
      Most of the operational flights by training units ceased after the invasion
      of Normandy in June 1944, but OTUs and HCUs sometimes provided
      aircraft for diversionary sweeps over the North Sea and over France in

1944 and 1945; details of these sweeps, however, are not included in the statistics because the German lines were never crossed, although there were occasional losses on the sweeps.' *The Bomber Command War Diaries: An Operational Reference Book 1939–1945* by Martin Middlebrook and Chris Everitt (Midland,1985, 1990, 1995).

2   In total, 47,268 airmen died in action or while prisoners of war.

3   On Saturday, 23 March at 15.30, eighty Lancasters bombed the little town of Wesel, which was an important troop centre behind the Rhine front in the area about to be attacked by the 21st Army Group massing for the Rhine crossings at dawn. More than 400 tons of bombs were dropped on the German troops and many strong points were destroyed. Five hours later, at 22.30, only a short time before Field Marshal Sir Bernard Montgomery's zero hour and as the 1st Commando Brigade followed by the 51st Highland Division closed in, 195 Lancasters and twenty-three Mosquitoes of 5 and 8 Groups followed it up with another attack to complete the work of the afternoon. In exactly nine minutes, well over 1,000 tons of bombs went down from 9,000ft on those troops who had crept back into the ruins to await the British commandos' attack. In all, more than 1,500 tons of bombs were dropped in the two attacks – a weight of bombs that had already almost completely wiped out cities eight times the size of Wesel. The effects on the defenders was devastating; the bombing was completed at approximately 22.39 hours and the British Army was crossing the river in assault craft, aided by searchlights, before the bombers had left the area. A message of appreciation from Montgomery to Sir Arthur Harris was received. It said: 'I would like to convey to you personally and all in Bomber Command my grateful appreciation for the magnificent co-operation you have given us in the battle of the Rhine. The bombing of Wesel last night was a masterpiece and was a decisive factor in making possible our entry into the town before midnight. Please convey my thanks to all your crews and ground staffs.'

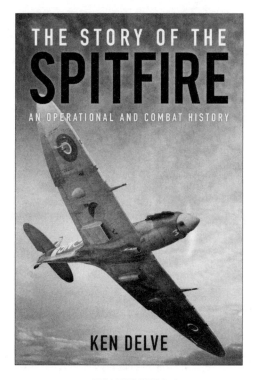

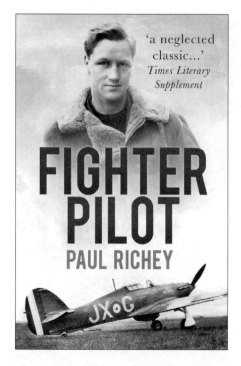